LIVING LANGUAGE®

JAPANESE
COURSEBOOK

REVISED & UPDATED

THE LIVING LANGUAGE® SERIES

**Living Language Basic Courses,
 Revised & Updated**

Spanish*	Japanese*
French*	Russian
German*	Italian*

Portuguese (Brazilian)
Portuguese (Continental)
Inglés/English for Spanish Speakers

Living Language Verb Courses

Spanish	French
German	Italian

**Living Language Advanced Courses,
 Revised & Updated**

Spanish 3	French 3

**Living Language Ultimate™
 (formerly All the Way™)**

Spanish*	Spanish 2*
French*	French 2*
German*	German 2*
Italian*	Italian 2*
Russian*	Russian 2*
Japanese*	Japanese 2*

Inglés/English for Spanish Speakers*
Inglés/English for Spanish Speakers 2*
Chinese (1999)

**Living Language® Essential Language
 Guides**

Essential Spanish for Healthcare
Essential Spanish for Social Services
Essential Spanish for Law Enforcement
Essential Language Guide for Hotel &
 Restaurant Employees

Living Language Fast & Easy™

Spanish	Italian	Portuguese
French	Russian	Czech
German	Polish	Hungarian
Japanese	Korean	Mandarin
Arabic	Hebrew	(Chinese)

Inglés/English for Spanish Speakers

Living Language All Audio™

Spanish   French   Italian   German

**Living Language Speak Up!®
 Accent Elimination Courses**

Spanish   American Regional
Asian, Indian and Middle Eastern

Fodor's Languages for Travelers

Spanish   French   Italian   German

**Living Language® Parent/Child
 Activity Kits**

Learn in the Kitchen: French, Italian,
 Spanish
Learn in the Car: French, Italian,
 Spanish
Learn Together: French, Italian, Spanish

**Living Language Conversational
 English**

for Chinese Speakers
for Japanese Speakers
for Korean Speakers
for Spanish Speakers
for Russian Speakers

*Available on Cassette and Compact Disc

If you're traveling, we recommend
Fodor's guides

Available in bookstores everywhere, or call 1-800-733-3000
for additional information.

Visit our website at: www.livinglanguage.com

JAPANESE
COURSEBOOK

REVISED & UPDATED

REVISED BY HIROKO STORM, PH.D.

University of Arizona

Assistant Professor of Japanese
Lafayette College

◆

Based on the original by Ichiro Shirato

LIVING LANGUAGE®
A Random House Company

This work was previously published under the titles *Conversation Manual Japanese* and *Living Language™ Conversational Japanese* by Ichiro Shirato, based on the method devised by Ralph Weiman. Special thanks to Gladys Heldman.

Published by Living Language, A Random House Company, New York, New York. Living Language is a member of the Random House Information Group.

Random House, Inc. New York, Toronto, London, Sydney, Auckland

www.livinglanguage.com

Living Language and colophon are registered trademarks of Random House, Inc.

Printed in the United States of America

Library of Congress Catalog Card Number: 60-15399

ISBN 0-609-80302-6

10   9   8   7

Living language ® publications are available at special discounts for bulk purchases for sales promotions or premiums, as well as for fund-raising or educational use. Special editions can be created in large quantities for special needs. For more information, write to Special Sales Manager, Living Language, 280 Park Avenue, New York, NY 10017.

CONTENTS

Introduction   xv
Course Material   xvii
Instructions   xix

LESSON 1   1
A. A Preliminary Note   1
B. The Alphabet: The Letters   2
C. Accent   3
D. The Alphabet: The Sounds   4
E. Loan Words: English Words
   Used in Japanese   4

LESSON 2   6
A. Vowels   6
B. Vowel Clusters   7
C. Devoiced Vowels   8

LESSON 3   9
A. Consonants I   9

LESSON 4   12
A. Consonants II   12
B. Semi-Vowels   16

LESSON 5   17
    A. The Japanese Syllabary   17
    B. General Sound Equivalents   18
    C. More Loan Words   20

LESSON 6   23
    A. Days and Months   23
    B. Numbers 1–10   23
    C. Colors   24
    D. North, South, East, West   24
    QUIZ 1   24
    E. Word Study   25

LESSON 7   25
    A. Greetings   25
    B. How's the Weather?   28
    QUIZ 2   28

LESSON 8   29
    A. Do You Have?   29
    B. In a Restaurant   30
    QUIZ 3   32
    C. Word Study   32

LESSON 9   33
    A. Pronouns   33
    B. To Be or Not to Be   34
    C. *Desu*   37
    QUIZ 4   39
    REVIEW QUIZ 1   40

LESSON 10   43
    A. Common Verb Forms   43
    B. Asking a Question I   46
    C. Where Is It?   47
    D. Here and There   48
    E. Near and Far   49
    QUIZ 5   50

LESSON 11   51
  A. Nouns and Noun Particles   51
  B. Common Adjective Forms   58
    QUIZ 6   65

LESSON 12   65
  A. Plain or Polite   65
  B. To Construct the Polite Form of a Verb   67
  C. The -*te* and -*ta* Forms   69
  D. Various Usages of the -*te* Form   73
    QUIZ 7   75

LESSON 13   75
  A. My, Your, His, Her, etc.   75
  B. Some Comparisons   77
  C. Asking a Question II   78
    QUIZ 8   80
  D. Word Study   81

LESSON 14   82
  A. To Have and Have Not   82
  B. Also   85
    QUIZ 9   85
  C. Word Study   86

LESSON 15   87
  A. I Have Been to . . .   87
  B. Sometimes I Go . . .   87
  C. I Can, I Am Able to . . .   88
  D. I've Decided to . . .   88
    QUIZ 10   89

LESSON 16   90
  A. Do You Speak Japanese?   90
  B. Please Speak a Little Slower   91
  C. Thanks!   92
    QUIZ 11   93
  D. Word Study   93

LESSON 17   94
  A. This and That   94
    QUIZ 12   96
  B. Not   96
  C. Isn't It? Aren't You? etc.   97
    QUIZ 13   98
  D. Word Study   98

LESSON 18   99
  A. It's Me (I), etc.   99
  B. It's Mine, etc.   99
  C. About Me, etc.   100
  D. To Me, etc.   100
  E. The Modifiers   100
  F. The Noun-Maker *No*   102
    QUIZ 14   103

LESSON 19   104
  A. Hello, How Are You?   104
  B. I'd Like You to Meet . . .   104
  C. What's New?   105
  D. See You Soon!   105
    QUIZ 15   106

LESSON 20   107
  A. Have You Two Met?   107
  B. Glad to Have Met You   108
    QUIZ 16   109
  C. Word Study   110
    REVIEW QUIZ 2   111

LESSON 21   114
  A. Numbers   114
  B. More Numbers   116
  C. Pronunciation of Numbers
    Before Certain Counters   117
  D. First, Second, Third   119

QUIZ 17 120
E. Two and Two 120

LESSON 22 121
  A. It Costs 121
  B. The Telephone Number Is 122
  C. My Address Is 123
  D. Some Dates 123
    QUIZ 18 124

LESSON 23 125
  A. What Time Is It? 125
  B. The Time Is Now 126
  C. When Will You Come? 126
  D. It's Time 127
    QUIZ 19 128
  E. Word Study 129

LESSON 24 130
  A. Ago 130
  B. Morning, Noon, and Night 130
  C. This Week, Next Month, etc. 131
  D. Expressions of Past, Present, and Future ... 133

LESSON 25 133
  A. Days of the Week 133
  B. Days of the Month 134
  C. What's the Date Today? 135
    QUIZ 20 136
  D. Months of the Year 137
  E. The Seasons 138
    QUIZ 21 139

LESSON 26 140
  A. *Iku:* To Go 140
  B. A Few Action Phrases 143
  C. Word Study 144
  D. *Shinbun Uriba De* 144

ix

LESSON 27   145
- A. They Say That . . .   145
- B. I Have to, I Must . . .   146
- C. Something to Drink   147
  - QUIZ 22   149
- D. Word Study   150

LESSON 28   150
- A. A Little and a Lot   150
- B. Too Much   151
- C. More or Less   151
- D. Enough and Some More   152
  - QUIZ 23   153

LESSON 29   154
- A. I Want to . . .   154
- B. I Intend to . . .   155
- C. It Is Supposed to . . .   156
- D. Something, Everything, Nothing   157
  - QUIZ 24   159
- E. Word Study   160

LESSON 30   161
- A. Of Course! It's a Pity!
  It Doesn't Matter!   161
  - QUIZ 25   162
- B. The Same   163
- C. Already   163
- D. Word Study   163

LESSON 31   164
- A. I Like It, It's Good   164
- B. I Don't Like It, It's Bad   165
  - QUIZ 26   166
  - REVIEW QUIZ 3   166
- C. Word Study   169
- D. *Waraibanashi*   170

x

LESSON 32   171
  A. Who? What? When? etc.   171
    QUIZ 27   175
  B. Word Study   177
  C. How Much?   177
  D. How Many?   177
    QUIZ 28   178

LESSON 33   179
  A. Some, Someone, Something   179
  B. Once, Twice   181
  C. Up to   181
  D. I Need It, It's Necessary   182
  E. I Feel Like   182
  F. At the Home of   183
    QUIZ 29   183
    REVIEW QUIZ 4   184

LESSON 34   187
  A. On the Road   187
  B. Bus, Train, Subway, Taxi   188
  C. Writing and Mailing Letters and Faxes   189
  D. Telephoning   190
  E. Word Study   191

LESSON 35   192
  A. What's Your Name?   192
  B. Where Are You From?
    How Old Are You?   193
  C. Professions   195
  D. Family Matters   195
    REVIEW QUIZ 5   196

LESSON 36   200
  A. *Kaimono:* Shopping   200
    QUIZ 30   204
  B. Word Study   206

LESSON 37   206
  A. *Asagohan:* Breakfast   206
  B. A Sample Menu   211
    REVIEW QUIZ 6   212

LESSON 38   214
  A. In, On, Under   214
  B. If, When   216
  C. Without   218
    QUIZ 31   219
    REVIEW QUIZ 7   220
  D. *Shakuya Sagashi:* House Hunting   223
    QUIZ 32   229

LESSON 39   231
  A. *Kuru:* To Come   231
  B. *Iu (yuu):* To Say   232
    QUIZ 33   234
  C. *Suru:* To Do   234
    QUIZ 34   236
    REVIEW QUIZ 8   237
  D. I'm a Stranger Here   240
    QUIZ 35   244

LESSON 40   246
  A. The Most Common Verb Forms   246
  B. *Kyuuyuu to No Saikai:* Meeting an
    Old Friend   256
    QUIZ 36   262
  C. The Most Common Verbs
    and Verb Phrases   264
    QUIZ 37   280
  D. Public Notices and Signs   281
    FINAL REVIEW QUIZ   286

SUMMARY OF JAPANESE GRAMMAR   291
  1. The Alphabet and Romanization   291
  2. Simple Vowels   295

3. Vowel Clusters 296
4. Consonants and Semi-Vowels 297
5. Double Consonants 299
6. The Syllabic *N* 299
7. Contractions 301
8. Accent 301
9. Intonation 302
10. Nouns 302
11. Counters 310
12. Pronouns 314
13. Prenouns 317
14. *Ko-So-A-Do* Words 318
15. Adjectives 319
16. Comparisons 321
17. The Classes and Forms of Verbs 324
18. Particles Used with Verbs 334
19. Negatives 340
20. Word Order 343
21. Questions 345
22. Question Words 346
23. Something, Everything,
    Nothing, Anything 348
24. Even If, Even Though 351
25. Hearsay 352
26. Seeming 353
27. Imminence 354
28. Obligation and Prohibition 355
29. Permission 357
30. Alternatives 358
31. Passive, Potential, and Respect 359
32. Causative 360
33. Desideratives 361
34. To Do (Something) for . . . 362
35. May, Perhaps, Probably 363
36. If and When 364
37. Whether . . . or . . . , If . . . or . . . 367
38. Noun-Makers 368
39. In Order to 369

40. Requests, Commands 371
41. Adverbial Expressions 373
42. The Writing System 376

LETTER WRITING 393
1. Formal Letters 393
2. Business Letters 396
3. Informal Letters 399
4. Addressing an Envelope 403

INTRODUCTION

Living Language® Japanese makes it easy to learn how to speak, read, and write Japanese. This course is a thoroughly revised and updated version of *Living Japanese: The Complete Living Language Course®*. The same highly effective method of language instruction is still used, but the content has been updated to reflect modern usage and the format has been clarified. In this course, the basic elements of the language have been carefully selected and condensed into forty short lessons. If you can study about thirty minutes a day, you can master this course and learn to speak Japanese in a few weeks.

You'll learn Japanese the way you learned English, starting with simple words and progressing to more complex phrases. Just listen and repeat after the native instructors on the recordings. To help you immerse yourself in the language, you'll hear only Japanese spoken. Hear it, say it, absorb it through use and repetition.

This *Living Language® Japanese Coursebook* provides English translations and brief explanations for each lesson. The first five lessons cover pronunciation, laying the foundation for learning the vocabulary, phrases, and grammar which are explained in the later chapters. If you already know a little Japanese, you can use the book as a phrase book and reference. In addition to the forty lessons, there is a summary of Japanese grammar, plus verb conjugations and a section on writing letters.

Also included in the course package is the *Living Language® Japanese Dictionary*. It contains more than 15,000 entries, with many of the definitions illustrated by phrases and idiomatic expressions. More than 1,000 of the most essential words are capitalized to make them easy to find. You can increase your vocabulary and range of expression just by browsing through the dictionary.

Practice your Japanese as much as possible. Even if you can't manage a trip abroad, watching Japanese movies, reading Japanese magazines, eating at Japanese restaurants, and talking with Japanese-speaking friends are enjoyable ways to help you reinforce what you have learned with *Living Language® Japanese*. Now, let's begin. The following instructions will tell you what to do.

COURSE MATERIAL

1. Two 90-minute cassettes or three 60-minute compact discs.

2. *Living Language® Japanese Coursebook*. This book is designed for use with the recorded lessons, but it may also be used alone as a reference. It contains the following sections: basic Japanese in forty lessons, a summary of Japanese grammar, verb conjugations, and a section on letter writing.

3. *Living Language® Japanese Dictionary*. The Japanese/English–English/Japanese dictionary contains more than 15,000 entries. Phrases and idiomatic expressions illustrate many of the definitions. More than 1,000 of the most essential words are capitalized.

INSTRUCTIONS

1. Look at page 5. The words in **boldface** type are the ones you will hear on the recording.

2. Now read Lesson 1 all the way through. Note the points to listen for when you play the recording. The first word you will hear is **Akira.**

3. Start the recording, listen carefully, and say the words aloud in the pauses provided. Go through the lesson once and don't worry if you can't pronounce everything correctly the first time around. Try it again and keep repeating the lesson until you are comfortable with it. The more often you listen and repeat, the longer you will remember the material.

4. Now go on to the next lesson. If you take a break between lessons, it's always good to review the previous lesson before starting a new one.

5. In the manual, there are two kinds of quizzes. With matching quizzes, you must select the English translation of the Japanese sentence. The other type requires you to fill in the blanks with the correct Japanese word chosen from the three given directly below the sentence. If you make any mistakes, reread the section.

6. Even after you have finished the forty lessons and scored 100 percent on the final quiz, keep practicing your Japanese by listening to the recordings and speaking with Japanese-speaking friends. For further study, try *Living Language® Ultimate Japanese* and *Ultimate Japanese Advanced.*

LIVING LANGUAGE®

JAPANESE
COURSEBOOK

REVISED & UPDATED

LESSON 1

DAI IKKA

A. A PRELIMINARY NOTE

Japanese, as spoken by the majority of Japan's 120 million people, is the language you will be learning in this course. Not only can it be used throughout Japan, but also, to a limited extent, in Korea, Taiwan, and some parts of Southeast Asia.

Japanese is peculiarly original among the world's languages. Despite the fact that more than half the words in Japanese were borrowed from Chinese, the linguistic structure of Japanese is quite different from that of Chinese. And although Japanese grammar is amazingly similar to Korean, and both languages share some vocabulary adopted from Chinese, the two differ from each other in all other respects.

There are several things you should know and remember to make your understanding of Japanese easier:

1. Japanese syllables can be classified into five kinds:

   a. a vowel by itself
   b. a consonant by itself
   c. a consonant + a vowel
   d. a semi-vowel + a vowel
   e. a consonant + *y* + a vowel

2. In Japanese, verbs, adjectives, copulas (linking words), and certain endings are inflected in a number of categories.

3. Japanese has many so-called "particles." They are used very frequently to show the grammatical relationship within a sentence of one word to another. Mastery of these particles is a key to the rapid learning of Japanese.

4. Punctuation is used in Japanese as it is in English. The use of punctuation marks in the Japanese writing system is relatively new, and rules governing punctuation usage have not yet been firmly established.

5. The word order of Japanese sentences differs from the word order of English sentences. In Japanese, verbs come at the end of a sentence, rather than following the subject and preceding the object as they do in English.

6. Japanese has a complex system of "honorifics," words that reflect the relationship between the speakers and whom they are speaking about. Different words and word forms are used to indicate the degrees of politeness. This concept is similar to the French differentiation between "vous" and "tu," but in Japanese, there are more than a dozen ways to say "you." This book uses the most standard forms of the language, so that, unless otherwise indicated, each phrase can be said by both men and women in most situations without sounding too casual or too formal.

B. THE ALPHABET: THE LETTERS

All Japanese words and sentences in this course have been transcribed into Roman letters, and all the letters of the English alphabet (except for "l,"[1] "q," and "x") appear in the transcription. Note, however, that the letter "c" appears only in combination with "h" and that these two letters together (ch) are *always treated as one letter*.

A comprehensive list of signs and instructions in Japanese characters (including their English meanings) appears in Lesson 40. An explanation of the traditional Japanese writing system and a description of Japanese characters appear in the section called "The Writing System." For a discussion of the Japanese Syllabary, see Lesson 5.

C. ACCENT

Regardless of their length, Japanese words may or may not be accented. When a word is accented, there is a drop in the pitch of the voice in the syllable that directly follows the accented syllable. If a word is unaccented, the pitch is always slightly lower on the first syllable, and thereafter the pitch is held at an even level. In accented words, the pitch drops directly after the accented syllable and then is held at an even level throughout the rest of the word. If a one-syllable word is accented, the drop in pitch occurs after that word.

Note that accents may be dropped in certain cases, depending on the placement of a word in a sentence and on the dialect of the speaker. The best way for a student to grasp the complex rules governing accentuation in Japanese is to listen closely to the recordings that accompany this course or to native speakers of Japanese.

---

[1] The sound of *l* is sometimes heard in the pronunciation of Japanese by Japanese nationals. But this sound is always interchangeable with the Japanese variety of *r*. For the sake of simplicity, all sounds that might sometimes be pronounced *l* are written throughout this course as *r*.

D. THE ALPHABET: THE SOUNDS

Many Japanese sounds are like sounds in English. Listen and repeat the following Japanese first names, and notice which sounds are similar and which are different:

Akira	Haruo	Noboru
Aiko	Hideko	Nobuko
Atsuko	Isoo	Osamu
Chieko	Itoko	Rentaroo
Emiko	Jiroo	Ryuuichi
Eijiroo	Jun	Shinzoo
Fusao	Kiyoshi	Susumu
Fusako	Kuniko	Takashi
Gantaroo	Makoto	Teruko
Giichi	Mariko	Umeko

NOTE

1. Each sound is pronounced clearly and crisply; sounds are not slurred over as they often are in English.

2. Each syllable is spoken evenly for almost an equal length of time.

3. Some names or words have an accented syllable and some don't.

E. LOAN WORDS: ENGLISH WORDS USED IN JAPANESE

Now listen to and repeat the following words. These are some of the thousands of English "loan words" used in Japan. While the meanings of these loan words

are the same as those of their English counterparts,
notice how the Japanese spelling and pronunciation
differ from the English:

akusento	accent
amachua	amateur
Amerika	America
baree	ballet
basu	bus
bataa	butter
beru	bell
booto	rowboat
chokoreeto	chocolate
daiyamondo	diamond
dansu	dance
dezaato	dessert
dezain	design
enameru	enamel
erebeetaa	elevator
esukareetaa	escalator
furanneru	flannel
gaido	guide (for travelers)
gasorin	gasoline
gareeji	garage
gorufu	golf
haihiiru	high heel
handobaggu	handbag
herikoputaa	helicopter
hisuterii	hysteria, hysterics
hoosu	water hose
hoomushikku	homesick
hoteru	hotel
infure	inflation
inku	ink
interi	intelligentsia
jaanarisuto	journalist

jamu	jam, jelly
jazu	jazz
kappu	cup (trophy, measuring)
koppu	drinking glass
karee raisu	curried rice
karendaa	calendar
maagarin	margarine
maaketto	market
maaku	mark
modan	modern
nairon	nylon

LESSON 2

DAI NIKA

A. VOWELS

The following groups of words will give you some additional practice in spelling and pronunciation. Listen to the vowel sounds in each word.

1. The sound *a* is pronounced as in the English word "ah" or "father," but short and crisp:

hanasu	tell	**kata**	shoulder
akai	red	*wakai*	young

2. The sound *i* is pronounced like the "e" in the English word "keep," but short and crisp:

i	stomach	**ni**	two
ki	tree	*hi*	fire

3. The sound *u* is pronounced as in the English word "put," but spoken without rounding the lips:

ushi	cow, bull	**kutsu**	shoes
kushi	comb	*tsukue*	desk

4. The sound *e* is pronounced like the "a" in the English word "may," but without the final "y":

e	picture	**te**	hand
ke	hair	*me*	eye

5. The sound *o* is pronounced as in the English word "go," but sharply cut off:

o	tail	**otoko**	male
oto	sound	*soto*	outside

B. VOWEL CLUSTERS

1. When two identical vowels such as *aa, ii, uu, ee,* or *oo* appear together, they form a sound twice as long as that of a single vowel. Compare the following pairs:

kado	corner	**kaado**	card
chizu	map	**chiizu**	cheese
su	nest	**suu**	number (*particle*)
deta	came out	**deeta**	data
to	door	**too**	ten

Sometimes a pair of identical vowels is called a "long vowel" or a "double vowel," and it can be written as a single letter with a macron over it, e.g., *ā, ū, ē,* and *ō*. However, "long" or "double" *i* is usually written *ii*:

koohii,	coffee	**kuuki,**	air
kōhii		*kūki*	
kaaten,	curtain	*keeki,*	cake
kāten		*kēki*	

2. In a succession of two or more different vowels, each vowel is pronounced clearly and distinctly, and each is articulated for the same length of time:

ue	top	**akai**	red
tsukue	desk	**aoi**	blue
chiisai	small	*aoi umi*	blue ocean
chiisai ie	small house	*aoi kao*	pale face

The combination *ei* forms an exception to this rule, for in everyday speech *ei* is often pronounced like *ee:*

keiko	practice	**Beikoku**	The United
(said		(said	States of
keeko)		*Beekoku*)	America
seito	pupil,	*seinen*	youth
(said	student	(said	
seeto)		*seenen*)	

C. Devoiced Vowels

The vowels *i* and *u* are "weak" or "devoiced" vowels. Unless they are accented, they sometimes disappear altogether or are whispered in rapid conversation. Devoicing usually occurs when these vowels are surrounded by such voiceless consonants as *ch, f, h, k, p, s, sh, t,* and *ts;* or in a word immediately following one of the voiceless consonants. In the following examples, the vowel with a circle underneath is a devoiced vowel:

ki̥tte	postage stamp	**zehi̥**	by all means
ku̥tsushi̥ta	socks	**su̥kkari**	entirely

However, the devoicing of vowels is not crucial. Unlike the case of single vowel vs. double vowel shown in B-1 above, voicing vs. devoicing does not change the meaning.

LESSON 3

DAI SANKA

A. CONSONANTS I

1. *B* is generally pronounced like the English "b," but less explosively:

bentoo	box lunch	*binsen*	writing pad
kaban	briefcase	*obon*	tray

2. *Ch* is pronounced like the English "ch" in "cheese":

ocha	tea	*uchi*	house
chotto	a little bit	*chuui*	caution

3. *D* is pronounced with the tip of the tongue touching the back of the upper teeth and is less explosive than the English "d":

| **dare** | who | *densha* | streetcar |
| **doko** | where | *kado* | corner |

4. *F* is usually pronounced by forcing the air out between the lips as though blowing out a candle. Note that this consonant resembles the English "wh."

| **fune** | ship | *furo* | bath |
| **fukai** | deep | *futatsu* | two |

5. The Japanese *g* has two sounds:

a. At the beginning of a word, it is pronounced like the English "g" in "go":

| **gaikoku** | foreign country | *genryoo* | raw material |
| **gin** | silver | *go* | five |

b. In the middle of a word, it usually has some nasal quality and sounds something like the "ng" of the English word "singer":

| **hagaki** | postcard | *kagi* | key |
| **kage** | shadow | *kagu* | household furniture |

6. The Japanese *h* has two sounds:

a. Before *a, e,* and *o,* it is pronounced like the English "h" in "high":

| **hai** | yes | **hon** | book |
| *hei* | fence | *hoo* | cheek |

b. Before *i* or *y*, it is pronounced like the English "h" in "hue":

higashi	east	**hyaku**	one hundred
hiru	noon	*hyooshi*	rhythm

7. *J* is pronounced like the English "j" in "jeep":

jagaimo	potato	**shookaijoo**	letter of introduction
jibiki	dictionary	*juku*	cram school

8. *K* is pronounced like the English "k" in "kite":

kasa	umbrella	**koya**	hut
kesa	this morning	*kutsu*	shoes

9. *M* is pronounced like an English "m," but without tightening the lips as much:

maiasa	every morning	**mikan**	tangerine
me	eye	*mushi*	bug

10. *N* has two sounds in Japanese:

a. Before *a*, *e*, *o*, and *u*, it is pronounced with the tip of the tongue touching the back of the upper teeth:

nashi	pear	**nodo**	throat
neko	cat	*numa*	marsh

b. Before *i* or *y*, it is pronounced like the "n" in the English word "news" (with the tip of the tongue touching the back of the lower teeth and the middle part of the tongue touching the roof of the mouth):

niku	meat	**gyuunyuu**	cow's milk
nishi	west	*nyuuin*	hospitalization

11. *P* is pronounced like the English "p," but less explosively:

pan	bread	**pin**	pin
pen	pen	*sanpun*	three minutes

12. *R* is pronounced by first placing the tip of the tongue at the back of the upper teeth and then flapping it.[1]

raigetsu	next month	**riku**	land
renga	brick	*roku*	six

LESSON 4

DAI YONKA

A. CONSONANTS II

1. *S* is pronounced like the English "s" in "song," but with less hiss:

saka	slope	**sora**	sky
sekai	world	*su*	vinegar

---

[1] For more on the sound of *r*, refer to the footnote on page 3.

2. *Sh* resembles the English "sh" in "she":

shashin	photograph	**shooko**	proof
shichi	seven	*shuto*	capital city

3. *T* is pronounced with the tip of the tongue touching the back of the upper teeth and is less explosive than the English "t":

tamago	egg	**te**	hand
takusan	a lot	*to*	door

4. *Ts* is pronounced like the English "ts" in "cats":

natsu	summer	*atsui*	hot
tsunami	tidal wave	*tsutsuji*	azalea

5. *V* is pronounced like the English "v" in "vain." This sound appears only in words borrowed from Occidental languages. Note that most Japanese do not use this sound at all but replace it with a *b*, as follows:

vaiorin	violin	**baiorin**	violin
veeru	veil	**beeru**	veil
viniiru	vinyl	*biniiru*	vinyl
revyuu	revue	*rebyuu*	revue

6. *Z* usually has two sounds in Japanese:

   a. At the beginning of a word it has a sound similar to the English "ds" in "beds":

zaisei	finance	**zoo**	elephant
zeitaku	luxury	*zutto*	by far

b. In the middle of a word it is pronounced like the English "z" in "zero":

kaze	wind	*mizu*	water
suzume	sparrow	*kazoku*	family

Note that some Japanese mix the *dz* and *z* sounds described above without regard to the position of the letter in the word.

7. *P, t, k,* or *s* can be a syllable by itself.[1] To pronounce such a syllabic consonant, hold the tongue position abruptly for one beat before the next syllable is pronounced.

a. When a syllabic consonant (*p, t, k,* or *s*) is followed by the same consonant, they are called "double consonants" and the sound is doubled in length. Note the differences in pronunciation between the following pairs of words. The first word in each pair contains a single consonant and the second contains double consonants:

haka	tomb	**hakka**	peppermint
kasai	fire damage	**kassai**	applause
moto	formerly	*motto*	more

b. Syllabic *t* can be followed by *ch* or *ts,* and *s* can be followed by *sh:*

itchi	agreement	**irasshai**	welcome
ittsuu	one letter	*kesshin*	determination

[1] In words borrowed from Western languages (loan words), *d* or *g* can also be a syllable by itself.

8. The syllabic *n* represents another group of sounds that is independent of the *n* described above in Item 10. In this manual, the syllabic *n* is written like the ordinary *n*. Remember, however, that it differs in pronunciation from the ordinary *n* as follows:

a. It is always held as long as one full syllable.
b. Its own sound value changes, depending on what follows.

   (1) Before *n*, *t*, and *d*, it is pronounced like the English "n" in "pen":

anna	that sort of	**santoo**	third class
onna	female	*kondo*	this time

   (2) Before *m*, *p*, or *b*, it is pronounced like the English "m":

SPELLED	PRONOUNCED	
sanmai	**sammai**	three sheets
shinpai	*shimpai*	worry
kanban	*kamban*	signboard

   (3) Before a vowel or a semi-vowel (*y* or *w*), it is pronounced somewhat like the English *ng* in "singer," but without finishing the *g* sound; the preceding vowel is often nasalized:

gen'an[1]	original plan
tan'i	unit
hon'ya	bookstore
minwa	folklore

[1] Notice that an apostrophe is placed after a syllabic *n* when it precedes a vowel or *y*.

Note that in the following pairs of words, the first has an ordinary *n* and the second has a syllabic *n:*

| **tani** | valley | **tan'i** | unit |
| *zenin* | approval | *zen'in* | all members |

(4) Before *k, g,* and *s,* or when it is the final letter in a word, the syllabic *n* sounds somewhat like the English "ng" in "singer" described in (3) above:

kankei	relationship	*sensei*	teacher
ningen	human beings	*san*	three
sen	one thousand	*kin*	gold

B. SEMI-VOWELS

1. *W* is pronounced somewhat like the English "w" in "want," but without rounding or protruding the lips:

| **watakushi**[1] | I (formal) | **kawa** | river |
| *watashi* | (informal) | *uwagi* | jacket |

2. *Y* occurs in two kinds of environments:

a. It occurs before a vowel (e.g., *ya, yu, yo*) and is pronounced like the English "y" in "yellow":

| **yama** | mountain | **hayai** | fast |
| *yoru* | night | *fuyu* | winter |

---

[1] The use of formal and informal forms is very complicated. It depends on the speaker and the particular situation. Women are more likely than men to use the formal form of the word.

b. It occurs between a consonant and a vowel. Then the consonant is palatalized (said with the tongue touching the palate):

kyaku	guest	**ryoodo**	territory
happyoo	announcement	*kyuu*	nine

LESSON 5

DAI GOKA

A. THE JAPANESE SYLLABARY

The traditional writing system used in Japan is based on two different types of symbols: phonetic and ideographic. (See "The Writing System" for a detailed explanation.) The phonetic symbols are the Japanese equivalents of our alphabet and are called *kana*. Each *kana* symbol stands for a syllable.

These are the basic syllables represented in *kana:*[1]

a	ka	sa	ta	na	ha	ma	ya	ra	wa	n (syllabic)
i	ki	shi	chi	ni	hi	mi		ri		
u	ku	su	tsu	nu	fu	mu	yu	ru		
e	ke	se	te	ne	he	me		re		
o	ko	so	to	no	ho	mo	yo	ro	o[2]	

[1] For non-basic syllables, see "The Writing System," page 376.
[2] These two *o* sounds are pronounced the same but their uses differ. For details, see "The Writing System," page 376.

B. GENERAL SOUND EQUIVALENTS

1. Japanese *aa* = English "ar," "er," "ir," "or":

apaato	apartment	*saakasu*	circus
pitchaa	pitcher (baseball)	*mootaa*	motor

2. Japanese *ee* = English "a":

geemu	game	*teeburu*	table
keeki	cake	*keeburu*	cable (car)

3. Japanese *oo* = English "o," "oa":

boonasu	bonus	*hoomuran*	home run
booto	boat	*koochi*	coach (athletic)

4. Japanese *ui* = English "ui," "wi":

kuizu	quiz (radio, TV program)	*uitto*	wit

5. Japanese *b* = English "v":

terebi	television	*shaberu*	shovel

6. Japanese *chi* = English "ti":

chippu	tip	*chiimu*	team

7. Japanese *ji* = English "di":

rajio	radio	*jirenma*	dilemma
sutajio	studio (art, broadcasting, movie)		

8. Japanese *k* = English "c":

kakuteru	cocktail	*kamera*	camera
Amerika	America	*konsarutanto*	consultant

9. Japanese *kku* = English "ack," "ock":

barakku	barrack
dokku	dock

10. Japanese *kki* = English "eck," "ick":

dekki	deck
sutekki	stick (walking)

11. Japanese *ru* = English "l," "rl":

hoteru	hotel	*kaaru*	curl
booru	ball		

12. Japanese *suto* = English "st":

sutoraiki,	strike	*jaanarisuto*	journalist
or **suto**	(labor)		
pianisuto	pianist		

13. Japanese *tto* = English "t":

maaketto	market	*soketto*	socket
pan-	pamphlet	*yotto*	yacht
furetto			

14. Japanese *tsu* = English "t":

jaketto,	jacket	*shatsu*	shirt
or **jaketsu**	(sweater)		
omuretsu	omelet		

15. Japanese *s* = English "th":

suriru thrill *oosoritii* authority

C. More Loan Words

As you have already observed, a great number of
English words have been adopted by the Japanese and
are in everyday use. The following is a list of some
more loan words.

apaato	apartment house	*geemu*	game
		gorira	gorilla
aribai	alibi	*guruupu*	group
arufabetto	alphabet	*haamonika*	harmonica
arukooru	alcohol	*hoomuran*	home run
asupirin	aspirin	*infuruenza*	influenza
batto	bat (base-ball)	*iyahoon*	earphone
		jiguzagu	zigzag
booi sukauto	boy scout	*jirenma*	dilemma
boonasu	bonus	*karorii*	calorie
booru	ball	*keeki*	cake (Occidental)
burashi	brush		
daasu	dozen	*konkuriito*	concrete
dainamaito	dynamite	*kooto*	coat
damu	dam	*koruku*	cork
dorama	drama	*kurabu*	club
doru	dollar	*kureyon*	crayon
emerarudo	emerald	*kuriimu*	cream
episoodo	episode	*kuriiningu*	cleaning
feruto	felt	*kuupon*	coupon
gaaru sukauto	girl scout	*makaroni*	macaroni
		massaaji	massage

masukotto	mascot	*ribon*	ribbon
medaru	medal	*roketto*	rocket
megahon	megaphone	*romansu*	romance
memo	memo	*saakasu*	circus
menyuu	menu	*sairen*	siren
mootaa	motor	*sakkarin*	saccharine
motto	motto	*sandoitchi*	sandwich
neonsain	neon sign	*sararii*	salary
onsu	ounce	*shaberu*	shovel
oosoritii	authority	*shoouindoo*	show
ootobai	motorcycle		window
	(auto-	*soketto*	socket
	bicycle)	*sooseeji*	sausage
ootomiiru	oatmeal	*supai*	spy
Orinpikku	Olympic	*supiido*	speed
	Games	*surippa*	slipper
paasento	percent	*sutereo*	stereo
pai	pie	*suutsu*	suitcase
painappuru	pineapple	*keesu*	
panfuretto	pamphlet	*taipuraitaa*	typewriter
panku	flat tire	*tairu*	tile
	(puncture)	*takushii*	taxi
panorama	panorama	*tanku*	tank
parupu	pulp	*taoru*	towel
pasupooto	passport	*teeburu*	table
pianisuto	pianist	*tonneru*	tunnel
poketto	pocket		(railroad)
raion	lion	*torakku*	truck
rajuumu	radium	*ueetoresu*	waitress
reinkooto	raincoat	*uranyuumu*	uranium
resutoran	restaurant	*yotto*	yacht
	(Occi-	*yuumoa*	humor
	dental)		

Note that when a word from English is used in Japanese, not only is the *sound* of the word changed to harmonize with the Japanese sound system, but the *length* of the word may be cut, as in the following examples:

infure	inflation
panku	puncture (flat tire)
pasokon	personal computer
terebi	television

Notice that some words are used in a more restricted sense in Japanese than in English. Here are some more words borrowed from English that are used in a restricted or altered sense in Japanese:

JAPANESE FORM	WORD OF ORIGIN	BUT MEANS IN JAPANESE
barakku	barrack	shack; shabby-looking, flimsy wooden house
biru *birudingu*	building	Occidental-style concrete office building
bisuketto	biscuits	tea biscuits and cookies
doa	door	Occidental-style door
doramu	drum	drum (musical only; refers mainly to types used in jazz)
jamu	jam	jam and jelly
kappu	cup	trophy, measuring cup
konpasu	compass	compass (instrument for drawing circles)
manshon	mansion	condominium (or high-class apartment)
mishin	machine	sewing machine
nooto	note	notebook
paipu	pipe	pipe (for smoking)
raitaa	lighter	cigarette lighter
sutoroo	straw	drinking straw

LESSON 6

DAI ROKKA

A. Days and Months

Getsuyoobi	Monday
Kayoobi	Tuesday
Suiyoobi	Wednesday
Mokuyoobi	Thursday
Kin'yoobi	Friday
Doyoobi	Saturday
Nichiyoobi	Sunday

Ichigatsu	January
Nigatsu	February
Sangatsu	March
Shigatsu	April
Gogatsu	May
Rokugatsu	June
Shichigatsu	July
Hachigatsu	August
Kugatsu	September
Juugatsu	October
Juuichigatsu	November
Juunigatsu	December

B. Numbers 1–10

ichi	one
ni	two
san	three
shi, yon	four
go	five
roku	six

shichi, nana	seven
hachi	eight
kyuu, ku	nine
juu	ten

C. Colors

ao	blue
aka	red
kiiro	yellow
midori	green
shiro	white
kuro	black
chairo	brown
nezumiiro, haiiro	gray

D. North, South, East, West

| kita | north | higashi | east |
| minami | south | nishi | west |

QUIZ 1

Match the Japanese and English words in these two columns:

1. *Nichiyoobi*   a. Thursday
2. *Hachigatsu*   b. brown
3. *Suiyoobi*   c. ten
4. *nezumiiro*   d. Sunday
5. *Mokuyoobi*   e. red
6. *ku*   f. August
7. *chairo*   g. Monday
8. *hachi*   h. July
9. *Shichigatsu*   i. five
10. *kiiro*   j. white

11. *aka*   k. gray
12. *Getsuyoobi*   l. nine
13. *go*   m. Wednesday
14. *shiro*   n. yellow
15. *juu*   o. eight

ANSWERS
1—d; 2—f; 3—m; 4—k; 5—a; 6—l; 7—b; 8—o;
9—h; 10—n; 11—e; 12—g; 13—i; 14—j; 15—c.

E. WORD STUDY

fiito	feet
garon	gallon
guramu	gram
inchi	inch
kiromeetoru	kilometer
mairu	mile
meetoru	meter
pondo	pound
rittoru	liter
yaado	yard

LESSON 7

DAI NANAKA

A. GREETINGS

Now let's study some of the greetings you'll use right from the start. The words in brackets are literal translations.

Ohayoo gozaimasu.	Good morning.
Yamada-san[1]	Mr. Yamada
Yamada-san, ohayoo gozaimasu.	Good morning, Mr. Yamada.
Konnichi wa.	Good afternoon. [Good day.]
Konban wa.	Good evening.
Oyasumi nasai.	Good night (*said just before going to bed*).
Ogenki desu ka?	How are you? [Are you in good spirits?]
genki	well [good spirits]
Genki desu.	I am very well.
Arigatoo gozaimasu.	Thank you.
Okagesama de.	Thank you. [Due to your kind thought, am well.]
Onamae wa nan to osshaimasu ka?	What is your name?
Onamae wa?	What is your name?
Yamada Masao to mooshimasu.[2]	My name is Yamada Masao.[2]
Yamada desu.	I am Yamada.
Watakushi no namae wa Yamada desu.	My name is Yamada.
Gomen nasai.	Excuse me. I'm sorry.
Ii desu.	That's all right.

[1] The suffix *-san* is used in Japanese as a term of respect meaning "Mr.," "Mrs.," "Miss," "Sir," or "Madam."

[2] Japanese people use their last names before their first names; therefore, Yamada is the last name of the person speaking. When giving their names in English, however, Japanese people usually adopt the Western order. For a Western name, even while speaking Japanese, the Western order is also usually used.

yukkuri	slowly
Yukkuri hanashite kudasai.	Please speak slowly.
doozo	please
Doozo yukkuri hanashite kudasai.	Please speak slowly.
moo ichido	once more
Itte kudasai.	Please say [it].
Moo ichido itte kudasai.	Please repeat that. [Say it once more, please.]
Doozo moo ichido itte kudasai.	Please repeat that. [Please say it once more.]
doomo	very much [indeed!]
Doomo arigatoo gozaimasu.	Thank you very much.
Doo itashimashite.	Not at all.
Arigatoo gozaimashita.	Thank you (*for what you have done*).
Kochira koso.	It was a pleasure. [It was my side (that should have thanked).]
Dewa ashita.	Till tomorrow. See you tomorrow. [Well, then, tomorrow.]
Dewa Doyoobi ni.	Till Saturday. See you Saturday. [Well, then, on Saturday.]
Dewa Getsuyoobi ni.	Till Monday. See you Monday.
Dewa Mokuyoobi ni.	Till Thursday. See you Thursday.
Dewa konban.	Till this evening. See you this evening.

Dewa ashita no ban.   Till tomorrow evening. See you tomorrow evening.

Dewa raishuu.   Till next week. See you next week.

Dewa mata.   See you later. [Well, then, again.]

Dewa sono uchi ni.   See you sometime.

Sayonara.   Good-bye.

B. How's the Weather?

Kyoo no tenki wa doo desu ka?   How's the weather today? What's the weather like today?

Ii tenki desu.   It's nice weather.

Kyoo wa tenki ga warui desu.   The weather is bad today.

Ame ga futte imasu.   It's raining.

Yuki ga futte imasu.   It's snowing.

Atsui desu.   It's hot.

Samui desu.   It's cold.

Suzushii desu.   It's cool.

QUIZ 2

1. *Genki desu.* a. Please speak.
2. *Konban wa.* b. once more
3. *Hanashite kudasai.* c. It's hot.
4. *Arigatoo gozaimasu.* d. See you tomorrow.
5. *moo ichido* e. How are you?
6. *Doozo.* f. I am very well.
7. *Atsui desu.* g. slowly
8. *Dewa ashita.* h. Thank you.
9. *Ogenki desu ka?* i. Please.
10. *yukkuri* j. Good evening.

ANSWERS
1—f; 2—j; 3—a; 4—h; 5—b; 6—i; 7—c; 8—d;
9—e; 10—g.

LESSON 8

DAI HACHIKA

A. DO YOU HAVE?

In the phrases below, you will see the particles *ka* and
ga. Particles are an important part of basic grammar
and will be studied in Lesson 11. For now, understand
that particles indicate the relationship between the
words or parts of a phrase. For example, the particle
ka is used at the end of an interrogative sentence and
shows that what precedes it is a question. The particle
ga is used to show that what precedes it is the grammatical subject of a verb. Also, note that there is usually no translation in Japanese for "some" or "any."

Arimasu ka?	Do you have . . . ? [Is there . . . ?]
mizu ga	some water *(as the subject of the verb)*
tabako ga	some (any) cigarettes
hi ga	a light
matchi ga	some matches
sekken ga	some soap
kami ga	some paper

Mizu ga¹ arimasu ka?   Do you have some water?
Tabako ga arimasu ka?   Do you have any cigarettes?

B. IN A RESTAURANT

asagohan	breakfast
hirugohan	lunch
bangohan	supper
Irasshaimase.	Welcome.
Nani o meshiagari-masu ka?	What would you like to eat?
Misete kudasai.	Show me . . . , please.
Menyuu o misete kudasai.	Show me a menu, please.
. . . kudasai.	I'd like [Please give me . . .]
Pan o kudasai.	I'd like some bread, please.
pan o	some bread
bataa o	some butter
suupu o	some soup
niku o	some meat
gyuuniku o	some beef
tamago o	some eggs
yasai o	some vegetables
jagaimo o	some potatoes
sarada o	some salad
miruku o	some milk
wain o	some wine
satoo o	some sugar
shio o	some salt
koshoo o	some pepper

¹ Note that in the English equivalent, "water" is the object of "have," but *mizu* (water) is followed by the particle *ga* (the subject marker; see above). This also holds true for the rest of the sentences in the section.

yakizakana o	some broiled fish
miso shiru o	some miso soup (made with bean paste)
sashimi o	some sashimi (raw fish)
tenpura o	some tempura (fritter; deep-fried food)
Motte kite kudasai . . .	Please bring me . . .
Suupu o motte kite kudasai.	Please bring me some soup.
tiisupuun o	a teaspoon
fooku o	a fork
naifu o	a knife
napukin o	a napkin
sara o	a plate
koppu o	a glass
. . . ippai kudasai.	I'd like [Please give me] a glass of . . .
. . . hitobin kudasai.	I'd like [Please give me] a bottle of . . .
Mizu o ippai kudasai.	Please give me a glass of water.
ocha o ippai	a cup of tea
koohii o ippai	a cup of coffee
wain o ippon	a bottle of wine
biiru o ippon	a bottle of beer
tamago o moo hitotsu	another egg
sore o sukoshi	a little of that
sore o moo sukoshi	a little more of that
pan o moo sukoshi	some more bread, a little more bread
niku o motto	some more meat
niku o moo sukoshi	a little more meat
Chekku o motte kite kudasai.	The check, please.

QUIZ 3

1. *niku o*	a. please bring me
2. *biiru o*	b. matches
3. *arimasu ka?*	c. please give me
4. *miruku o*	d. meat
5. *bataa o*	e. some water
6. *kudasai*	f. a light
7. *matchi o*	g. milk
8. *niku o moo sukoshi*	h. eggs
9. *motte kite kudasai*	i. beer
10. *mizu o*	j. the check
11. *hi o*	k. Do you have . . .
12. *shio o*	l. butter
13. *tamago o*	m. a cup of coffee
14. *koohii o ippai*	n. some more meat
15. *chekku o*	o. salt

ANSWERS
1—d; 2—i; 3—k; 4—g; 5—l; 6—c; 7—b; 8—n;
9—a; 10—e; 11—f; 12—o; 13—h; 14—m; 15—j.

C. WORD STUDY

burausu	blouse
hankachi	handkerchief
nekutai	necktie
oobaakooto	overcoat
seetaa	sweater
shatsu	shirt
sukaafu	scarf
sukaato	skirt
surippu	slip

LESSON 9

DAI KYUUKA

This lesson and several of the following lessons are longer than the others. They contain the grammatical information you need to know from the start. Don't try to memorize anything; just read each section until you understand every point. Then, as you continue with the course, try to observe examples of the points mentioned. Refer back to these sections and to the Summary of Japanese Grammar at the back of the book as necessary. In this way you will eventually find that you have a good grasp of the basic features of Japanese grammar without any deliberate memorizing of rules.

A. PRONOUNS

Personal pronouns are used much less frequently in Japanese than in English. The context clarifies what or who is being referred to or addressed. In addition, in Japanese there are more varieties of words that correspond to English pronouns. The list below will help you follow the sections to come, but be sure to study Section 12 of the Summary of Japanese Grammar for more information.

I	**watashi**, watakushi[1]
you	**anata**[2]
he/she	**ano hito**
he	**kare**

[1] The form *watakushi*, while official, is less conversational than *watashi*.
[2] *Anata* and *anatagata* are usually to be avoided. It is more polite to use the person's name.

she	**kanojo**
we	**watashitachi,** watakushitachi
you (*pl.*)[1]	**anatagata**[2]
they	**ano hitotachi,** karera

B. To Be or Not to Be

1. There is more than one way to say "is" in Japanese. A different word is used for this English verb in each of the following sentences:

Enpitsu desu.	It is a pencil.
Enpitsu ga arimasu.[3]	There is a pencil.
Nyuu Yooku ni imasu.	He is in New York.

a. When you say that one thing is equal to another, you use *desu*. Its meaning roughly corresponds to "am, is, are."

b. When you are talking about something being located or situated in a place, use *arimasu* if the thing referred to is inanimate.

c. Use *imasu* if the thing referred to is animate.

Note that *desu* is called the *copula*. *Arimasu* and *imasu* are ordinary verbs and are inflected like other verbs, which you will begin to study in Lesson 10. Also, the negative of *desu* has its own particular forms; see below.

---

[1] Throughout this book *pl.* stands for "plural" and *sg.* stands for "singular."

[2] *Anata* and *anatagata* are usually to be avoided. It is more polite to use the person's name.

[3] This sentence is ambiguous; it can also mean "(I) have a pencil." See Lessons 8 and 14 for phrases with "have."

2. Study these examples with *desu, arimasu,* and *imasu:*

a. *Sore wa enpitsu desu.*

That is a pencil. (A equals B.)

b. *Soko ni enpitsu ga arimasu.*

There is a pencil there. (A—inanimate—is located at B.)

c. *Soko ni kodomo ga imasu.*

There is a child there. (A—animate—is located at B.)

a. *Sore wa tabako desu ka?*

Is that a cigarette?

b. *Tabako ga arimasu ka?*

Is a cigarette there?

c. *Yamada-san wa soko ni imasu ka?*

Is Mr. Yamada there?

a. *Shikago wa ookii machi desu.*

Chicago is a big city.

b. *Shikago wa Irinoishuu ni arimasu.*

Chicago is in the state of Illinois.

c. *Yamada-san wa Shikago ni imasu.*

Mr. Yamada is in Chicago.

3. Listen for examples of these forms in the phrases below. Notice that the word or phrase that equals the element "A" (as used in the phrases above) is marked with the particle *wa* or *ga. Wa* is used when the emphasis in the sentence is not on "A." *Ga* is used to emphasize "A." The word or phrase equaling the element "B" always comes immediately before *desu.* (If no specific noun is used for "B," use *soo* in its place, for *desu* can never be used alone.)

Anata wa Amerikajin desu ka?	Are you an American?
Hai, soo desu.	Yes, I am. [Yes, am so.]
tatemono	building
taishikan	embassy
Dono tatemono ga Amerika Taishikan desu ka?	Which building is the American Embassy?
Ano tatemono wa Amerika Taishikan desu.	That building is the American Embassy.
Ano tatemono ga soo desu.	That building is. [That building is so.]
Ano tatemono ga Amerika Taishikan desu ka?	Is that building the American Embassy?
Hai, soo desu.	Yes, it is. [Yes, is so.]
Sumisu-san wa Amerika Taishikan ni imasu.	Mr. Smith is in the American Embassy.
Tanaka-san wa Too-kyoo ni imasu.	Ms. Tanaka is in Tokyo.
Okinawa wa doko ni arimasu ka?	Where is Okinawa?
Nippon to Taiwan no aida ni arimasu.	It is between Japan and Taiwan.
Dono kata ga Tanaka-san desu ka?	Which person is Ms. Tanaka?
Watashi ga Tanaka desu.	I am. [Am Tanaka.]
Watashi ga soo desu.	I am [so].
Sore wa tabako desu.	That is a cigarette.
Enpitsu ga arimasu ka?	Do you have a pencil? Is there a pencil?

Kodomo wa Tookyoo ni   The child is in Tokyo.
imasu.

Tabako ga arimasu.   I have a cigarette.
                             There is a cigarette.

C. DESU

1. Compare the following different forms of *desu* in the affirmative:

present or future	*A wa B desu.*	A is B.
past	*A wa B deshita.*	A was B.
tentative	*A wa B deshoo.*	A is probably B.
tentative past	*A wa B datta deshoo.*	A was probably B.

2. The negative forms of the above are:

present or future	*A wa B* $\begin{Bmatrix} ja \\ dewa \end{Bmatrix}$	*arimasen.*	A is not B.
	A wa B $\begin{Bmatrix} ja \\ dewa \end{Bmatrix}$	*nai desu.*	
past	*A wa B* $\begin{Bmatrix} ja \\ dewa \end{Bmatrix}$	*arimasen deshita.*[1]	A was not B.
	A wa B $\begin{Bmatrix} ja \\ dewa \end{Bmatrix}$	*nakatta desu.*	
tentative	*A wa B* $\begin{Bmatrix} ja \\ dewa \end{Bmatrix}$	*nai de- shoo.*	A is prob- ably not B.
tentative past	*A wa B* $\begin{Bmatrix} ja \\ dewa \end{Bmatrix}$	*nakatta deshoo.*	A was probably not B.

[1] This form of the negative is not heard in colloquial conversation as often as the second form, below. However, it is included here for reference, since some forms of adjectives follow this pattern, as you will see in Lesson 11.

Ja is a contraction of *dewa* that you will hear in conversation, while you are more likely to see *dewa* in written material. Their meaning is the same. Most of the examples in this book will use *ja,* since our focus is on conversational Japanese.

3. Study these examples with *desu* and its forms:

gakusei	student
Watashi wa gakusei desu.	I'm a student.
kaishain[1]	businessperson
Watashi wa kaishain desu.	I'm a businessperson.
Watakushi wa Amerika-jin desu.	I'm American.
Kono tatemono wa Igirisu Taishikan desu ka?	Is that building the British Embassy?
Igirisu Taishikan ja arimasen.	It is not the British Embassy.
Watashi wa gakusei ja arimasen.	I'm not a student.
Ano hito wa kaishain ja arimasen.	He [that person] is not a businessperson.
Ano hito wa Nihonjin ja arimasen.	She [that person] is not Japanese.
Watashi wa gakusei deshita.	I was a student.
sensei	teacher
Tanaka-san wa sensei deshita.	Ms. Tanaka was a teacher.
hoteru	hotel

[1] *Kaishain* actually means "employee of a business firm." You will often hear *bijinesuman* for "businessman" or *sarariiman* for "a person earning a salary."

Ano tatemono wa hoteru deshita.	That building was a hotel.
Kare wa gakusei ja arimasen deshita.	He was not a student.
Yamada-san wa kaishain ja arimasen deshita.	Ms. Yamada was not a businessperson.
Amerika Taishikan ja arimasen deshita.	That was not the American Embassy.
Kore wa hoteru deshoo.	This is probably a hotel.
Ano hito wa Amerikajin deshoo.	She is probably American.
Ano hito wa sensei ja nai deshoo.	He is probably not a teacher.
kuruma	car
Kuruma wa Nihonsei ja nai deshoo.	The car is probably not Japanese.
Igirusu Taishikan ja nai deshoo.	That is probably not the British Embassy.
Ano hito wa sensei ja nakatta deshoo.	He was probably not a teacher.
Kuruma wa Nihonsei ja nakatta deshoo.	The car was probably not Japanese.

QUIZ 4

1. *Tabako ga arimasu ka?*
2. *Watashi wa gakusei ja arimasen.*
3. *Sore wa enpitsu desu.*
4. *Kono tatemono wa Igirusu Taishikan desu ka?*

a. Is this building the British Embassy?
b. Mr. Yamada is a businessperson.
c. Ms. Tanaka was not a teacher.
d. It's a car.

5. *Tanaka-san wa*   e. The child is in
   sensei ja arimasen   Tokyo.
   deshita.
6. *Nyuu Yooku ni*   f. This is probably a
   imasu.   hotel.
7. *Kuruma desu.*   g. Do you have a ciga-
                               rette?
8. *Kore wa hoteru*   h. I'm not a student.
   deshoo.
9. *Kodomo wa*   i. That is a pencil.
   Tookyoo ni imasu.
10. *Yamada-san wa*   j. I'm in New York.
    kaishain desu.

ANSWERS
1—g; 2—h; 3—i; 4—a; 5—c; 6—j; 7—d; 8—f;
9—e; 10—b.

REVIEW QUIZ 1
Choose the correct Japanese equivalent for the English
word or phrase:

1. five =
   a. *roku*
   b. *shichi*
   c. *go*

2. eight =
   a. *hachi*
   b. *ku*
   c. *shi*

3. Tuesday =
   a. *Suiyoobi*
   b. *Kayoobi*
   c. *Kin'yoobi*

4. Sunday =
    a. *Nichiyoobi*
    b. *Doyoobi*
    c. *Getsuyoobi*

5. March =
    a. *Sangatsu*
    b. *Kugatsu*
    c. *Shigatsu*

6. June =
    a. *Shichigatsu*
    b. *Rokugatsu*
    c. *Gogatsu*

7. red =
    a. *ao*
    b. *kiiro*
    c. *aka*

8. green =
    a. *kiiro*
    b. *midori*
    c. *haiiro*

9. black =
    a. *kuro*
    b. *chairo*
    c. *shiro*

10. brown =
    a. *kuro*
    b. *aka*
    c. *chairo*

11. Good morning =
     a. *Ohayoo gozaimasu.*
     b. *Konban wa.*
     c. *Genki desu.*

12. I'm not a student =
     a. *Kare wa Kaishain desu.*
     b. *Watashi wa gakusei ja arimasen.*
     c. *Igirisu Taishikan ja arimasen.*

13. Thank you =
     a. *Itte kudasai.*
     b. *Arigatoo gozaimasu.*
     c. *Doo itashimashite.*

14. Please =
     a. *Hanashite kudasai.*
     b. *Arigatoo gozaimasu.*
     c. *Doozo.*

15. Good-bye =
     a. *Dewa ashita.*
     b. *Sayonara.*
     c. *Konnichi wa.*

16. car =
     a. *kuruma*
     b. *kaishain*
     c. *kodomo*

17. She's probably American =
     a. *Ano hito wa Amerikajin ja arimasen.*
     b. *Ano hito wa Amerikajin deshita.*
     c. *Ano hito wa Amerikajin deshoo.*

18. businessperson =
    a. *kaishain*
    b. *hoteru*
    c. *kodomo*

19. There's a cigarette =
    a. *Tabako ga arimasu.*
    b. *Tabako desu.*
    c. *Tabako ga imasu.*

20. He is in New York =
    a. *Nyuu Yooku ga arimasu.*
    b. *Nyuu Yooku ni imasu.*
    c. *Nyuu Yooku desu.*

ANSWERS
1—c; 2—a; 3—b; 4—a; 5—a; 6—b; 7—c; 8—b;
9—a; 10—c; 11—a; 12—b; 13—b; 14—c; 15—b;
16—a; 17—c; 18—a; 19—a; 20—b.

LESSON 10

DAI JIKKA

A. COMMON VERB FORMS

In Japanese, main verbs come at the ends of sentences
(similarly to *desu*). You will also see that Japanese
verbs make no distinction between persons and numbers; the same forms are used for first, second, and
third persons in both the singular and plural. And, as
you have probably noticed, in Japanese it is the verb
endings that determine tenses.[1]

[1] You will learn more about verb forms in Lesson 12.

1. I speak, I spoke, I'm speaking, etc.

Hanashimasu.	I speak. I will speak.
Hanashimashita.	I spoke. I have spoken.
Hanashimashoo.	Let's talk. I think I'll talk.
Hanashite imasu.	I am talking.
Hanashite imashita.	I was speaking.
Hanashite kudasai.	Please speak.

NOTE

a. The endings denoting tense are:

present or future	*(hanashi)masu*
past	*(hanashi)mashita*
tentative	*(hanashi)mashoo*
present progressive	*(hanashi)te imasu*
past progressive	*(hanashi)te imashita*
polite request	*(hanashi)te kudasai*

b. The same forms are used for singular and plural and for the first, second, and third persons. The subject of a sentence does not have to be mentioned when the context clarifies who is speaking or what is being spoken about.

Hanashimasu.	I speak.
Hanashimasu.	You (*sg.*) speak.
Hanashimasu.	He/she speaks.
Hanashimasu.	We speak.
Hanashimasu.	You (*pl.*) speak.
Hanashimasu.	They speak.

2. I don't speak, I didn't speak, I wasn't speaking, etc.

Hanashimasen.	I don't speak. I will not speak.
Hanashimasen deshita.	I didn't speak.
Hanashite imasen.	I am not speaking.
Hanashite imasen deshita.	I wasn't speaking.
Hanasanaide kudasai.	Please don't speak.

NOTE

a. The negative is formed as follows:

negative present or future	*(hanashi)masen*
negative past	*(hanashi)masen deshita*
negative present progressive	*(hanashi)te imasen*
negative past progressive	*(hanashi)te imasen deshita*
negative polite request	*(hanasa)naide kudasai*

  b. Note, again, that the subject of each of these sentences could be "I," "you," "he/she," "we," or "they." "I" is arbitrarily used as the subject in the English translations.

3. Study these examples:

Tabemasu.	I eat. I will eat.
Tabete imasu.	I am eating.
Tabemashita.	I ate.

Tabete imashita.	I was eating.
Tabete kudasai.	Please eat.
Tabemashoo.	Let's eat.
Tabemasen.	I do not eat. I will not eat.
Tabete imasen.	I am not eating.
Tabemasen deshita.	I did not eat.
Tabete imasen deshita.	I was not eating.
Tabenaide kudasai.	Please don't eat.
Donna mono o tabemashita ka?	What kinds of things did you eat?
Sukiyaki ya tenpura o tabemashita.	We ate sukiyaki, tempura, and things like that.
koohii	coffee
Koohii o nomimasu.	I drink coffee.
ocha	tea
Ocha o nomimashoo.	Let's drink green tea.
Ocha o nomimashita.	They drank green tea.

As the lessons proceed, you'll see more verbs in these forms and after a while you'll become more familiar with them. Be sure to refer to Lesson 40 for more on verbs as well.

B. ASKING A QUESTION I

1. As we have seen, one way to ask a question is to add the particle *ka* to the end of the sentence and use either a rising or falling intonation:

Naraimasu.	You learn.
Naraimasu ka?	Do you learn?
Naraimashita.	You learned. You have learned.

Naraimashita ka?	Did you learn? Have you learned?
Naratte imasu.	You are learning.
Naratte imasu ka?	Are you learning?
Naratte imashita.	You were learning.
Naratte imashita ka?	Were you learning?

2. To ask a question with a negative, use the particle *ka* in the same way:

Naraimasen ka?	Don't you learn?
Naraimasen deshita ka?	Didn't you learn?
Naratte imasen ka?	Aren't you learning?
Naratte imasen deshita ka?	Weren't you learning?

C. WHERE IS IT?

Chotto sumimasen.	Excuse me for a moment. [I am asking a question, but . . .]
doko	where
arimasu	there is
Doko ni arimasu ka?	Where is it?
Hoteru wa doko ni arimasu ka?	Where is there a hotel?
resutoran	restaurant
Resutoran wa doko ni arimasu ka?	Where is there a restaurant?
denwa	telephone
Denwa wa doko ni arimasu ka?	Where is there a telephone?
uketsuke	reception desk
Uketsuke wa doko ni arimasu ka?	Where is the reception desk?
eki	station

Eki wa doko ni arimasu ka?	Where is the station?
yuubinkyoku	post office
Yuubinkyoku wa doko ni arimasu ka?	Where is the post office?

D. HERE AND THERE

koko	here, this place
soko	there, that place (near to person addressed by speaker)
asoko	there, that place over there (far from both speaker and person addressed)
doko	where, which place
Doko desu ka?	Where is it? Which place is it?
kochira	this way
sochira	that way
achira	that way over there
dochira	which way
Dochira desu ka?	Which way is it?
Achira desu	It is over that way.
Kochira desu.	It's this way.
migi no hoo ni	to the right [in the direction of the right]
hidari no hoo ni	to the left [in the direction of the left]
Migi no hoo ni arimasu.	It's to the right. [It is in the direction . . .]
Hidari no hoo ni arimasu.	It's to the left.

Migi e magarimasu.	You turn right.
Hidari e magarimasu.	You turn left.
Massugu ikimasu.	You go straight ahead.
Massugu saki desu.	It's straight ahead.
Choodo hantaigawa desu.	It's directly opposite.
Kado ni arimasu.	It's on the corner.
Koko ni wa arimasen.	It's not here.
Soko ni wa arimasen.	It's not there.
Asoko ni arimasu.	It's over there.
Koko ni imasu.	He is here.
Koko ni kite kudasai.	Come here, please.
Koko ni ite kudasai.	Stay here, please.
Soko de matte ite kudasai.	Wait there, please.
Kochira e itte kudasai.	Go this way, please.
Achira e itte kudasai.	Go that way, please.
Soko ni dare ga imasu ka?	Who's there?
Koko ni oite kudasai.	Put it here, please.
Soko ni oite kudasai.	Put it there, please.

E. NEAR AND FAR

Chikai desu.	It's near.
Koko kara chikai desu.	It's near here. [Near from here.]
Totemo chikai desu.	It's very near. It's quite close.
Mura no chikaku[1] desu.	It's near the village.
Michi no chikaku desu.	It's near the road.
Sono hito no uchi no chikaku desu.	It's near his house.

[1] *chikaku:* nearby place (*a noun*).

Koko kara totemo chikai desu.	It's very near here.
tooi	far
Tooi desu ka?	Is it far?
Tooi desu.	It's far.
Tooku arimasen.	It's not far.
Koko kara tooi desu.	It's far from here.

QUIZ 5

1. *Denwa wa doko ni arimasu ka?*   a. It's this way.

2. *Hanashimasu.*   b. It's to the right.

3. *Kochira desu.*   c. He's/I'm turning left.

4. *Massugu saki desu.*   d. It's directly opposite.

5. *Migi no hoo ni arimasu.*   e. It's straight ahead.

6. *Mura no chikaku desu.*   f. Where is there a telephone?

7. *Soko de matte ite kudasai.*   g. He speaks.

8. *Kochira e itte kudasai.*   h. It's near the village.

9. *Hidari e magarimasu.*   i. It's not here.

10. *Choodo hantaigawa desu.*   j. Stay here, please.

11. *Tooku arimasen.*   k. Wait there, please.

12. *Soko ni oite kudasai.*   l. Go this way, please.

13. *Koko ni arimasen.*   m. Who's there?

14. *Koko ni ite kudasai.*   n. Put it there, please.

15. *Soko ni dare ga imasu ka?*   o. I'm eating.

16. *Hoteru wa doko ni arimasu ka?*   p. Let's eat.

17. *Naraimashita ka?*   q. I drink coffee.
18. *Tabete imasu.*   r. Where is there a
                                hotel?
19. *Tabemashoo.*   s. It's not far.
20. *Koohii o nomimasu.*   t. Did you learn?

ANSWERS
1—f; 2—g; 3—a; 4—e; 5—b; 6—h; 7—k; 8—l;
9—c; 10—d; 11—s; 12—n; 13—i; 14—j; 15—m;
16—r; 17—t; 18—o; 19—p; 20—q.

LESSON 11

DAI JUUIKKA

A. NOUNS AND NOUN PARTICLES

In Japanese, the form of a noun remains the same no
matter where it appears in a sentence. Normally, every
noun is followed by at least one particle when it is
used in a sentence.[1] A particle, which is often not
translatable, is the "tag" or "signpost" that tells what
relation the word it accompanies has to another word
or part of a sentence. For instance, one particle may
show that the noun it follows is the *subject* of the sentence, another may show that the noun it follows is the
object of the sentence, and still another may show that
the noun it follows is the *modifier of another noun.*
Remember, however, that *all* particles must follow the
words with which they are used.

Following is a list of important noun particles with
a brief description of their use:[2]

---

[1] There are some exceptions to this rule, but only a few.
[2] See the Summary of Japanese Grammar for a more complete list
of particles and their uses.

1. *Wa* shows that the noun it follows is the topic of the sentence. Here the word "topic" is deliberately employed as a contrast to the word "subject," which we often use in grammar. A topic in Japanese—that is, a word or group of words that is followed by the particle *wa*—serves as advance notice of what the speaker will talk about. This practice of isolating a topic and setting it off with the particle *wa* is frequently used to start a sentence in Japanese, and can be compared to the occasional practice in English of beginning a sentence with "As for . . ." or "Speaking of . . ." For instance, in Japanese you would say:

As for Mr. Yoshida, (he) came to this country again this year.
Talking about this morning's *New York Times*, have (you) read (it)?

Notice how a topic is first singled out and then followed by a simplified statement. Note also that a topic can be either an *implied subject* or an *implied object* of the verb, and that it may even specify a *time* or *place*.

Further examples with *wa:*

Kabukiza wa Tookyoo ni arimasu.	(The) Kabuki Theatre is in Tokyo. [As for the Kabuki Theatre, (it) is in Tokyo.]
Bunraku wa mimasen deshita.	I didn't see (the) Bunraku (Puppet Play). [As for Bunraku, I didn't see (it).]

Boardman-san wa Amerika e kaerimashita.	Speaking of Mr. Boardman, he returned to America.
Kinoo wa Tanaka-san no uchi e ikimashita.	Speaking of yesterday, I went to Tanaka's house.

2. *Ga* shows that the noun it follows is both the grammatical subject of a verb and also an "emphatic" subject. In English, you place emphasis on a subject by raising your voice. In Japanese you can create the same emphasis, usually without raising the voice, by using the particle *ga*.

   If you do *not* want to emphasize the subject, you can either introduce the subject with the topic particle *wa* or avoid mentioning it altogether. In English you always mention the subject, except when using the imperative. In Japanese you may omit specifically naming the subject when you feel that the person you are speaking to already knows what the subject is.

Watashi ga ikimashita.	I (not he) *(spoken with emphasis)* went. [(It) was I who went.]
Tanaka-san ga kimashita.	*Ms. Tanaka (spoken with emphasis)* came.
Jikan ga arimasen.	There isn't *time*.

3. *O* shows that the noun it follows is *the thing acted on* by the verb. It roughly corresponds to the direct object of a transitive verb. Yet, *O* also implies the notion of a place in which movements (transitions) such as going, coming, passing, walking, running, swimming, flying, and departing take place.

Kippu o kaimashita.	I bought some tickets.
Tegami o dashimashita.	I sent a letter.
Ginza Doori o arukimashita.	We walked on Ginza Street.
Saka o hashirimashita.	We ran on the slope.

4. *No* shows that the noun it follows modifies (i.e., explains, characterizes) another noun that comes after it. It is most frequently used for the possessive ("of"):

Tookyoo no machi desu.	It is the city of Tokyo.
Yamada-san no uchi desu.	It is Mr. Yamada's house. [(It) is the house of Mr. Yamada.]
Tanaka-san no kodomo desu.	He is Ms. Tanaka's child. [He is the child of Ms. Tanaka.]

5. *Ni* is used in the following ways:

  a. The noun with *ni* may tell *where* a thing or person is (in the sense of being "in" or "at" a place):

Tanaka-san wa Tookyoo ni imasu.	Ms. Tanaka is in Tokyo.
Ginza wa Chuuoo-ku ni arimasu.	Ginza is in the Chuo ward (of Tokyo).

  b. The noun with *ni* may tell the *purpose* for which the action is performed (in the sense of "for" or "in order to"):

Nihon e benkyoo ni   I came to Japan to
   kimashita.   study.

    c. The noun with *ni* may tell the *person* or *thing*
       to which the action of the verb is directed (in
       the sense of "to," "from," or "of"):

Yamada-san ni   I gave it to Mr. Yamada.
   agemashita.

    d. The noun with *ni* may tell the *thing into*
       which something changes (there is usually no
       translation for this usage):

Tookyoo Daigaku no   I became a student at
   gakusei ni   [of] Tokyo University.
   narimashita.

    e. The noun with *ni* is the direction toward
       which a motion takes place ("to," "toward"):

Nara ni ikimashita.   I went to Nara.
Amerika ni okurimashita.   I sent it to America.

   6. *De* signifies that the noun preceding it is:

    a. The *place* of action ("at," "in"):

Kyooto de kaimashita.   I bought it in Kyoto.

    b. The *means* of action ("by," "through"):

Hikooki de   I went by [means of a]
   ikimashita.   plane.

    c. The *limit* to which the predicate is restricted
       ("in," "within"):

Nihon de ichiban   takai yama desu.

It is the highest mountain in Japan. [Restricting ourselves to Japan, (it) is the highest mountain.]

7. *Kara* shows that the noun it follows is the *beginning point* in space or time of an action or state ("from," "since"):

Amerika kara   kimashita.

I came from America.

Nigatsu kara koko ni   sunde imasu.

I have been living here since February.

8. *Made* shows that the noun it follows is the *ending point* of an action or event ("up to," "by," "until"):

Hiroshima made   ikimashita.

I went as far as Hiroshima.

Juugatsu made   Kyooto ni imasu.

I'll be in Kyoto until October.

Kara and *made* are often used together:

Tookyoo kara Oosaka   made ikimashita.

I went from Tokyo to Osaka.

9. *E* shows that the noun it follows is the *direction toward which* a motion takes place ("to," "toward"). *E* and *ni* (in 5-e above) are usually interchangeable:

Nara e ikimashita.   I went to Nara.

Amerika e okurimashita.   I sent it to America.

10. *To* shows that the preceding noun is one of the following:

   a. A part of a complete list ("and"):

Tookyoo to Kyooto to Oosaka e ikimashita.	I went to Tokyo, Kyoto, and Osaka. (These are the places I went to.)
Yamada-san to Tanaka-san to Takeda-san ga kimashita.	Mr. Yamada, Ms. Tanaka, and Ms. Takeda came. (These are the people who came.)

   b. The one with whom the action of the verb is performed ("with"):

Kanai to ikimashita.	I went with my wife.
Tanaka-san to hanashi-mashita.	I spoke with Mr. Tanaka.

   c. The thing into which something or somebody changes:

Ano tatemono wa Tanaka-san no mono to narima-shita.	That building became Ms. Tanaka's (property).
Nihon no daihyoo to narimashita.	She became the representative of Japan.
Daigishi to narimashita.	He became a member of Parliament.

Note that in this usage *to* is often interchangeable with *ni* (shown above).

11. *Ya* shows, as *to* sometimes does, that the noun it follows is part of a list; however, the fact that *ya* is used implies that the list is not a complete one:

Niku ya pan ya sarada o tabemashita.	I ate meat, bread, and salad (and some other things).

B. COMMON ADJECTIVE FORMS

There are two types of adjectives in Japanese: *i-* adjectives and *na-* adjectives.

1. *I-* adjectives
   I- adjectives all end in *-i*. They are used very much like verbs. They have their own forms for present, past, etc., and they have "plain" and "polite" forms, as do verbs (see Lesson 12).

   a. Below are some commonly used conjugations of the *i-* adjective *takai* (expensive):

Takai desu.	It is expensive. It will be expensive.
Takakatta desu.	It was expensive.
Takai deshoo.	It is probably expensive.
Takakatta deshoo.	It was probably expensive.
Takaku arimasen. ⎱ *Takaku nai desu.* ⎰	It is not expensive.
Takaku arimasen deshita. ⎱ *Takaku nakatta desu.* ⎰	It was not expensive.
Takaku nai deshoo.	It is probably not expensive.

Takaku nakatta deshoo.   It was probably not
                            expensive.

(1) Notice how the endings differ for affir-
    mative and negative forms (parentheses
    set off the adjectival root "expensive"
    from the ending):

	AFFIRMATIVE
present	*(taka)i desu*
past	*(taka)katta desu*
tentative	*(taka)i deshoo*
tentative past	*(taka)katta deshoo*

	NEGATIVE
present	*(taka)ku arimasen*
	(taka)ku nai desu
past	*(taka)ku arimasen deshita*
	(taka)ku nakatta desu
tentative	*(taka)ku nai deshoo*
tentative past	*(taka)ku nakatta deshoo*

(2) Notice how the same forms are used for
    both singular and plural in all persons (I,
    you, he, she, it, we, you, they):

Takai desu.	It is expensive.
Takai desu.	They are expensive.
Takakatta desu.	It was expensive.
Takakatta desu.	They were expensive.
Kashikoi desu.	You are wise.
Kashikoi desu.	She is wise.

(3) Notice that the present negative and the
    past negative of *i-* adjectives have two
    forms. The *-ku nai* (present) and *-ku*

nakatta (past) forms are used more often in colloquial conversation:

Takaku nai desu.	It is not expensive.
Hoteru wa takaku na-katta desu.	The hotel was not expensive.

See d and f below as well.

b. *I-* adjectives modifying a noun:

takai kuruma	expensive car
Takai kuruma desu.	It is an expensive car.
Takai kuruma ja nai desu.	It is not an expensive car.
ookii	big
ookii hoteru	big hotel
Ookii hoteru deshita.	It was a big hotel.

c. Sentences with present, affirmative *i-* adjectives:

Yasui desu.	It's inexpensive/cheap.
Oishii desu.	It's delicious/tasty.
Ookii desu.	It's big.
Chiisai desu.	It's small.
Ii desu. Yoi desu.[1]	It's good/nice.
Warui desu.	It's bad.
Warui tenki desu.	It's bad weather.
Tenki wa warui desu.	The weather is bad.
Chiisai hon desu.	It's a small book.
Ookii kuruma desu.	It's a big car.

[1] Both *ii* and *yoi* mean "good," but *ii* is more colloquial and more commonly used. However, conjugations, such as the negative or past, are based on *yoi* and not *ii*.

Oishii koohii desu.	It's delicious coffee.
Yasui hon desu.	It's an inexpensive book.

d. Sentences with present, negative *i*- adjectives:

Takaku nai desu. **Takaku arimasen.**	It is not expensive.
Yoku nai desu. **Yoku arimasen.**	It is not good.
omoshiroi	interesting
Omoshiroku nai desu. **Omoshiroku ari-** **masen.**	It is not interesting.
atarashii	new
Atarashiku nai desu. *Atarashiku ari-* *masen.*	It is not new.
furui[1]	old
Furuku nai desu. *Furuku arimasen.*	It is not old.
tooi	far
Tooku nai desu. *Tooku arimasen.*	It is not far.
atsui	hot
Atsuku nai desu. *Atsuku arimasen.*	It is not hot.
Tenki wa waruku nai desu.	The weather is not bad.
Kuruma wa yoku nai desu.	The car is not good.
Furui kuruma wa takaku arimasen.	The old cars are not expensive.

[1] *Furui*, "old," is used to describe inanimate things and not animate beings.

e. Sentences with past, affirmative *i-* adjectives:

Ookikatta desu.	It was big.
Atsukatta desu.	It was hot.
Atarashikatta desu.	It was new.
Yokatta desu.	It was good.
Kuruma wa takakatta desu.	The car was expensive.
Heya wa chiisakatta desu.	The room was small.
Tenki wa warukatta desu ka.	Was the weather bad?

f. Sentences with past, negative *i-* adjectives:

Takaku nakatta desu. **Takaku arimasen deshita.**	It was not expensive.
Omoshiroku nakatta desu. *Omoshiroku arimasen deshita.*	It was not interesting.
Ooikiku nakatta desu.	It was not big.
Kuruma wa ookiku nakatta desu.	The car was not big.
Koohii wa oishiku nakatta desu.	The coffee was not tasty.
Hoteru wa yoku nakatta desu.	The hotel was not good.
Resutoran wa atarashiku nakatta desu.	The restaurant was not new.

2. *Na-* adjectives

Na- adjectives are used very much like nouns. Unlike *i-* adjectives, they do not conjugate—that is, change their forms according to tense, etc.

Instead, the copula *desu* that follows *na-* adjectives conjugates.

a. Below are some sentences with *na-* adjectives. Notice that the sentence patterns are just like those with nouns (see Lesson 9):

shizuka	quiet
Shizuka desu.	It is quiet.
Shizuka deshita.	It was quiet.
Shizuka deshoo.	It is probably quiet.
Shizuka datta deshoo.	It was probably quiet.

Shizuka $\begin{Bmatrix} ja \\ dewa \end{Bmatrix}$ arimasen.

Shizuka $\begin{Bmatrix} ja \\ de(wa) \end{Bmatrix}$ nai desu.

It is not quiet.

Shizuka $\begin{Bmatrix} ja \\ dewa \end{Bmatrix}$ arimasen deshita.

Shizuka $\begin{Bmatrix} ja \\ de(wa) \end{Bmatrix}$ nakatta desu.

It was not quiet.

Shizuka $\begin{Bmatrix} ja \\ de(wa) \end{Bmatrix}$ nai deshoo.

It is probably not quiet.

Shizuka $\begin{Bmatrix} ja \\ de(wa) \end{Bmatrix}$ nakatta deshoo.

It was probably not quiet

kirei	pretty/clean
Kirei ja arimasen.	It is not pretty/clean.
fukuzatsu	complicated
Fukuzatsu ja arimasen.	It is not complicated.
Fukuzatsu de nakatta desu.	It was not complicated.
Kono mondai wa fukuzatsu desu.	This problem is complicated.

Shigoto wa fukuzatsu ja nai desu.	The job is not complicated.
shinsetsu	kind
Yamada-san wa shinsetsu desu.	Mr. Yamada is kind.
Tanaka-san wa shinsetsu deshita.	Ms. Tanaka was kind.
kantan	simple/brief
Kantan deshita.	It was simple/brief.
Shigoto wa kantan deshita.	The job was simple.

b. *Na-* adjectives modifying a noun
   Na- adjectives are used with *na* before a noun:

shizuka na apaato	quiet apartment
kirei na shashin	pretty photograph
fukuzatsu na mondai	complicated problem
shinsetsu na sensei	kind teacher
taisetsu	important
taisetsu na mono	important thing
genki	healthy
genki na kodomo	healthy child
rippa	magnificent
rippa na tatemono	magnificent building
raku	easy/comfortable
raku na shigoto	easy task
Kantan na setsumei deshita.	It was a brief explanation.
Taisetsu na mono ja nai desu.	It is not an important thing.

QUIZ 6

1. Takai desu.	a. It's not a good car.
2. *Omoshiroku nai desu.*	b. It's delicious.
3. *Yoi hoteru desu.*	c. It was good.
4. *Ii kuruma ja nai desu.*	d. It is probably expensive.
5. *Yokatta desu.*	e. It was probably expensive.
6. *Ii eiga deshita.*	f. It's a good hotel.
7. *Takai deshoo.*	g. It is pretty.
8. *Takakatta deshoo.*	h. It is expensive.
9. *Oishii desu.*	i. It's not interesting.
10. *Kirei desu.*	j. It was a good movie.

ANSWERS
1—h; 2—i; 3—f; 4—a; 5—c; 6—j; 7—d; 8—e; 9—b; 10—g.

LESSON 12

DAI JUUNIKA

A. PLAIN OR POLITE

For each of the forms of *i-* adjectives, verbs, and copulas used at the end of sentences, there is an additional form called a "plain form." The forms we have seen at the end of a sentence are called "polite forms." The polite forms are derived from plain forms and are characterized by ending with -*desu* or -*masu* or a form derived from one of these. The plain form is usually used in the *middle* of a sentence, while the polite form is usually at the *end* of a sentence. However, the plain form, too, can be used at the end of a sentence, but only when the speaker is very familiar with and has a casual relationship to the person he/she is speaking to. A husband, for example, may use this form with his wife, or a high-school boy with his classmates. But for anyone learning Japanese as a foreign language, it is best to use the polite form at the end of a sentence.

Dictionaries and glossaries usually list the plain present affirmative form of *i-* adjectives, verbs, and the copula. Here is a table showing the plain and polite present affirmative forms of some words that you have already seen:

PLAIN PRESENT AFFIRMATIVE	POLITE PRESENT AFFIRMATIVE	MEANING
	I- ADJECTIVES	
takai	*takai desu*	it is expensive
tooi	*tooi desu*	it is far
	VERBS	
hanasu	*hanashimasu*	I speak
kau	*kaimasu*	I buy
aru	*arimasu*	there is
taberu	*tabemasu*	I eat
kuru	*kimasu*	I come
	COPULA	
da[1]	*desu*	A is B

To construct the polite present affirmative form of an *i-* adjective, add *desu* to the plain present affirmative.

Construct the polite present affirmative of a verb according to the rules set forth in the next section.

---

[1] *Na* or *no* is used in place of *da* in certain environments.

The polite present affirmative of the copula *da* is *desu*. Rarely, *de arimasu* can also be used, but this form is considered very formal.

B. To Construct the Polite Form of a Verb

In order to construct the polite form of a verb from its plain present form, you must learn to identify the class or conjugation to which the verb belongs. To do so, you need to know the following basic facts:

1. The plain present affirmative form of all verbs ends in -*u*.

2. All verbs belong to one of three classes: *consonant, vowel,* or *irregular.* Consonant verbs make up the largest group and irregular verbs the smallest.

3. There are only two verbs that are really irregular, and they are the most common: *suru* [do] and *kuru* [come]. Although there are a few other verbs that are somewhat irregular, they are basically consonant verbs. Two examples are *iku* [go] and *kudasaru* [give].

4. The vast majority of verbs that end in -*eru* or -*iru* are vowel verbs—for example, *taberu* [eat] and *miru* [see]—so called because the base[1] (which remains unchanged most of the time) ends in a vowel. However, there are a few verbs that end in -*eru* or -*iru* that are not vowel verbs; for example: *keru* [kick], *kaeru* [return], *hairu* [enter].

---

[1] The base of a vowel verb is that part remaining after the final -*ru* is dropped; i.e., *tabe(ru), mi(ru)*.

Since the bases of these verbs end in *-r* (*ker-*, *kaer-*, *hair-*, respectively) they are classified as consonant verbs.

5. All other verbs are consonant verbs—so called because the base ends in a consonant.[1] Verbs that end in two vowels, such as *kau* [buy], or *iu*, which is *yuu* [say], are also included in this class because they add *-w* at the end of the base when appending an ending that begins with *-a*, e.g., *-anai* [not], *-areru* (*passive*), or *-aseru* (*causative*).

Once you can identify the class to which a given verb belongs, you can form the polite, present affirmative forms as follows:

I. Consonant verbs

Add *-imasu* to the base, with two exceptions:

a. When the base ends in *s*, the letter is changed to *sh* before adding *-imasu*. For example: *hanasu* becomes *hanashimasu*.

b. When the base ends in *ts*, the latter is changed to *ch* before adding *-imasu*. For example: *tatsu* becomes *tachimasu*.

II. Vowel verbs

Add *-masu* to the base.

---

[1] The base of a consonant verb is that part remaining after the final *u* has been dropped. For example: *das(u)* [put out, send out], *ar(u)* [there is], *ka(w)(u)* [buy], *kak(u)* [write].

III. Irregular verbs

Learn the polite form of each individually.

Note: In the following examples, the end of the base has been marked with a hyphen:

PLAIN PRESENT AFFIRMATIVE	POLITE PRESENT AFFIRMATIVE	MEANING
	CONSONANT VERBS	
kak-u	*kakimasu*	writes
kas-u	*kashimasu*	lends
mats-u	*machimasu*	waits
mots-u	*mochimasu*	holds
hair-u	*hairimasu*	enters
ka(w)-u	*kaimasu*	buys
	VOWEL VERBS	
tabe-ru	*tabemasu*	eats
tome-ru	*tomemasu*	stops
mi-ru	*mimasu*	sees
oki-ru	*okimasu*	gets up
	IRREGULAR VERBS	
suru	*shimasu*	does
kuru	*kimasu*	comes

C. THE *-TE* AND *-TA* FORMS

When the *-te* form of a verb appears in a sentence, it signifies that one or more additional verbs will also appear in that sentence.

The *-te* form of a verb is used in such expressions as *hanashite kudasai* [please speak] and *hanashite imasu* [I'm speaking]. Although the verb in such a construction most often ends in *-te,* it can also end in *-tte* or *-de.* The way the *-te* form ends or the way it is formed from the plain, present, affirmative (which is the dictionary form) depends on (a) the *class of verb* to which it belongs, and (b) if it is a consonant verb, the *pronunciation of the last syllable* of the plain present.

The -*te* form is sometimes called a "gerund," but unlike a proper gerund, this form is never used as a noun. (See page 73 for uses of the -*te* form.)

The -*ta* form is another way to refer to the plain past affirmative as opposed to the polite past affirmative. However, in dependent clauses, the -*ta* form is usually used in place of the polite form.

Remember that the polite past affirmative always ends in -*mashita*, whereas the -*ta* form can end not only in -*ta* but also in -*tta* or -*da*. The -*ta* form is derived from the plain present affirmative in exactly the same way as the -*te* form.

When using either of these forms, be careful not to interchange the final -*e* and -*a*. Follow these instructions:

1. For consonant verbs:

    a. When the last syllable of the plain present is -*u*, -*tsu*, or -*ru*, drop that syllable and add -*tte* or -*tta*:

PLAIN PRESENT AFFIRMATIVE	-*TE* FORM	-*TA* FORM	MEANING OF PLAIN PRESENT AFFIRMATIVE
kau	**katte**	**katta**	buy
omou	*omotte*	*omotta*	think
matsu	**matte**	**matta**	wait
motsu	*motte*	*motta*	hold
okuru	**okutte**	**okutta**	send
toru	*totte*	*totta*	take

Note: To learn this rule it might be helpful to memorize the following fictitious word, which is made up by stringing together the three final syllables involved and the -tta:

u-tsu-ru-tta (utsurutta)

b. If the last syllable of the plain present affirmative is -*mu*, -*nu*, or -*bu*, drop it and replace it with -*nde* or -*nda*:

PLAIN PRESENT AFFIRMATIVE	-*TE* FORM	-*TA* FORM	MEANING OF PLAIN PRESENT AFFIRMATIVE
yomu	**yonde**	**yonda**	read
nomu	*nonde*	*nonda*	drink
shinu	**shinde**	**shinda**	die
yobu	**yonde**	**yonda**	call
tobu	*tonde*	*tonda*	fly

Mnemonic device: *mu-nu-bu-nda (munubunda).*

c. If the last syllable of the plain present affirmative is -*ku*, drop it and replace it with -*ite* or *ita*. If the last syllable is -*gu*, drop it and replace it with -*ide* and -*ida*:

PLAIN PRESENT AFFIRMATIVE	-*TE* FORM	-*TA* FORM	MEANING OF PLAIN PRESENT AFFIRMATIVE
kaku	**kaite**	**kaita**	write
saku	*saite*	*saita*	bloom
oyogu	**oyoide**	**oyoida**	swim
kagu	*kaide*	*kaida*	smell

Mnemonic device: *ku-gu-ita-ida (kuguitaida).*

Note: *iku* [go] is one exception. Its *-te* and *-ta* forms are *itte* and *itta*, respectively.

d. When the last syllable of the plain present is *-su,* drop it and add *-shite* or *-shita:*

PLAIN PRESENT AFFIRMATIVE	*-TE* FORM	*-TA* FORM	MEANING OF PLAIN PRESENT AFFIRMATIVE
hanasu	**hanashite**	**hanashita**	speak
kasu	**kashite**	**kashita**	lend
hosu	*hoshite*	*hoshita*	dry
moyasu	*moyashite*	*moyashita*	burn

Mnemonic device: *su-shita (sushita).*

2. For vowel verbs:

Simply drop the final syllable *-ru* and add *-te* or *-ta.*

PLAIN PRESENT AFFIRMATIVE	*-TE* FORM	*-TA* FORM	MEANING OF PLAIN PRESENT AFFIRMATIVE
taberu	**tabete**	**tabeta**	eat
akeru	**akete**	**aketa**	open
miru	*mite*	*mita*	see
kiru	*kite*	*kita*	wear

3. For irregular verbs:

PLAIN PRESENT AFFIRMATIVE	*-TE* FORM	*-TA* FORM	MEANING OF PLAIN PRESENT AFFIRMATIVE
suru	**shite**	**shita**	do
kuru	**kite**	**kita**	come

D. Various Usages of the *-TE* Form

The basic function of a *-te* form is to name an action or condition. It serves to show that the sentence is not complete. That is why, as a rule, it does not appear at the end of a sentence.

The *-te* form verb is used in many ways. Some of the more important follow:

1. When a sentence contains several different verbs, the *-te* form is usually used for all but the last:

Nippon e itte kaima-shita.	I bought it in Japan. [(I) went to Japan and bought it (there).]
Eiga o mite Ginza de gohan o tabete uchi e kaerimashita.	I saw a movie, ate [my meal] on Ginza, and returned home.

Notice that the tense is expressed in *the terminal verb only* and not in the *-te* form verbs. In translation, however, the tense is expressed for the *-te* form verbs as well.

2. Sometimes the function of a *-te* form verb is merely to explain *how* the action of the following verb is performed:

Hashitte[1] ikimashita.	He went running.
Isoide[2] kimashita.	He came hurriedly.

---

[1] *hashiru* = run.
[2] *isogu* = hurry.

3. The phrase -*te imasu* is used to express an action going on or a state or condition resulting from an action that occurred in the past:

Ame ga futte imasu.	It is raining. [The rain is falling.]
Ima gohan o tabete imasu.	We are eating [the meal] now.
Okyaku sama ga kite imasu.	We have a visitor. [(A) visitor came and is with us.]

4. The phrase -*te arimasu* is used to express a state or condition that is the result of the past action of a transitive verb. In English it is often translated by the passive voice.

Sore wa haratte arimasu.	That has been paid for. That is paid. [That is in the state of my having paid for it.]
Sono tegami wa moo kaite arimasu.	That letter (you are speaking of) is already written. [The letter is already in the state of my having written it.]

5. The phrase -*te kudasai* is used to express a request and corresponds most closely to the imperative in English:

Kippu o katte kudasai.	Please buy a ticket.
Doyoobi ni kite kudasai.	Come on Saturday, please.

QUIZ 7

1. *Nippon e itte kaimashita.*	a. He came hurriedly.
2. *Isoide kimashita.*	b. I went to Japan and bought it there.
3. *Ame ga futte imasu.*	c. That letter is already written.
4. *Doyoobi ni kite kudasai.*	d. Come on Saturday, please.
5. *Hashitte ikimashita.*	e. We have a visitor.
6. *Sono tegami wa moo kaite arimasu.*	f. He went running.
7. *Okyaku sama ga kite imasu.*	g. It is raining.
8. *Sore wa haratte arimasu.*	h. That has been paid for.
9. *Ima gohan o tabete imasu.*	i. We are eating now.
10. *Eiga o mite Ginza de gohun o tabete uchi e kaerimashita.*	j. I saw a movie, ate on Ginza, and returned home.

ANSWERS
1—b; 2—a; 3—g; 4—d; 5—f; 6—c; 7—e; 8—h; 9 i; 10—j.

LESSON 13

DAI JUUSANKA

A. MY, YOUR, HIS, HER, ETC.

There are no separate words for "my," "your," "his," "her," etc. To express the idea of these words, add the particle *no* to the words for "I," "you," "he," "she."

Watashi no hon wa doko ni arimasu ka?	Where is my book?
Anata no hon wa doko ni arimasu ka?	Where is your book?
Sono hito no hon wa doko ni arimasu ka?	Where is his/her [that person's] book?
Sono hitotachi no hon wa doko ni arimasu ka?	Where are their [those people's] books?
Anata no tegami wa doko ni arimasu ka?	Where is your letter?
Sono hito no tegami wa doko ni arimasu ka?	Where is his/her [that person's] letter?
Sono hitotachi no tegami wa doko ni arimasu ka?	Where are their [those people's] letters?

Sometimes the idea of "your" may be suggested by prefixing the noun referred to with *o-* or *go-*. In such cases, *anata no* [your] is usually not used. Notice that the nouns to which *o-* or *go-* can be added are limited in number.

Gokazoku[1] wa?	How about your family?
Okuni[2] wa dochira desu ka?	Where are you from?
Onamae[3] wa nan desu ka?	What is your name?

---

[1] *kazoku* = family.
[2] *kuni* = country, hometown.
[3] *namae* = name.

B. SOME COMPARISONS

Here are a few forms of comparisons. Refer to Section 16 in the Summary of Japanese Grammar for more information.

1. More . . . than:

Sono densha wa hayai desu.	That train is fast.
Sono densha wa basu yori hayai desu.	That train is faster than the bus.
Sono kuruma wa atarashii desu.	That car is new.
Sono kuruma wa watashi no kuruma yori atarashii desu.	That car is newer than my car.
Tanaka-san no heya wa shizuka desu.	Ms. Tanaka's room is quiet.
Tanaka-san no heya wa kono heya yori shizuka desu.	Ms. Tanaka's room is more quiet than this room.

2. The most . . .

Kono kuruma ga ichiban atarashii desu.	This car is the newest.
Watashi no shigoto ga ichiban raku desu.	My job is the easiest.
Kono resutoran ga ichiban kirei desu.	This restaurant is the cleanest.
Kono mondai ga ichiban fukuzatsu desu.	This problem is the most complicated.

3. Not as . . . as . . .

Tanaka-san wa Harada-san hodo[1] sei ga takaku arimasen.	Ms. Tanaka is not as tall as Ms. Harada.
Nara wa Kyooto hodo ookiku arimasen.	Nara is not as big as Kyoto.
Watashi no heya wa Tanaka-san no heya hodo kirei ja arimasen.	My room is not as clean as Ms. Tanaka's room.
Kyoo no shiken wa mae no shiken hodo kantan dewa nakatta desu.	Today's test was not as simple as the previous test.

4. As . . . as possible:

Dekiru dake kuwashiku kaite kudasai.	Please write it as detailed (with as much detail) as possible.
Dekiru dake kitsuku shimete kudasai.	Please tie it as tightly as possible.
Dekiru dake hayaku shite kudasai.	Do it as soon as possible.

C. ASKING A QUESTION II

There are several ways to ask a question:

1. Add the particle *ka* at the end of a declarative sentence, and either raise the pitch of your voice at the end (i.e., use the "question intonation"), or not, as you like.

[1] *hodo* = not as . . . as

2. Phrase the sentence like a declarative statement and use the question-intonation but do not use the particle *ka* at the end. This is a very informal usage.

3. When you ask a question that demands an answer, and the answer can be one of several alternatives, add *ka* to each of the alternatives you offer.

Kore desu ka?	Is it this?
Kore desu.	It's this.
Sore desu ka?	Is it that?
Kore desu ka sore desu ka?	Is it this or is it that?
Koko ni imasu ka?	Is he here?
Asoko ni imasu ka?	Is he over there?
Koko ni imasu ka asoko ni imasu ka?	Is he here or is he over there?
Doko ni imasu ka?	Where is he?
Doko desu ka?	Where is it? [Which place is (it)?]
Dare desu ka?	Who is it?
Donata¹ desu ka?	Who is it *(respect)?*
Nan desu ka?	What is it?
Itsu desu ka?	When is it?
Ikura desu ka?	How much is it?
Ikutsu desu ka?	How many? How old is he?
Naze desu ka?	Why is it?

¹ *Donata* is more polite than *dare*. *Donata* is called the "respect" form of *dare*. The respect form of words is used only when someone is talking about someone else in a more polite way. The "humble" form, as opposed to respect, is used to demote one's status.

Dooshite[1] desu ka?	Why is it?
Doo desu ka?	How is it?
Dochira desu ka?	Which of the two is it? Which way is it?
Dore desu ka?	Which is it *(used for more than two)?*
Dono tatemono desu ka?	Which building is it?
Dono hito desu ka?	Which person is it?
Ikimashita ka?	Did you go?
Dare ga ikimashita ka?	Who went?
Naze ikimashita ka?	Why did you go?
Itsu ikimashita ka?	When did you go?
Nan de ikimashita ka?	How did you go? [By what means (of transportation) did (you) go?]
Dare to ikimashita ka?	With whom did you go?
Itsu dare to ikimashita ka?	When and with whom did you go?
Dooshite Tanaka-san to ikimashita ka?	Why did you go with Ms. Tanaka?
Kabuki wa doo deshita ka?	How was the Kabuki play?
Bunraku wa dooshite mimasen deshita ka?	Why didn't you see the Bunraku (puppet play)?
Kabuki e dare to iki-mashita ka?	With whom did you go to the Kabuki?

QUIZ 8

1. *Watakushi no hon wa doko ni ari-masu ka?*

a. Where is your book?

---

[1] *Dooshite* is less formal than *naze.*

2. *Anata no hon wa doko ni arimasu ka?*

b. What is your name?

3. *Sono hitotachi no tegami wa doko ni arimasu ka?*

c. That train is not as fast as this train.

4. *Onamae wa nan desu ka?*

d. Which building is it?

5. *Sono densha wa kono densha hodo hayaku arimasen.*

e. Where are their [those people's] letters?

6. *Kono kuruma no hoo ga ano ji-doosha yori atarashii desu.*

f. Where is my book?

7. *Dono tatemono desu ka?*

g. When is it?

8. *Dekiru dake haya-ku shite kudasai.*

h. This car is newer than that one.

9. *Kore desu ka?*

i. Do it as soon as possible, please.

10. *Itsu desu ka?*

j. Is it this?

ANSWERS
1—f; 2—a; 3—c; 4—b; 5—c; 6—h; 7—d; 8—i; 9—j; 10—g.

D. WORD STUDY

aisukuriimu	ice cream
bifuteki	beefsteak
chiizu	cheese
kechappu	catsup
mayoneezu	mayonnaise
omuretsu	omelet
sarada	salad

soosu	sauce (Worcestershire)
suupu	soup
toosuto	toast

LESSON 14

DAI JUUYONKA

A. To Have and Have Not

1. I (you, he, she . . .) have:

Motte imasu.[1]
{
I have. [Am holding.]
You have. [Are holding.]
He has. [Is holding.]
They have. [Are holding.]
}

2. I (you, he, she . . .) don't have:

Motte imasen.	I don't have. You don't have, etc.
Nani mo motte imasen.	I have nothing. I don't have anything.
Okane o motte imasu.	I have money.
Okane o juubun motte imasu.	I have enough money.
Okane o sukoshi mo motte imasen.	I don't have any money. [I don't have even a little bit of money.]

[1] Another expression for "have" was introduced in Lesson 8.

3. Do I (you, he, she . . .) have?

Motte imasu ka?   Do I have (it)?

4. Don't I (you, he, she . . .) have?

Motte imasen ka?	Don't you have (it)?
Okane o motte imasu ka?	Does he have (any) money?
Okane o juubun motte imasu ka?	Does he have enough money?
Enpitsu o motte imasu ka?	Do you have a pencil?
Pen o motte imasu ka?	Do you have a pen?
Okane o juubun motte imasen ka?	Don't you have enough money?
Enpitsu o motte imasen ka?	Don't you have a pencil?
Pen o motte imasen ka?	Don't you have a pen?

5. I (you, he, she . . .) have to have:

Motte inakereba narimasen.   I have to have (it). [If (I) don't have (it), it won't do.]

6. Do I (you, he, she . . .) have to have?

Motte inakereba narimasen ka?   Do I have to have (it)?

7. I (you, he, she . . .) don't have to have:

Motte inakute mo ii desu.	I don't have to have (it). [Even if (I) don't have (it), I will be all right.]

8. Don't I (you, he, she . . .) have to have?

Motte inakute mo ii desu ka?	Don't I have to have it?
Pasupooto o motte inakereba narimasen.	You have to have a passport.
Kippu o motte inakereba narimasen.	You have to have a ticket.
Shookaijoo o motte inakereba narimasen.	You have to have a letter of introduction.
Pasupooto o motte inakereba narimasen ka?	Do you have to have a passport?
Kippu o motte inakereba narimasen ka?	Do you have to have a ticket?
Shookaijoo o motte inakereba narimasen ka?	Do you have to have a letter of introduction?
Pasupooto o motte inakute mo ii desu.	You don't have to have a passport.
Kippu o motte inakute mo ii desu.	You don't have to have a ticket.
Shookaijoo o motte inakute mo ii desu.	You don't have to have a letter of introduction.
Pasupooto o motte inakute mo ii desu ka?	Don't I have to have a passport? [Is it all right (to go) even if I don't have a passport?]

9. I (you, he, she . . .) may have it:

Motte iru ka mo shiremasen.	I may have (it). [I cannot tell if I have (it).]

10. I (you, he, she . . .) may not have it:

Motte inai ka mo shiremasen.	I may not have (it).
Okane o motte iru ka mo shiremasen.	He may have (some) money.
Kippu o motte iru ka mo shiremasen.	He may have the ticket.
Okane o motte inai ka mo shiremasen.	He may not have any money.
Kippu o motte inai ka mo shiremasen.	He may not have the ticket.

B. ALSO

mo	also, too
watashi mo	I also, I too
anata mo	you also
ano hito mo	he/she also
watashitachi mo	we also
anatatachi mo	you also
ano hitotachi mo	they also
Ano hitotachi mo kimasu.	They are coming too.
Watashi mo kimasu.	I'm coming too.

QUIZ 9

1. *Oishii desu.*   a. He may have a ticket.

2. *Atarashii desu.*

   b. I don't have any money.

3. *Nan desu ka?*

   c. You don't have to have a ticket.

4. *Dono tatemono desu ka?*

   d. You have to have a passport.

5. *Okane o juubun motte imasu.*

   e. I have enough money.

6. *Enpitsu o motte imasu ka?*

   f. It's delicious.

7. *Pasupooto o motte inakereba narimasen.*

   g. Which building is it?

8. *Okane o sukoshi mo motte imasen.*

   h. It's new.

9. *Kippu o motte inakute mo ii desu.*

   i. Do you have a pencil?

10. *Kippu o motte iru ka mo shiremasen.*

   j. What is it?

ANSWERS

1—f; 2—h; 3—j; 4—g; 5—e; 6—i; 7—d; 8—b; 9—c; 10—a.

C. WORD STUDY

burausu	blouse
mafuraa	muffler (heavy scarf)
nekutai	necktie
oobaakooto	overcoat
seetaa	sweater
shatsu	shirt
sukaafu	scarf
sukaato	skirt
surippu	slip

LESSON 15

DAI JUUGOKA

A. I HAVE BEEN TO . . .

Hakone e itta koto[1] ga arimasu.	I have been to Hakone. [(I) have the experience of having gone to Hakone.]
Taiwan e itta koto ga arimasu.	I have been to Taiwan.
Nihon ryoori o tabeta koto ga arimasu.	I have eaten Japanese cooking. [(I) have had the experience of eating Japanese cooking.]
Kabuki o mita koto ga arimasu.	I have seen (the) Kabuki.

B. SOMETIMES I GO . . .

Hakone e iku koto ga arimasu.	Sometimes I go to Hakone. [The act of my going to Hakone exists.]
Taiwan e iku koto ga arimasu.	Sometimes I go to Taiwan.

---

[1] *koto* = act, event, experience.

Nihon ryoori o taberu koto ga arimasu.	Sometimes I eat Japanese cooking.
Kabuki o miru koto ga arimasu.	Sometimes I see Kabuki plays.

C. I CAN, I AM ABLE TO . . .

Ashita wa Hakone e iku koto ga dekimasu.	Tomorrow I can go to Hakone. [The act of my going to Hakone tomorrow is possible.]
Rainen wa Taiwan e iku koto ga dekimasu.	Next year I can go to Taiwan.
Nihon ryoori o taberu koto ga dekimasu.	I can eat Japanese cooking.
Nyuu Yooku de Kabuki o miru koto ga dekimashita.	I got to see the Kabuki in New York.

D. I'VE DECIDED TO . . .

Ashita wa Hakone e iku koto ni shimashita.	I've decided to go to Hakone tomorrow.
Rainen wa Taiwan e iku koto ni shimashita.	I've decided to go to Taiwan next year.
Nihon ryoori o taberu koto ni shimashita.	I've decided to have [eat] Japanese cooking.
Kabuki o miru koto ni shimashita.	We've decided to see the Kabuki plays.

QUIZ 10

1. *Sore desu ka?*   a. We've decided to see the Kabuki plays.

2. *Doko ni imasu ka?*   b. Please do it as soon as possible.

3. *Ookii deshoo.*   c. I have seen (the) Kabuki.

4. *Itsu desu ka?*   d. Why didn't you see the Bunraku?

5. *Dare to ikimashita ka?*   e. That one isn't as big as this one.

6. *Ookiku arimasen deshita.*   f. I was able to eat Japanese cooking.

7. *Kabuki wa doo deshita ka?*   g. When is it?

8. *Itsu ikimashita ka?*   h. It is probably big.

9. *Dare ga ikimashita ka?*   i. Where is he?

10. *Sore wa kore hodo ookiku arimasen.*   j. Is it that?

11. *Kabuki o mita koto ga arimasu.*   k. It wasn't big.

12. *Nihon ryoori o taberu koto ga de-kimashita.*   l. When did you go?

13. *Dekiru dake ha-yaku shite kudasai.*   m. Who went?

14. *Bunraku wa doo shite mimasen deshita ka?*   n. With whom did you go?

15. *Kabuki o miru koto ni shimashita.*   o. How was the Ka-buki play?

ANSWERS

1—j; 2—i; 3—h; 4—g; 5—n; 6—k; 7—o; 8—l; 9—m; 10—e; 11—c; 12—f; 13—b; 14—d; 15—a.

LESSON 16

DAI JUUROKKA

A. DO YOU SPEAK JAPANESE?

Nihongo ga dekimasu ka?	Do you speak Japanese? [Is Japanese possible?]
Iie, dekimasen.	No, I don't speak Japanese.
heta desu.	speak poorly [be poor (in skill)]
taihen heta desu	speak very poorly [be very poor]
Taihen heta desu.	I (speak) very poorly.
sukoshi	a little
Hai, sukoshi dekimasu.	Yes, I speak a little.
honno sukoshi	just a little
Honno sukoshi dekimasu.	I speak just a little.
amari . . . dekimasen	not much (*used with a negative verb*)
wazuka dake	just a little
Wakarimasu ka?	Do you understand (it)?
Iie, wakarimasen.	No, I don't understand (it).
Amari yoku wakarimasen.	I don't understand (it) very well.
Nihongo wa amari yoku wakarimasen.	I don't understand Japanese very well.
Hai, wakarimasu.	Yes, I understand.
Hai, sukoshi wakarimasu.	Yes, I understand a little.

Yomemasu[1] ga[2] hanasemasen.	I can read but I can't speak.
Wakarimasu ka?	Do you understand?
Sukoshi mo wakarimasen.	Not at all.
Yoku wakarimasen.	I don't understand very well.
Kaite kudasai.	Write it, please.
Doo kakimasu ka?	How do you write it?
Sono kotoba wa shirimasen.	I don't know that word.
Sore wa Nihongo de doo iimasu ka?	How do you say that in Japanese?
"Thank you" wa Nihongo de doo iimasu ka?	How do you say "Thank you" in Japanese?

B. PLEASE SPEAK A LITTLE SLOWER

Yukkuri hanashite kudasareba . . .	If you speak slowly (for me) . . .
Yukkuri hanashite kudasareba wakarimasu.	If you speak slowly, I'll be able to understand you.
Yukkuri hanashite kudasai.	Please speak slowly.
Nan to osshaimashita ka?	What did you say?

---

[1] *Yomemasu* = can read; *hanasemasu* = can speak. These examples present a way of saying "can . . ." different from the one introduced in Section C of Lesson 15. See also Section C (p. 264) of Lesson 40 and Section 31 of the Summary of Japanese Grammar.

[2] *ga* = but.

Doo yuu imi desu ka?	What do you mean?
. . . kudasaimasen ka?	Wouldn't you . . . ?
hanasu	speak
motto yukkuri	slower
Motto yukkuri hanashite kuda-saimasen ka?	Would you please speak slower? [Wouldn't you speak . . .]
doozo	please
Doozo motto yukkuri hanashite kudasai-masen ka?	Would you mind speaking a little slower, please?
Moo ichido itte kuda-saimasen ka?	Would you please say (that) again?

C. THANKS!

Arigatoo.	Thanks.
Doomo arigatoo gozaimasu.	Thank you very much.
Doo itashimashite.	Don't mention it.
Arigatoo gozaimasu.	Thanks. [(I) thank (you).]
Doo itashimashite.	You're welcome.
Gomennasai.	Excuse me.
Doozo.	Certainly. [Please (go ahead).]
Doozo osaki ni.	Go ahead!
Sumimasen. Nan to osshaimashita ka?	Pardon? What did you say?
Dewa mata.	See you soon.
Dewa nochihodo.	See you later.
Dewa konban.	See you this evening.

QUIZ 11

1. *Kaite kudasai.*	a. I don't speak Japanese.
2. *Nihongo wa dekimasen.*	b. Just a little.
3. *Nihongo wa yoku wakarimasen.*	c. Do you understand?
4. *Wakarimasu ka?*	d. I don't understand Japanese very well.
5. *Honno sukoshi.*	e. Write it down, please.
6. *Moo ichido itte kudasaimasen ka?*	f. How do you write it?
7. *"Thank you" wa Nihongo de doo iimasu ka?*	g. I don't know that word.
8. *Doo yuu imi desu ka?*	h. How do you say "Thank you" in Japanese?
9. *Doo kakimasu ka?*	i. What do you mean?
10. *Sono kotoba wa shirimasen.*	j. Would you please say that again?

ANSWERS
1—e; 2—a; 3—d; 4—c; 5—b; 6—j; 7—h; 8—i; 9—f; 10—g.

D. WORD STUDY

banana	banana
karifurawaa	cauliflower
kyabetsu	cabbage
meron	melon
orenji	orange

paseri	parsley
remon	lemon
retasu	lettuce
serori	celery
tomato	tomato

LESSON 17

DAI JUUNANAKA

A. THIS AND THAT

1. *Kono:* This

kono hon	this book
kono hito	this person
kono hoteru	this hotel
kono tegami	this letter
kono hanashi	this story

2. *Sono:* That

Sono refers to a thing or place that is nearby.

sono hon	that book
sono hi	that day
sono kotoba	that word
sono hito	that person
sono hoteru	that hotel
sono tegami	that letter

3. *Ano:* That

Ano refers to something outside of immediate reach.

ano uchi	that house (over there)
ano ki	that tree (over there)
ano neko	that cat (over there)

The distinction among *kono, sono,* and *ano* holds true with the distinction among *kore, sore,* and *are,* respectively. The difference between the *kono-sono-ano* series and the *kore-sore-are* series below is that a member of the former series must be followed by a noun (e.g., *kono hon* [this book]), and a member of the latter series cannot be followed by a noun.

4. *Kore:* This

Kore wa doo yuu imi desu ka?	What does this mean?
Kore wa watakushi no desu.	This is mine.

5. *Sore:* That

Sore desu.	That's it. It's that.
Sore o totte kudasai.	Please pick that one.
Sore wa ii kangae desu ne.	That is a good idea.
Kore mo sore mo dame desu.	Both this one and that one are no good.

6. *Are:* That

Are desu.	It's that (over there).
Are ja arimasen.	It isn't that. That's not it.
Are o kudasai.	Give me that (over there), please.
Kore wa watakushi no desu; are wa anata no desu.	This one is mine; that one (over there) is yours.

QUIZ 12

1. *Are wa anata no desu ka?*	a. What does this mean?
2. *Kore wa doo yuu imi desu ka?*	b. It isn't that.
3. *Are o kudasai.*	c. That is mine.
4. *Ano hon o kudasai.*	d. This one is mine; that one is yours.
5. *Sore desu.*	e. This is mine.
6. *Kore wa watakushi no desu.*	f. Give me that, please.
7. *Are desu.*	g. It's that.
8. *Sore wa watakushi no desu.*	h. Please give me that book (over there).
9. *Kore wa watakushi no desu; are wa anata no desu.*	i. It's that.
10. *Are ja arimasen.*	j. Is that yours?

ANSWERS
1—j; 2—a; 3—f; 4—h; 5—g; 6—e; 7—i; 8—c; 9—d; 10—b.

B. NOT

Yoku arimasen.	It's not good.
Waruku arimasen.	It's not bad.
Sore ja arimasen.	It's not that.
Koko ni arimasen.	It's not here.
Amari takusan de naku.	Not too much.
Amari hayaku naku.	Not too fast.
Mada desu.	Not yet. [It's yet (to come).]

Sukoshi mo ... masen.	Not at all *(with a negative predicate).*
Sukoshi mo jikan ga arimasen.	I don't have any time.
Doo suru ka shirimasen.	I don't know how to do it.
Itsu ka shirimasen.	I don't know when.
Doko ka shirimasen.	I don't know where.
Nani mo shirimasen.	I don't know anything.
Nani mo iimasen deshita.	He didn't say anything.
Nani mo arimasen.	Nothing. [There is nothing.]
Nani mo motte imasen.	I don't have anything.
Kesshite.	Never *(with a negative predicate).*
Kesshite kimasen.	She never comes.
Dare ga kimashita ka?	Who came?
... Dare mo kimasen deshita.	... Nobody came.
Dare mo miemasen.	I don't see anyone. [No one is in sight.]
Moo soko e ikimasen.	I don't go there anymore.
Moo kimasen.	She doesn't come anymore.
Hyakuen shika arimasen.	I have only a hundred yen. [(I) don't have but a hundred yen.]
Ichijikan shika arimasen.	You have only one hour.

C. ISN'T IT? AREN'T YOU? ETC.

Hontoo desu ne?	It's true, isn't it?
Kimasu ne?	You are coming, aren't you?

Juubun motte imasu ne?	You have enough of it, don't you?
Sukoshi mo motte imasen ne?	You don't have any of it, do you?
Sansei desu ne?	You agree, don't you?

QUIZ 13

1.	*Sore ja arimasen.*	a.	I don't see anyone.
2.	*Itsu ka shirimasen.*	b.	I have only a hundred yen.
3.	*Sukoshi mo jikan ga arimasen.*	c.	You have only one hour.
4.	*Nani mo arimasen.*	d.	You are coming, aren't you?
5.	*Kimasu ne?*	e.	You don't have any of it, do you?
6.	*Ichijikan shika arimasen.*	f.	It's not that.
7.	*Dare mo miemasen.*	g.	I don't have any time.
8.	*Hyakuen shika arimasen.*	h.	I don't know when.
9.	*Sukoshi mo motte imasen ne?*	i.	He didn't say anything.
10.	*Nani mo iimasen deshita.*	j.	There's nothing.

ANSWERS
1—f; 2—h; 3—g; 4—j; 5—d; 6—c; 7—a; 8—b; 9—e; 10—i.

D. WORD STUDY

baree booru	volleyball
basuketto booru	basketball
bokushingu	boxing

gorufu	golf
haikingu	hiking
pinpon	Ping-Pong (table tennis)
resuringu	wrestling
sukeeto	skating
sukii	ski, skiing
tenisu	tennis

LESSON 18

DAI JUUHACHIKA

A. IT'S ME (I), ETC.

Watashi desu.	It's me (I).
Anata desu.	It's you.
Ano hito desu.	It's him/her (he/she).
Watashitachi desu.	It's us.

B. IT'S MINE, ETC.

Notice that when a noun appears together with *no* but the combination is not followed by another noun, it often means, literally, "a thing pertaining to (that noun)." For example:

watakushi no	a thing pertaining to me; my thing; mine
Watashi no desu.	It's mine.
Anata[1] no desu.	It's yours.

---

[1] It is more polite to use the person's name rather than the personal pronoun "you" *(anata, anatagata)*. If you want to say "it's yours" and you are speaking to Mr. Yamada, you would say *Yamada-san no desu.*

Ano hito no desu.	It's his (hers).
Watashitachi no desu.	It's ours.
Anatagata no desu.	It's yours *(pl.)*.
Ano hitotachi no desu.	It's theirs.

C. ABOUT ME, ETC.

Anata no koto o hanashite iru no desu.[1]	I'm talking about you. [(I'm) talking of things pertaining to you.]
Watashi no koto o hanashite iru no desu ne?	You are talking about me, aren't you? [. . .that's what it is, isn't it?]

D. TO ME, ETC.

Watashi ni kudasai.	Give it to me, please.
Watashitachi ni kudasai.	Give it to us, please.
Watashi ni kudasaimashita.	She gave it to me.
Watashitachi ni kudasaimashita.	She gave it to us.

E. THE MODIFIERS

In Japanese, a modifier *always* precedes the word modified, whether the modifier is a single word, a

---

[1] Notice that when the sequence *no desu* (or *n desu*) immediately follows a predicate, it means, "That's what it is," or "It's a fact that," and the predicate itself is usually in the plain form.

phrase, or a clause. An adjective that modifies a noun is always placed before the noun, and an adverb that modifies a verb is always placed before the verb. Even a long clause, which in English would follow the noun, precedes it in Japanese. In fact, the very act of placing a clause before a noun makes it a modifier of that noun.

Here are some examples:

ie	a house
akai	it is red *(plain)*
akai ie	a red house
yane	a roof
Yane ga akai.	The roof is red.
yane ga akai ie ⎤ yane no akai ie ⎦	the house whose roof is red [the-roof-is-red house]
Yane no akai ie ni sunde imasu.	He lives in a house with a red roof.
hito	a person
sunde imasu	he lives [is residing]
sunde iru	he lives *(plain)*
sunde iru hito	the person who lives (there)
sono ie ni sunde iru hito	the person who lives in that house
yane no akai ie ni sunde iru hito	the person who lives in the house with a red roof
Ano yane no akai ie ni sunde iru hito ga kyonen Amerika kara kita hito desu.	The person who lives in that house with a red roof is the person who came from America last year.

F. The Noun-Maker *No*

In addition to the particle *no* that follows a noun and links it to another noun, there is a "noun-maker" *no* which appears only *after* a clause. (As you have already seen, a clause *can* be a single adjective or a verb or a series of words ending in an adjective or verb.) This *no* makes a noun out of the clause and is usually translated "one who," "one which," "the act of doing," "the time when," or "the place where."

Akai no o kudasai.	Please give me one that is red. Please give me a red one.
Akaku nai no o kuda-sai.	Give me one that is not red, please.
Yane ga akai no ga watashi no ie desu.	The one (house) with a red roof is my house. [The-roof-is-red one (house) is my house.]
Tabemashita.	I ate.
Tabeta.	I ate *(plain)*.
sakana	fish
Tabeta no wa sakana deshita.	The food [thing] that I ate was fish.
Sakana o tabeta.	I ate fish *(plain)*.
Sakana o tabeta no wa kinoo deshita.	It was yesterday that I ate fish. [The day that (I) ate fish was yesterday.]

QUIZ 14

1. *Watashi no desu.*	a. It was yesterday that I ate fish
2. *Tabeta no wa sakana deshita.*	b. Give me one that is not red, please.
3. *Anata no koto o hanashite iru no desu.*	c. Give it to us, please.
4. *Anatagata no desu.*	d. Give me one that is red, please.
5. *Watashitachi ni kudasai.*	e. He lives in a house with a red roof.
6. *Watashi ni kudasaimashita.*	f. It's yours.
7. *Yane no akai ie ni sunde imasu.*	g. He gave it to me.
8. *Akaku nai no o kudasai.*	h. The food that I ate was fish.
9. *Akai no o kudasai.*	i. It's mine.
10. *Sakana o tabeta no wa kinoo deshita.*	j. I'm talking about you.

ANSWERS
1—i; 2—h; 3—j; 4—f; 5—c; 6—g; 7—e; 8—b;
9—d; 10—a.

LESSON 19

DAI JUUKYUUKA

A. HELLO, HOW ARE YOU?

Konnichi wa.	Hello. Good afternoon.
Ohayoo gozaimasu.	Good morning.
Ogenki desu ka?	How are you?
Okagesama de genki desu.	Very well, thanks. [Thanks to your thinking of me . . .]
Betsu ni kawari arimasen.	So-so. [No special change.]
Anata wa?	And how are you? [And you?]
Doo ni ka yatte orimasu.	Not bad.
Okagesama de doo ni ka yatte orimasu.	Not bad, thanks.

B. I'D LIKE YOU TO MEET . . .

Sakata-san o goshookai itashimasu.	Allow me to present Ms. Sakata. [May (I) introduce Ms. Sakata.]
Hajimemashite.	Glad to meet you. [It is a pleasure to meet you.]
Sakata desu. Doozo yoroshiku.	I am Sakata. Glad to meet you.
Doozo yoroshiku.	Glad to meet you.

C. What's New?

Konnichi wa.	Hello.
Ogenki desu ka?	How are you?
Okage sama de.	Fine, thanks.
Kawatta koto wa ari-masen ka?	What's new?
Betsu ni arimasen.	Nothing much. [There isn't anything especially.]
Nisannichi shitara denwa o kakete ku-dasai.	Call me one of these days, please.
Wasurenaide kudasai.	Please don't forget.
Kashikomarimashita.	I'll certainly do so.
Daijoobu desu ne?	Are you sure it's OK? You're sure it's OK?
Daijoobu desu.	Sure!

D. See You Soon!

Dewa mata.	See you soon. [Well, then, again.]
Getsuyoobi ni ome ni kakarimasu.	See you on Monday.
Isshuukan shitara ome ni kakarimasu.	I'll see you in a week.
Nishuukan shitara ome ni kakarimasu.	I'll see you in two weeks.
Kin'yoobi no yoru ome ni kakarimasu.	I'll see you Friday night.
Kono Mokuyoobi ni ome ni kakarimasu.	I'll see you this coming Thursday.

Kono Mokuyoobi no ban hachiji ni ome ni kakarimasu.	I'll see you this coming Thursday at eight o'clock in the evening. [This coming Thursday evening at eight o'clock (I'll) see you.]
Kon'ya ome ni kakarimasu.	I'll see you tonight.

QUIZ 15

1. *Ogenki desu ka?*   a. So-so.
2. *Ashita ome ni*   b. Very well, thanks.
   kakarimasu.
3. *Doozo yoroshiku.*   c. Not too bad.
4. *Kawatta koto wa*   d. How are you?
   arimasen ka?
5. *Mokuyoobi ni ome*   e. I'll see you tomor-
   ni kakarimasu.   row.
6. *Okagesama de.*   f. I'm happy to know
                                            you.
7. *Betsu ni arimasen.*   g. What's new?
8. *Konnichi wa.*   h. I'll see you on
                                            Thursday.
9. *Doo ni ka yatte*   i. Good afternoon.
   orimasu.   Hello.
10. *Betsu ni kawari*   j. Nothing much.
    arimasen.
11. *Isshuukan shitara*   k. Allow me . . . (I
    ome ni kakarimasu.   would like to intro-
                                            duce . . .)
12. *Nisannichi shitara*   l. Call me one of
    denwa o kakete   these days, please.
    kudasai.

13. *Dewa mata.*   m. See you Monday.
14. *Goshookai itashi-* n. See you soon.
    masu.
15. *Getsuyoobi ni ome* o. See you in a week.
    ni kakarimasu.

ANSWERS
1—d; 2—e; 3—f; 4—g; 5—h; 6—b; 7—j; 8—i;
9—c; 10—a; 11—o; 12—l; 13—n; 14—k; 15—m.

LESSON 20

DAI NIJIKKA

A. HAVE YOU TWO MET?

Kono kata o gozonji desu ka?	Do you know my friend [this person]?
Iie, kyoo hajimete ome ni kakarimasu.	No, I don't think so. [Am meeting him for the first time today.]
Iie, ome ni kakatta koto wa arimasen.	No, I haven't had the pleasure of meeting [this person].
Mae kara gozonji desu ne?	I believe you already know one another.
Hai, mae kara zonjiagete orimasu.	Yes, we've already met. [Have known him from before.]
Iie, zonjiagete orimasen.	No, I don't believe we've met before. [No, (I) don't know (the gentleman.)]

B.   GLAD TO HAVE MET YOU

Hajimemashite.	Glad to meet you. [It's a pleasure to meet you.]
Ome ni kakarete yokatta desu.	Glad to have met you. [Has been good fortune (for me) to have been able to see you.]
Mata zehi oai shitai to omoimasu.	Hope to see you soon.
Doozo yoroshiku.	Same here.
Moo ichido sono uchi ni hi o kimete oai shimashoo.	Let's get together again one of these days.
Arigatoo gozaimasu.	Fine. [Thank you.]
Watakushi no juusho to denwa bangoo wa omochi deshoo ka?	Do you have my address and telephone number?
Iie, motte orimasen.	No, I don't.
Itadakemasu ka?	Let me have it. [Can I have it?]
Banchi wa Bunkyoo-ku Oiwake-choo[1] ni-choome[2] juugo banchi desu.	My address is 15 2-choome, Oiwake-choo, Bunkyo-ku.

---

[1] *Choo* is a word for "street" or "block," and is sometimes added to the name proper, as in *Oiwake-choo*.
[2] *Choome* is a word for "street." *Me* in "*choome*" signifies that the street is an ordinal (e.g., *Ginza yon choome* = Ginza Fourth Street).

Denwa bangoo wa san yon hachi san no roku yon roku san ban desu.
My telephone number is 3483-6463.

Jimusho no banchi mo itadakemasu ka?
Give me your office address, too. [Can I have . . .]

Okaki shimashoo. Ginza yon choome no ni banchi desu.
I'll write it for you. It's 2 Ginza Fourth Street.

Asa wa kuji mae deshitara uchi ni orimasu.
You can get me at home before nine in the morning. [If it is before nine (I'll) be at home.]

Sono ato wa jimusho no hoo ni orimasu.
Otherwise [afterward] at the office.

Aa soo desu ka. Dewa, tashika ni gorenraku shimasu.
Good. I'll be sure to get in touch with you.

Dewa shitsurei shimasu. Odenwa o omachi shite orimasu.
Good-bye. [And] (I) will be waiting for your phone call.

Dewa mata.
See you soon.

QUIZ 16

1. *Iie, kyoo hajimete ome ni kakarimasu.*

2. *Hai, mae kara zonjiagete orimasu.*

3. *Iie, motte orimasen. Itadakemasu ka?*

a. Yes, we've already met.

b. No, I haven't had the pleasure of meeting (this person).

c. No, not yet. [I am meeting him for the first time today.]

4. *Jimusho no banchi mo itadakemasu ka?*

d. Glad to have met you.

5. *Dewa mata.*

e. I hope to see you soon.

6. *Aa soo desu ka. Dewa tashika ni gorenraku shimasu.*

f. Give me your office address, too.

7. *Watakushi no juusho to denwa bangoo wa omochi deshoo ka?*

g. No, let me have it.

8. *Iie, ome ni kakatta koto wa arimasen.*

h. Do you have my address and telephone number?

9. *Mata zehi oai shitai to omoimasu.*

i. Good. I will be sure to get in touch with you.

10. *Ome ni kakarete yokatta desu.*

j. See you soon.

ANSWERS
1—c; 2—a; 3—g; 4—f; 5—j; 6—i; 7—h; 8—b; 9—e; 10—d.

C. WORD STUDY

baiorin	violin
furuuto	flute
gitaa	guitar
haapu	harp
kurarinetto	clarinet
mandorin	mandolin
paipu orugan	pipe organ
piano	piano
sakisofon	saxophone
chero	cello

REVIEW QUIZ 2

1. *Doozo moo sukoshi yukkuri* _____ (speak)
   kudasaimasen ka?
   a. *kaite*
   b. *hanashite*
   c. *kakete*

2. *Doozo* _____ (slowly) *hanashite kudasai.*
   a. *hakkiri*
   b. *yoku*
   c. *yukkuri*

3. *Kodomo* _____ (direction-particle) *hon o yari-*
   mashita.
   a. *ga*
   b. *ni*
   c. *no*

4. *Yamada-san ni tegami* _____ (object-particle)
   kakimashita.
   a. *o*
   b. *ga*
   c. *no*

5. *Sonna ni* _____ (far) *arimasen.*
   a. *tooku*
   b. *chikaku*
   c. *takaku*

6. *Ano hito* _____ (topic-particle) *kodomo ni*
   okane o yarimashita.
   a. *o*
   b. *wa*
   c. *to*

7. *Watashi wa jimusho ni* _____ (am).
   a. *desu.*
   b. *imasu.*
   c. *arimasu.*

8. _____ (Late) *kimashita.*
   a. *Hayaku*
   b. *Tooku*
   c. *Osoku*

9. *Sono hon wa doko ni* _____ (is) *ka?*
   a. *imasu*
   b. *arimasu*
   c. *desu*

10. *Koppu o* _____ (bring) *kudasai.*
    a. *katte*
    b. *totte*
    c. *motte kite*

11. *Sore wa* _____ (easy) *desu.*
    a. *yasashii*
    b. *muzukashii*
    c. *ookii*

12. *Kodomo no* _____ (room) *desu.*
    a. *mono*
    b. *heya*
    c. *hon*

13. *Okane ga* _____ (there isn't).
    a. *arimasen.*
    b. *imasen.*
    c. *kimasen.*

14. *Tabako o* _____ (have) *imasu ka?*
    a. *mite*
    b. *kaite*
    c. *motte*

15. *Nihongo wa yoku* _____ (don't understand).
    a. *wakarimasen.*
    b. *kakemasen.*
    c. *shimasen.*

16. *Doo mo* _____ (thank) *gozaimasu.*
    a. *osamuu*
    b. *arigatoo*
    c. *otakoo*

17. _____ (Here) *ni imasu ka?*
    a. *Doko*
    b. *Soko*
    c. *Koko*

18._____ (A little) *wakarimasu.*
    a. *Yoku*
    b. *Takusan*
    c. *Sukoshi*

ANSWERS
1—b; 2—c; 3—b; 4—a; 5—a; 6—b; 7—b; 8—c;
9—b; 10—c; 11—a; 12—b; 13—a; 14—c; 15—a;
16—b; 17—c; 18—c.

LESSON 21

DAI NIJUU IKKA

A. NUMBERS

1. For 1 to 10 only, there are two sets of numbers:

ichi	one
ni	two
san	three
shi, yon	four
go	five
roku	six
shichi, nana	seven
hachi	eight
ku, kyuu	nine
juu	ten

hitotsu	one
futatsu	two
mittsu	three
yottsu	four
itsutsu	five
muttsu	six
nanatsu	seven
yattsu	eight
kokonotsu	nine
too	ten

juuichi	eleven
juuni	twelve
juusan	thirteen

juushi, juuyon	fourteen
juugo	fifteen
juuroku	sixteen
juushichi, juunana	seventeen
juuhachi	eighteen
juuku	nineteen
nijuu	twenty
nijuu ichi	twenty-one
nijuu ni	twenty-two
nijuu san	twenty-three
sanjuu	thirty
sanjuu ichi	thirty-one
sanjuu ni	thirty-two
sanjuu san	thirty-three
yonjuu, shijuu	forty
yonjuu ichi	forty-one
yonjuu ni	forty-two
yonjuu san	forty-three
gojuu	fifty
gojuu ichi	fifty-one
gojuu ni	fifty-two
gojuu san	fifty-three
rokujuu	sixty
rokujuu ichi	sixty-one
rokujuu ni	sixty-two
rokujuu san	sixty-threc
nanajuu, shichijuu	seventy
nanajuu ichi	seventy-one
nanajuu ni	seventy-two
nanajuu san	seventy-three

hachijuu	eighty
hachijuu ichi	eighty-one
hachijuu ni	eighty-two
hachijuu san	eighty-three
kyuujuu	ninety
kyuujuu ichi	ninety-one
kyuujuu ni	ninety-two
kyuujuu san	ninety-three

B. MORE NUMBERS

hyaku	one hundred
hyaku ichi	one hundred one
hyaku ni	one hundred two
hyaku san	one hundred three
hyaku nijuu	one hundred twenty
hyaku nijuu ichi	one hundred twenty-one
hyaku sanjuu	one hundred thirty
hyaku yonjuu	one hundred forty
hyaku gojuu	one hundred fifty
hyaku rokujuu	one hundred sixty
hyaku nanajuu	one hundred seventy
hyaku nanajuu ichi	one hundred seventy-one
hyaku hachijuu	one hundred eighty
hyaku kyuujuu	one hundred ninety
hyaku kyuujuu hachi	one hundred ninety-eight
hyaku kyuujuu ku	one hundred ninety-nine

nihyaku	two hundred
sanbyaku¹ nijuu shi	three hundred twenty-four
happyaku nanajuu go	eight hundred seventy-five
sen	one thousand
sen ichi	one thousand one
sen ni	one thousand two
sen san	one thousand three
ichi man	ten thousand
juu man	one hundred thousand
hyaku man	one million
sanzen sanbyaku san-juu san	three thousand three hundred thirty-three

C. PRONUNCIATION OF NUMBERS BEFORE CERTAIN COUNTERS

The pronunciation of numbers often differs before "counters" beginning with certain consonants. "Counters" are words like "sheet" in "ten sheets of paper" or "cup" in "ten cups of water." Most things have to be counted with a counter in Japanese.

Before a counter beginning with *h, f, k, s, sh, t, chi,* or *ts,* the pronunciation of the *ichi* [one], *hachi* [eight], and *juu* [ten] usually changes. When a

¹ Notice the *b* in *sanbyaku*, the *p* in *happyaku*, and the *z* in *sanzen*. See Section 4 of the Summary of Japanese Grammar.

counter begins with *h* or *f*, the *h* or *f* changes to *p*.
Before a counter beginning with *h, f,* or *k*, the numbers *roku* [six] and *hyaku* [one hundred] also change
form. Following are some examples of these changes
in form:

COUNTER: -*FUN*	MINUTE
ichi, ippun	one, one minute
roku, roppun	six, six minutes
hachi, happun (or) hachifun	eight, eight minutes
juu, juppun (or) jippun	ten, ten minutes
hyaku, hyappun	one hundred, one hundred minutes

COUNTER: -*KEN*	HOUSE
ichi, ikken	one, one house
roku, rokken	six, six houses
hachi, hakken (or) hachiken	eight, eight houses
juu, jukken (or) jikken	ten, ten houses
hyaku, hyakken	one hundred, one hundred houses

COUNTER: -*SATSU*	VOLUME
ichi, issatsu	one, one volume
hachi, hassatsu	eight, eight volumes
juu, jussatsu (or) jissatsu	ten, ten volumes

COUNTER: *-TEN* POINT

ichi, itten	one, one point
hachi, hatten	eight, eight points
juu, jutten (or) jitten	ten, ten points

D. First, Second, Third

dai ichi[1]	first
dai ni	second
dai san	third
dai yon	fourth
dai go	fifth
dai roku	sixth
dai nana	seventh
dai hachi	eighth
dai kyuu	ninth
dai juu	tenth
Dai Ichiji Taisen	World War I
dai ni maku	the second act
san too	the third class
yon kai	the fourth floor
dai go ka	the fifth lesson
dai rokkai	the sixth time
dai nana shuu	the seventh week
hachikagetsume[2]	the eighth month
dai kyuu nen	the ninth year
dai juu	the tenth
juuichi ninme no hito	the eleventh person
dai juuni shoo	the twelfth chapter
juusan nichime	the thirteenth day
juuyon seiki	the fourteenth century

[1] When *dai* precedes a numeral, it shows that the number which follows is an ordinal. Occasionally, an ordinal is used without *dai*.
[2] *-me* is another way to indicate an ordinal number.

juugo kenme no uchi	the fifteenth door, the fifteenth house
juuroku banme no fune	the sixteenth boat
juunana choome	the seventeenth street
dai juuhappan	the eighteenth edition
juuku banme no kuruma	the nineteenth car
nijikkenme no ie	the twentieth house

QUIZ 17

1. *rokkiro*	a. the third class
2. *yon kai*	b. the eighth month
3. *jippun*	c. the ninth year
4. *santoo*	d. six kilometers
5. *juuyon seiki*	e. the fourth floor
6. *juuichi ninme no hito*	f. ten minutes
7. *dai go ka*	g. the eleventh person
8. *hachikagetsume*	h. the thirteenth day
9. *juusan nichime*	i. the fifth lesson
10. *dai kyuunen*	j. the fourteenth century

ANSWERS
1—d; 2—e; 3—f; 4—a; 5—j; 6—g; 7—i; 8—b; 9—h; 10—c.

E.   TWO AND TWO

Ichi to ni de san ni narimasu.	Two and one are [become] three.
Ni tasu ichi wa san desu.	Two and [plus] one are three.
Ni to ni wa yon desu.	Two and two are four.
Ni tasu ni wa yon desu.	Two and [plus] two are four.

Yon to san wa shichi desu.	Four and three are seven.
Yon tasu san wa shichi desu.	Four and [plus] three are seven.
Go to ni de shichi ni narimasu.	Five and two are [become] seven.
Go tasu ni wa shichi desu.	Five and [plus] two are seven.
Shichi to ichi de hachi ni narimasu.	Seven and one are [become] eight.
Shichi tasu ichi wa hachi desu.	Seven and [plus] one are eight.

LESSON 22

DAI NIJUU NIKA

A. It Costs . . .

Kore wa . . . shimasu.	This costs . . .
Kore wa gosen en shimasu.	This costs five thousand yen.
Kono nooto wa gohyaku gojuu en shimasu.	This notebook costs five hundred fifty yen.
Kono booshi wa gosen en shimashita.	This hat cost me five thousand yen.
Kono doresu ni ichi man gosen en haraimashita.	I paid fifteen thousand yen for this dress.

Kono kuruma o sanbyakuman en de kaimashita.	I bought this car for three million yen.
Ichi rittoru nisen en desu.	It's two thousand yen a liter.
Ichi meetoru nihyaku gojuu en desu.	That costs two hundred fifty yen a meter.
Sen nihyaku en shimasu.	The price is twelve hundred yen. It costs twelve hundred yen.
Hitotsu gojuu en desu.	They cost fifty yen a piece.

B. THE TELEPHONE NUMBER IS . . .

Watashi no denwa bangoo wa san yon hachi san no san roku yon hachi ban desu.	My telephone number is 3483-3648.
San san san yon no goo nii¹ san roku ban ni kakete mite kudasai.	Try number 3334-5236.
Denwa bangoo ga kawarimashita. Ima no wa san nii roku yon no nii nii nii yon ban desu.	My telephone number has been changed; it's now 3264-2224.
Denwa wa san kyuu nii nii no san san rei nana ban desu.	Their phone number is 3922-3307.

¹ When giving phone numbers, numerals with one syllable can be pronounced with long vowels: *goo* and *nii*.

C. My Address Is . . .

Yoyogi juuni-choome juunana banchi ni sunde imasu.	I live at 17, 12-chome (street), Yoyogi.
Yamada-san wa doko ni sunde imasu ka?	Where does Mr. Yamada live? [Where is Mr. Yamada residing?]
Kono machi ni sunde imasu.	He lives in this town.
Asakusa san-choome yon banchi ni sunde imasu.	She lives at 4, 3-chome, Asakusa.
Ikebukuro yon-choome juuni banchi desu.	Our address is 12, 4-chome, Ikebukuro.
Ogikubo go-choome nihyaku rokujuu san banchi ni sunde imasu.	We live at 263, 5-chome, Ogikubo.
Heya no bangoo wa yonjuu ni desu.	My room number is 42.

D. Some Dates

Amerika wa sen yon-hyaku kyuujuu ni nen ni hakken sare-mashita.	America was discovered in 1492.
Sen happyaku kyuu-juu ichi nen ni oko-rimashita.	It happened in 1891.
Sen kyuuhyaku juuni nen ni umaremashita.	I was born in 1912.

Nyuu Yooku no Sekai hakurankai wa sen kyuuhyaku sanjuu kyuu nen ni arimashita.	The New York World's Fair took place in 1939.
Kore wa mina sen kyuuhyaku hachijuu nen ni okorimashita.	All this happened in 1980.
Watashi wa sen kyuuhyaku kyuujuu nen ni wa Tookyoo ni imashita.	I was in Tokyo in 1990.

QUIZ 18

1. *Kore wa gosen en shimasu.*

a. This costs five thousand yen.

2. *Denwa bangoo wa san nana nii kyuu no san san rei nana ban desu.*

b. I bought this car for five million yen.

3. *Kono kuruma o go-hyakuman en de kaimashita.*

c. Their phone number is 3729-3307.

4. *Watashi wa sen kyuuhyaku kyuujuu nen ni Tookyoo ni imashita.*

d. They cost fifty yen apiece.

5. *Sore wa hitotsu gojuu en desu.*

e. I was in Tokyo in 1990.

ANSWERS
1—a; 2—c; 3—b; 4—e; 5—d.

LESSON 23

DAI NIJUU SANKA

A. WHAT TIME IS IT?

Nanji desu ka?	What time is it?
Nanji ka oshiete ku-dasaimasen ka?	Do you have the time, please?
Ichiji desu.	It's one o'clock.
Niji desu.	It's two o'clock.
Sanji desu.	It's three o'clock.
Yoji desu.	It's four o'clock.
Goji desu.	It's five o'clock.
Rokuji desu.	It's six o'clock.
Shichiji desu.	It's seven o'clock.
Hachiji desu.	It's eight o'clock.
Kuji desu.	It's nine o'clock.
Juuji desu.	It's ten o'clock.
Juuichiji desu.	It's eleven o'clock.
Juuniji desu.	It's noon. It's twelve o'clock.
Gogo ichiji desu.	It's 1:00 p.m.
Gogo niji desu.	It's 2:00 p.m.
Gogo sanji desu.	It's 3:00 p.m.
Gogo yoji desu.	It's 4:00 p.m.
Gogo goji desu.	It's 5:00 p.m.
Gogo rokuji desu.	It's 6:00 p.m.
Gogo shichiji desu.	It's 7:00 p.m.
Gogo hachiji desu.	It's 8:00 p.m.
Gogo kuji desu.	It's 9:00 p.m.
Gogo juuji desu.	It's 10:00 p.m.
Gogo juuichiji desu.	It's 11:00 p.m.
Gogo juuniji desu.	It's 12:00 p.m.
Yoru no juuniji desu.	It's midnight.

B. The Time Is Now . . .

byoo	second
fun, pun	minute
ji	hour
Niji juu gofun desu.	It's two fifteen.
Niji juu gofun sugi desu.	It's a quarter after two.
Niji juu gofun mae desu.	It's a quarter to two.
Sanji yonjuu gofun desu.	It's three forty-five.
Niji-han desu.	It's half-past two.
Niji sanjippun desu.	It's two thirty.
Goji nijippun mae desu.	It's twenty to five.
Kuji sanjuu gofun desu.	It's nine thirty-five.
Shoogo desu.	It's noon.
Juuniji gofun mae desu.	It's five to twelve.
Juuniji gofun sugi desu.	It's five past twelve.
Gozen ichiji desu.	It's one o'clock in the morning.
Goji goro desu.	It's about five.
Shichiji goro desu.	It's about seven.
Juuichiji sukoshi mae desu.	It's almost eleven.
Mada rokuji-han desu.	It's only half-past six.
Goji sugi desu.	It's after five.

C. When Will You Come?

Itsu oide ni narimasu ka?	When will you come *(respect)?* What time will you come?

Sanji ni soko e iki-masu.	I'll be there at three o'clock.
Sanji nijuppun mae ni kimashita.	She came at twenty to three.
Gogo niji ni kimasu.	He'll come at 2:00 p.m.
Kuji nijuu gofun goro ni soko e ikimasu.	We'll be there about nine twenty-five.
Konban no juuji-han ni kaette kimasu.	He'll be back at ten thirty this evening.
Hachiji juu gofun goro ni soko de ome ni kakari-mashoo.	I'll see you there about eight fifteen.
Rokuji ni aimasu.	We'll meet at six.
Yoji ni dekakemasu.	I'm going out at four o'clock.
Shichiji to hachiji no aida ni kite kuda-sai.	Come between seven and eight, please.
Yoru no rokuji ni ki-masu.	He'll come at six in the evening.
Konban juuji ni kite kudasai.	Come at ten o'clock tonight, please.
Densha wa shichiji nijuu sanpun ni tsukimasu.	The train arrives at seven twenty-three.
Densha wa kuji yon-jippun ni demasu.	The train leaves at nine forty.

D. IT'S TIME

Jikan desu.	It's time.
Sore o suru jikan desu.	It's time to do it. [(It) is to-do-it time.]
Deru jikan desu.	It's time to leave.

Uchi e kaeru jikan desu.	It's time to go home.
Jikan ga arimasu.	I have time.
Juubun jikan ga arimasu.	I have enough time.
Jikan ga arimasen.	I don't have the time.
Dono kurai nagaku soko ni iru tsumori desu ka?	How long do you intend to stay here?
Dono kurai nagaku koko ni imashita ka?	How long have you been here?
Jikan no muda o shite imasu.	He's wasting his time.
Suru jikan o agete kudasai.	Give her time to do it, please.
Kimono o kigaeru aida dake matte kudasai.	Just give me enough time to change my clothes. [Please wait just for the duration that I am changing clothes.]
Tokidoki kimasu.	He comes from time to time.

QUIZ 19

1. *Niji-han desu.*

2. *Niji juu gofun desu.*

3. *Jikan desu.*

4. *Jikan no muda o shite imasu.*

a. I'll see you there about eight fifteen.

b. The train arrives at seven twenty-three.

c. He's wasting his time.

d. Come at ten o'clock this evening, please.

5. *Soko de hachiji juu gofun goro ni ome ni kakarimasu.*

e. It's one o'clock in the morning.

6. *Densha wa shichiji nijuu sanpun ni tsukimasu.*

f. He'll come at 2:00.

7. *Konban juuji ni kite kudasai.*

g. We'll be there about nine twenty-five.

8. *Gozen ichiji desu.*

h. It's two fifteen. It's a quarter after two.

9. *Kuji nijuu gofun goro ni soko e iki-masu.*

i. It's half-past two. It's two thirty.

10. *Niji ni kimasu.*

j. It's time.

ANSWERS

1—i; 2—h; 3—j; 4—c; 5—a; 6—b; 7—d; 8—e; 9—g; 10—f.

E. Word Study

anpaia	umpire
baatendaa	bartender
dezainaa	designer
konsarutant	consultant
enjinia	engineer
maneejaa	manager
sarariiman	salaried man
seerusuman	salesman
suponsaa	sponsor
taipisuto	typist

LESSON 24

DAI NIJUU YONKA

A. Ago

mae	ago
ichijikan mae	an hour ago
nijikan mae	two hours ago
sanjikan mae	three hours ago
ichinichi mae	a day ago
futsuka mae	two days ago
sanshuukan mae	three weeks ago
gokagetsu mae	five months ago
gonen mae	five years ago
juunen mae	ten years ago
zutto mae	a long time ago
kanari mae	a rather long time ago, quite a long time ago
sukoshi mae	a short time ago

B. Morning, Noon, and Night

asa	morning
hiru	noon
shoogo	noon
gogo	afternoon
ban	evening
yoru	night
hi	the day
shuu	the week
isshuukan	a week
nishuukan	two weeks
tsuki	month
toshi	year

kinoo	yesterday
kyoo	today
ashita	tomorrow
ototoi	the day before yesterday
tsugi no hi	the next day
asatte	the day after tomorrow
ima	now
sugu	in a moment, soon
kesa	this morning
kinoo no asa	yesterday morning
ashita no asa	tomorrow morning
kyoo no gogo	this afternoon [today's afternoon]
kinoo no gogo	yesterday afternoon
ashita no gogo	tomorrow afternoon
konban	this evening, tonight
kinoo no ban sakuban	yesterday evening
ashita no ban	tomorrow evening
kinoo no yoru sakuya yuube	last night
ashita no yoru	tomorrow night

C. THIS WEEK, NEXT MONTH, ETC.

konshuu	this week
senshuu	last week
raishuu	next week
saraishuu	in two weeks, the week after next
kongetsu	this month
sengetsu	last month
raigetsu	next month
saraigetsu	the month after next

sensengetsu	two months ago, the month before last
kotoshi	this year
kyonen } sakunen }	last year
rainen	next year
sarainen	in two years, the year after next
issakunen } otototoshi }	the year before last
asa	in the morning
ban	in the evening
hiru goro	around noon
yuushokugo	after dinner (the evening meal)
shuumatsu	at the end of the week
getsumatsu	at the end of the month
konshuu no owari goro ni	toward the end of the week
ichijikan mae	an hour ago
juu gofun inai ni	in a quarter of an hour
sono uchi ni	one of these days
Sono uchi ni ome ni kakarimasu.	See you one of these days.
mainichi	every day
ichinichi juu	all day (long)
hitoban juu	all night (long)
Asa kara ban made hatarakimasu.	He works from morning to night.
Kyoo wa nannichi desu ka?	What's the date?

D. EXPRESSIONS OF PAST, PRESENT, AND FUTURE

PAST	PRESENT	FUTURE
tsui sakki	**ima**	**sugu ato de**
a moment ago	now	in a moment
kinoo no asa	**kesa**	**ashita no asa**
yesterday morning	this morning	tomorrow morning
kinoo no gogo	**kyoo no gogo**	**ashita no gogo**
yesterday afternoon	this afternoon	tomorrow afternoon
sakuban	**konban**	**ashita no ban**
yesterday evening	this evening	tomorrow evening
sakuya	**kon'ya**	**ashita no yoru**
last night	tonight	tomorrow night
senshuu	**konshuu**	**raishuu**
last week	this week	next week
sengetsu	**kongetsu**	**raigetsu**
last month	this month	next month
sakunen[1]	**kotoshi**	**rainen**
last year (official)	this year	next year

LESSON 25

DAI NIJUU GOKA

A. DAYS OF THE WEEK

Getsuyoobi	Monday
Kayoobi	Tuesday

---

[1] *Sakunen* is an official way to say "last year." *Kyonen* is a more colloquial form.

Suiyoobi	Wednesday
Mokuyoobi	Thursday
Kin'yoobi	Friday
Doyoobi	Saturday
Nichiyoobi	Sunday

B. DAYS OF THE MONTH

In Japanese, each day of the month has a name, and these, except for the word for the first day, are also used to count the *number* of days.[1] For example, *futsuka*, "second day," can also mean "two days"; whereas, to count "one day," you say *ichinichi*.

tsuitachi	first day (of the month)
futsuka	second day
mikka	third day
yokka	fourth day
itsuka	fifth day
muika	sixth day
nanoka, nanuka	seventh day
yooka	eighth day
kokonoka	ninth day
tooka	tenth day
juuichinichi	eleventh day
juuninichi	twelfth day
juusannichi	thirteenth day
juuyokka	fourteenth day
juugonichi	fifteenth day
juurokunichi	sixteenth day
juushichinichi	seventeenth day
juuhachinichi	eighteenth day
juukunichi	nineteenth day
hatsuka	twentieth day

[1] For counters, see Section 11 of the Summary of Japanese Grammar.

nijuu ichinichi	twenty-first day
nijuu ninichi	twenty-second day
nijuu sannichi	twenty-third day
nijuu yokka	twenty-fourth day
nijuu gonichi	twenty-fifth day
nijuu rokunichi	twenty-sixth day
nijuu shichinichi	twenty-seventh day
nijuu hachinichi	twenty-eighth day
nijuu kunichi	twenty-ninth day
sanjuunichi	thirtieth day
sanjuu ichinichi	thirty-first day

C. What's the Date Today?

Kyoo wa nannichi desu ka?	What's the date today?
Doyoobi wa nannichi desu ka?	What will the date be on Saturday? [As for Saturday, what is the date?]
Kyoo wa tooka desu.	Today's the tenth.
Kyoo wa hatsuka desu.	Today's the twentieth.
Kyoo wa Kayoobi desu ka Suiyoobi desu ka?	Is today Tuesday or Wednesday?
Kyoo wa Suiyoobi desu.	Today's Wednesday.
Kyoo wa Getsuyoobi desu.	Today's Monday.
Raishuu no Doyoobi ni kite kudasai.	Come next Saturday, please.
Raishuu no Kayoobi ni tachimasu.	She's leaving next Tuesday.

Senshuu no Getsu-yoobi ni tsu-kimashita.	She arrived last Monday. [She arrived last week's Monday.]
Raishuu no Getsu-yoobi ni tsu-kimasu.	She's arriving next Monday.
Soko ni mikka ima-shita.	I was there three days.
Soko ni ichinichi shika imasen de-shita.	I was there only one day. [(I) wasn't there any more than one day.]

QUIZ 20

1. *ototoi*
2. *kyoo*

3. *gogo*
4. *tsui sakki*
5. *ashita no gogo*
6. *kyoo no gogo*
7. *asatte*
8. *Jikan o muda ni shite imasu.*
9. *hitoban juu*
10. *Dono kurai nagaku koko ni imashita ka?*

11. *raishuu*

12. *senshuu*

13. *sensenshuu*
14. *saraigetsu*
15. *ototoshi*

a. afternoon
b. day before yesterday
c. today
d. day after tomorrow
e. a moment ago
f. tomorrow afternoon
g. all night long
h. He's wasting his time.
i. this afternoon
j. How long have you been here?
k. the month after next
l. the week before last
m. next week
n. the year before last
o. last week

16. *Jikan desu*   p. It's time to go
                             home.
17. *Jikan ga arimasu.*   q. tomorrow night
18. *Uchi e kaeru jikan* r. this evening
    desu.
19. *ashita no yoru*   s. It's time.
20. *konban*   t. I have time.

ANSWERS

1—b; 2—c; 3—a; 4—e; 5—f; 6—i; 7—d; 8—h;
9—g; 10—j; 11—m; 12—o; 13—l; 14—k; 15—n;
16—s; 17—t; 18—p; 19—q; 20—r.

D. MONTHS OF THE YEAR

Ichigatsu	January
Nigatsu	February
Sangatsu	March
Shigatsu	April
Gogatsu	May
Rokugatsu	June
Shichigatsu	July
Hachigatsu	August
Kugatsu	September
Juugatsu	October
Juuichigatsu	November
Juuinigatsu	December

Kyoo wa Rokugatsu tsuitachi desu.

Today is the first of June.

Watashi wa Shigatsu juuninichi ni umaremashita.

I was born on April twelfth.

Imooto wa Gogatsu itsuka ni umaremashita.

My sister was born on May fifth.

Watashi no tan-joobi wa Nigatsu futsuka desu.	My birthday is February second.
Shichigatsu juuyokka ni kimasu.	I'll come on the fourteenth of July.
Gakkoo wa Kugatsu hatsuka ni hajima-rimasu.	School begins on the twentieth of September.
Sangatsu nijuu ninichi ni kaerimasu.	I'll be back on March twenty-second.
Juuichigatsu juuichi-nichi wa yasumi desu.	November eleventh is a holiday.
Shichigatsu mikka ni tachimasu.	She's leaving on July third.
Tegami wa Rokugatsu muika zuke desu.	The letter is dated June sixth.
Gogatsu juuichinichi ni otazune shimasu.	We'll come to see you on May eleventh.
Kyoo wa sen kyuuhyaku kyuujun ninen Gogatsu itsuka desu.	Today is May fifth, 1992.

E. THE SEASONS

haru	spring
natsu	summer
aki	autumn
fuyu	winter
fuyu ni	in winter
natsu ni	in summer
aki ni	in autumn, in fall
haru ni	in spring

QUIZ 21

1. *Kyoo wa nan' yoobi desu ka?*
   a. Sunday
2. *Sono uchi ni ome ni kakarimasu.*
   b. in a quarter of an hour
3. *ichinichi juu*
   c. See you one of these days.
4. *natsu ni.*
   d. all day
5. *juugo fun de*
   e. What's today?
6. *Raishuu no Getsu-yoobi ni tsukimasu.*
   f. in the summer
7. *Kyoo wa Getsu-yoobi desu.*
   g. winter
8. *Raishuu no Doyoobi ni kite kudasai.*
   h. What's the date Saturday?
9. *fuyu*
   i. Today's the twentieth.
10. *Nichiyoobi*
    j. Today's Monday.
11. *Kyoo wa hatsuka desu.*
    k. Come next Saturday, please.
12. *Doyoobi wa nanni-chi desu ka?*
    l. He'll arrive next Monday.
13. *Shichigatsu no juuyokka ni kimasu.*
    m. The letter is dated June sixth.
14. *Kyoo wa Roku-gatsu no tsuitachi desu.*
    n. I'll come on the fourteenth of July.
15. *Tegami wa Roku-gatsu muika zuke desu.*
    o. Today is the first of June.

ANSWERS

1—e; 2—c; 3—d; 4—f; 5—b; 6—l; 7—j; 8—k; 9—g; 10—a; 11—i; 12—h; 13—n; 14—o; 15—m.

LESSON 26

DAI NIJUU ROKKA

A. *IKU:* To Go[1]

1. I go, I don't go:

PLAIN	POLITE	
iku	ikimasu	I, you, we, they go; he, she goes[1]
itta	ikimashita	I went
itte	itte	I go and ...
ikanai	ikimasen	I don't go
ikitai	ikitai desu	I wish to go
ikeba ⎱ ittara ⎰		if I go
ikanakereba ⎱ ikanakattara ⎰		if I don't go
ittari[2]		sometimes I go
ikoo	ikimashoo	I think I'll go. Let's go.
ike		Go! *(sharp command)*

2. Study these phrases with forms of *iku:*

Kodomotachi wa doko e ikimasu ka? Where are the children going?

---

[1] Remember that in Japanese the same forms are used for first, second, and third persons in both the singular and plural.

[2] See footnote 3, page 143.

Doobutsuen e iki-masu.	They are going to the zoo.
Kinoo wa doko e iki-mashita ka?	Where did you go yesterday?
Umi e ikimashita.	I went to the beach [sea].
Kono densha wa doko made ikimasu ka?	How far does this train go?
Koobe made ikimasu.	It goes as far as Kobe.

3. Some common expressions with *iku:*

Itte kudasai!	Please go!
Ikanaide kudasai.	Please don't go.
Yukkuri itte kudasai.	Go slowly, please.
Itte sagashite kudasai.	Go look for it, please. [Go and look for (it), please.]
Soko e ikanakereba narimasen.	We have to go there. [If (I) don't go, (it) won't do.]
Itte wa ikemasen.	You must not go.
Ikanakute mo ii desu.	We don't have to go. [Even if (we) don't go (it) will be all right.]
Itte mo ikanakute mo ii desu.	It doesn't matter whether we go or not. [Even if (we) go, even if we don't go, (it) will be all right.]
Itte mo ii desu.	You may go. You have my permission to go. [Even if (you) go (it) will be all right.]
Ikitai desu ga iku koto ga dekimasen.	I want to go but I can't [go].

Itta koto ga arimasu.   I have been there.
Itta koto wa arimasen.   I have never been there.
Iku koto ga arimasu.   I sometimes go.

4. Verb particles with *iku:*

Soko e iku to[1] kau   If you go there, you
  koto ga dekimasu.   can buy (them).
Ashita iku to[2]   I said I would go to-
  iimashita.   morrow.
Itta keredomo[3] au koto   I went, but couldn't
  ga dekimasen de-   meet her/him.
  shita.
Kinoo wa ikimashita   I went yesterday, but I
  ga[4] kyoo wa   am not going today.
  ikimasen.
Takushii de itta kara[5]   I went by taxi and so I
  ma ni aimashita.   was able to make it.
Tookyoo e itte kara[6]   I went to Tokyo and
  Kyooto e ikimashita.   then [after that] I
                             went to Kyoto. After
                             I went to Tokyo, I
                             went to Kyoto.
Ame ga futta node[7]   It rained and so [be-
  ikimasen deshita.   cause of that fact] I
                             didn't go.

---

[1] *to* = if, when.
[2] *to* marks the end of a quote.
[3] *keredomo* = but.
[4] *ga* (particle) = but.
[5] *kara* (when it follows a sentence-ending form) = and so, and there-fore, because of that.
[6] *kara* (when it follows a *-te* form) = and after that, and subse-quently.
[7] *node* = and because of that fact, the situation being what it is.

Hiroshima e ikimashita | I went to Hiroshima
shi[1] Nagasaki e mo | and, in addition [not
ikimashita. | only that], I even
 | went to Nagasaki.

Hanashinagara[2] | Let's go as we talk.
ikimashoo.

Nichiyoobi ni wa | On Sundays I some-
Enoshima e ittari | times go to Eno-
Hakone e ittari[3] | shima and sometimes
shimasu. | [go] to Hakone.

B. A Few Action Phrases

Abunai! | Watch out! [(It) is
 | dangerous!]
Ki o tsukete kudasai! | Be careful! Pay atten-
 | tion!
Hayaku itte kudasai. | Please go fast.
Motto hayaku itte | Please go faster.
kudasai.
Sonna ni hayaku | Do not go so fast,
ikanaide kudasai. | please.
Anmari hayaku | Don't go too fast,
ikanaide kudasai. | please.
Motto yukkuri itte | Go slower, please.
kudasai.
Motto hayaku kite | Please come sooner.
kudasai.
Motto osoku kite ku- | Please come later.
dasai.
Isoide kudasai. | Please hurry up.

[1] *shi* = and not only that, and in addition to that.
[2] *-nagara* = as, while (denotes simultaneous actions by the same subject).
[3] *-tari . . . -tari* when followed by *suru* = sometimes do A, sometimes do B; do such things as A and B.

Isoganaide kudasai.	Please don't hurry.
Isoide imasu.	I'm in a hurry.
Isoide imasen.	I'm not in a hurry.
Doozo goyukkuri.	Take your time.
Chotto matte kudasai.	Just a minute!
Sugu mairimasu.[1]	I'm coming right away.

C. WORD STUDY

biiru	beer
juusu	juice
kakuteru	cocktail
kokoa	cocoa
koohii	coffee
miruku	milk
shanpen	champagne
sooda	soda
uisukii	whiskey
yooguruto	yogurt

D. *SHINBUN URIBA DE*

Kyaku: **Japan Taimuzu o kudasai. Komakai okane o motte inai n desu ga, sen en de totte morae-masu ka?**

Ten'in: **Ashita de kekkoo desu.**

Kyaku: **Demo kon'ya kuruma ka nan ka ni hikarete shinde shimattara doo shimasu?**

Ten'in: **Kamaisen. Taishita koto ja arimasen kara.**

AT THE NEWSTAND

Customer: Give me the *Japan Times,* please. However, I don't have any small change. Can you give me change for one thousand yen?

---

[1] *mairu* (humble verb) = come, go.

Dealer: Pay me tomorrow.

Customer: But suppose I get run over by a car or something tonight?

Dealer: So what! It wouldn't be a great loss.

NOTE

totte moraemasu ka = can I have you take it (from)?

Ashita de kekkoo desu. = Tomorrow will do.

hikarete shinde shimattara: hikareru is a passive form of *hiku* [run over]; *shinde shimau* = (and) die [end up in death]; *-tara* = if, suppose.

kara = and so, and therefore (when used after a sentence-ending form of a verb or an adjective).

LESSON 27

DAI NIJUU NANAKA

A. THEY SAY THAT . . .

-soo desu	They say that . . . It's said that . . . People say that . . . I understand that . . . I hear . . .
Soko wa taihen kirei da soo desu.[1]	They say that the place is very pretty.
Sore wa hontoo da soo desu.	They say that it is true.
Yamada-san no piano wa taihen yokatta soo desu.	People say that Mr. Yamada played the piano very well.

[1] Notice that the predicate appearing before *soo desu* is in the plain form.

[Talking about Mr. Yamada's piano (-playing), it was very good, so I hear.]

Tanaka-san wa kinoo Yokohama ni tsuita soo desu. — I understand that Ms. Tanaka arrived in Yokohama yesterday.

Tanaka-san wa kinoo konakatta soo desu. — I understand that Ms. Tanaka did not come yesterday.

Tanaka-san wa ima Tookyoo ni inai soo desu. — I hear that Ms. Tanaka is not in Tokyo now.

Takeda-san wa rainen Amerika e iku soo desu. — I hear that Mr. Takeda will be going to America next year.

B. I HAVE TO, I MUST . . .

Gohan o tabenakereba narimasen. — I must eat [my meal].

Kisoku o yoku oboenakereba narimasen. — You have to remember the regulations well.

Isoganakereba narimasen. — I have to hurry.

Yukkuri arukanakereba narimasen. — You must walk slowly.

Nihongo de hanasanakereba narimasen. — You have to speak Japanese.

Nihon de kawanakereba narimasen. — I have to buy it in Japan.

Yamada-san ni awanakereba narimasen.	I have to see Mr. Yamada.
Yamada-san ni denwa o kakenakereba narimasen.	I have to telephone Mr. Yamada.
Keikan ni kikanakereba narimasen.	I have to ask a policeman.
Tookyoo e kuruma de ikanakereba narimasen deshita.	I had to go to Tokyo by car.
Eki de Yamada-san ni awanakereba narimasen deshita.	I had to see Mr. Yamada at the station.
Eki kara Yamada-san ni denwa o kakenakereba narimasen deshita.	I had to phone Mr. Yamada from the station.
Beru o narashite hito ga dete kuru no o matanakereba narimasen deshita.	I had to ring the bell and wait for someone to answer.
Doa ga shimatte ita node soko ni tatte matte inakereba narimasen deshita.	The door was closed, so I had to stand there and wait.
Okane o motte inakatta node karinakereba narimasen deshita.	I had no money, (and) so I had to borrow (some).

C. SOMETHING TO DRINK

Mizu ga hoshii desu.	I want some water. [Water is wanted.]

Mizu ga hoshii desu ka?
Do you want some water? [Is water wanted?]

Mizu wa hoshiku arimasen.
I don't want any water.

Ocha wa ikaga desu ka?
How about some green tea?

Koohii wa ikaga desu ka?
How about some coffee?

Kuriimu wa ikaga desu ka?
How about some cream?

Osatoo wa ikaga desu ka?
How about some sugar?

Kuriimu wa dono kurai iremashoo ka?
How much cream should I put in?

Osatoo wa dono kurai iremashoo ka?
How much sugar should I put in?

Ocha wa dono kurai kaimashoo ka?
How much green tea should I buy?

Koohii wa dono kurai kaimashoo ka?
How much coffee should I buy?

Donna ocha o kaimashoo ka?
What kind of green tea should we buy?

Donna koohii o kaimashoo ka?
What kind of coffee should we buy?

Dono koohii o kaimashoo ka?
Which coffee should we buy?

Dono koohii ga hoshii desu ka?
Which coffee do you want?

Donna koohii ga suki desu ka?
What kind of coffee do you like?

Dono koohii ga ichiban suki desu ka?
Which coffee do you like best?

Dono koohii ga ichiban hoshii desu ka?
Which coffee do you want most?

QUIZ 22

1. *Tookyoo e kuruma de ikanakereba narimasen deshita.*
2. *Ocha wa ikaga desu ka?*
3. *Isoganakereba narimasen.*
4. *Yukkuri arukanakereba narimasen.*
5. *To ga shimatte ita node soko ni tatte matte inakereba narimasen deshita.*
6. *Yamada-san ni denwa o kakenakereba narimasen.*
7. *Okane ga nakatta node karinakereba narimasen deshita.*
8. *Gohan o tabenakereba narimasen.*
9. *Keikan ni kikanakereba narimasen deshita.*
10. *Eki de Yamada-san ni awanakereba narimasen deshita.*

a. I have to hurry.
b. You have to walk slowly.
c. I had to go to Tokyo by car.
d. How about some green tea?
e. I have to phone Mr. Yamada.
f. The door was closed, so I had to stand there and wait.
g. I must eat.
h. I had no money, so I had to borrow some.
i. I had to see Mr. Yamada at the station.
j. I had to ask a policeman.

ANSWERS
1—c; 2—d; 3—a; 4—b; 5—f; 6—e; 7—h; 8—g; 9—j; 10—i.

D. WORD STUDY

firutaa	filter
fookasu	focus
fuirumu	film
furasshu ranpu	flash lamp
kamera	camera
nega	negative
renzu	lens
serufu taimaa	self-timer
shattaa	shutter
suraido	slide

LESSON 28

DAI NIJUU HACHIKA

A. A LITTLE AND A LOT

Sukoshi.	A little.
Sukoshi desu ka takusan desu ka?	A lot or a little. [Is (it) a little or is (it) a lot?]
Honno sukoshi.	Just a little.
Sukoshi zutsu.	Little by little.
Moo sukoshi kudasai.	A little bit more. [Give (me) a little bit more.]
Sukoshi shika hanashimasen.	He doesn't talk much. [(He) doesn't talk except a little.]
Sukoshi hoshii desu ka takusan hoshii desu ka?	Do you want a little or a lot of it?

Sukoshi koko de yasunde ikimashoo.	Let's rest here a little and (then) go.
Sukoshi kudasai.	Give me a little of it, please.
Sukoshi mizu o kudasai.	Give me a little water, please.
Honno sukoshi dake desu.	It's only a very little bit.
Nihongo wa sukoshi shika dekimasen.	I speak very little Japanese. [(I) can't speak Japanese except a little.]
takusan	a lot, much
Okane wa takusan arimasen.	I don't have much money.
Jikan wa takusan arimasen.	I don't have much time.

B. TOO MUCH

amari	too
amari takusan	too much
Amari takusan desu.⎤	It's too much.
Amari oosugimasu.⎦	
Amari takusan ja arimasen.	It's not too much.
Amari atsusugimasu.	It's too hot.
Amari samusugimasu.	It's too cold.
Amari mizu ga oosugimasu.	There is too much water.

C. MORE OR LESS

tashoo	more or less
ookute mo	at the most
sukunakute mo	at the least
motto motto	more and more

motto motto suku- naku	less and less
moo rokubai	six times more
motto hayaku	earlier *(adv.)*
motto osoku⎤ *motto ato de* ⎦	later *(adv.)*
motto atsuku	hotter
Motto atsuku shite kudasai.	Please make it hotter.
motto takaku	more expensive
Motto takaku nari- mashita.	It became more expensive.
Moo arimasen.	There is no more of it. There is no more of it left.
Sore ijoo desu.	It's more than that.
Sore ika desu.	It's less than that.
Ichiban omoshiroi hon desu.	This is the most inter- esting book.
Ano hito wa oniisan yori se ga takai desu.	He is taller than his older brother.
Watashi hodo se ga takaku arimasen.	She isn't as tall as I am.
Watashi yori hikui desu.	She is shorter than I am.

D. ENOUGH AND SOME MORE

juubun	enough
Juubun desu ka?	Is it enough?
Juubun desu.	It's enough.
Juubun ja arimasen.	It's not enough.
Juubun ookii desu.	It's large enough.
Okane wa juubun motte imasu ka?	Do you have enough money?

motto	some more
Motto desu ka?	(Do you want) some more?
moo sukoshi	a little more
Mizu o moo ippai kudasai.	Give me another glass of water, please.
Pan o moo sukoshi kudasai.	Please give me some/a little more bread.
Niku o moo sukoshi kudasai.	Please give me some/a little more meat.
motto motto	much more, lots more
Moo ichido kite kudasai.	Come again [visit us once more], please.
Moo ichido itte kudasai.	Say it again [once more], please.
Moo ichido kurikaeshite kudasai.	Please repeat it [Repeat it once more . . .].

QUIZ 23

1. *Sukoshi hoshii desu ka takusan hoshii desu ka?*
2. *Eigo wa sukoshi shika hanasemasen.*
3. *Amari atsusugimasu.*
4. *Amari mizu ga oosugimasu.*
5. *Motto takaku narimashita.*
6. *Watashi hodo se ga takaku arimasen.*

a. I can speak little English.

b. It became more expensive.

c. She is not as tall as I am.

d. He doesn't talk much.

e. I don't have much money.

f. There is too much water.

7. *Okane wa juubun motte imasu ka?*

g. Do you want a little or do you want a lot?

8. *Moo ichido itte kudasai.*

h. It's too hot.

9. *Okane wa takusan arimasen.*

i. Do you have enough money?

10. *Sukoshi shika hanashimasen.*

j. Say it again, please.

ANSWERS

1—g; 2—a; 3—h; 4—f; 5—b; 6—c; 7—i; 8—j; 9—e; 10—d.

LESSON 29

DAI NIJUU KYUUKA

A. I WANT TO . . .

When you want to *have* something you say *ga hoshii desu*. When you want to *do* something, you use *o* (for the object) plus a pre-*masu* form plus *tai desu*.

The combination of a pre-*masu* plus *tai* acts exactly like an *i*- adjective. The item involved in the action that you want to perform is normally marked by *o*, but the use of *ga* is acceptable in limited cases. Usually, *ga* can be used with daily actions, such as "eat" or "drink."

Nomitai desu. I want to drink it.
Tabetai desu. I want to eat it.
Kaitai desu. I want to buy it.
Mitai desu. I want to see it.

Nomitaku arimasen.	I don't want to drink it.
Tabetaku arimasen.	I don't want to eat it.
Kaitaku arimasen.	I don't want to buy it.
Mitaku arimasen.	I don't want to see it.
Koohii o nomitai desu.	I'd like some coffee. [(I) want to drink coffee.]
Kudamono o tabetai desu.	I'd like some fruit. [(I) want to eat fruit.]
Kutsu o kaitai desu.	I want to buy (a pair of) shoes.
Eiga o mitai desu.	I want to see a movie.
Koohii o nomitaku narimashita.	I want to drink coffee now (though I didn't before). [(I) became desirous of drinking coffee.]
Kudamono o tabetaku narimashita.	I want to eat fruit now. [I became desirous of . . .]
Kutsu o kaitaku narimashita.	I want to buy shoes now. [I became desirous of . . .]
Eiga o mitaku narimashita.	I want to see a movie now. [I became desirous of . . .]

B. I INTEND TO . . .

Iku tsumori desu.	I intend to go.
Ryokoo suru tsumori desu.	I intend to travel.
Benkyoo suru tsumori desu.	I intend to study.
Kekkon suru tsumori desu.	I intend to marry.

Iku tsumori desu ka? Do you intend to go?

Iku tsumori deshita ka? Did you intend to go?

Iku tsumori ja arimasen ka? Don't you intend to go?

Iku tsumori ja arimasen deshita ka? Didn't you intend to go?

Ryokoo suru tsumori deshita ga shimasen deshita. I (had) intended to travel, but didn't.

Ryokoo suru tsumori deshita ga dekimasen deshita. I (had) intended to travel, but couldn't.

Ryokoo suru tsumori deshita ga akiramemashita. I (had) intended to travel, but I gave it up [the idea].

Ryokoo suru tsumori deshita ga dekiru ka doo ka wakarimasen. I (had) intended to travel, but I can't tell (now) if I can or not.

C. IT IS SUPPOSED TO . . .

Kuru hazu desu. It is supposed to come.

Tegami ga kuru hazu desu. A letter is supposed to come.

Tomodachi ga kuru hazu desu. A friend of mine is supposed to come.

Denwa ga aru hazu desu. There is supposed to be a telephone. He is supposed to have a telephone.

Shiranai hazu desu. He is not supposed to know it.

Kita hazu desu.	It is supposed to have come.
Tegami o uketotta hazu desu.	He is supposed to have received a letter.
Tomodachi ga shiraseta hazu desu.	My friend is supposed to have notified (him about it).
Tomodachi kara denwa ga atta hazu desu.	There is supposed to have been a phone call from a friend of mine.
Minna yonda hazu desu.	He is supposed to have read all of it.
Minna dekite iru hazu desu.	Everything is supposed to have been done.

D. SOMETHING, EVERYTHING, NOTHING

nani = what

nani ka[1] = something

nan de mo (used with affirmative) = everything, anything at all

nani mo (used with negative) = nothing, not anything

Nani ka kaimashita ka?	Did you buy something?
Dare ka kimashita ka?	Did someone come?
Itsu ka ikimashoo.	Let's go sometime.
Doko ka de kikimashita.	I heard it somewhere.
Nan de mo kaimashita.	I bought everything.

---

[1] See Section 23 of the Summary of Japanese Grammar for uses of question words with particles.

Dare de mo hairemasu.	Anybody at all can enter.
Itsu de mo ikimasu.	I go anytime.
Doko de mo kaemasu.	You can buy it at any place.
Nani mo kaimasen deshita.	I didn't buy anything.
Dare mo kimasen deshita.	Nobody came.
Itsu mo imasen deshita.	He wasn't there at any time. He was always absent.
Doko mo mimasen deshita.	I didn't see any place.
Nani ka tsumetai mono o nomimashoo.	Let's drink something cold.
Dare ka Nihongo no yoku dekiru hito ni kikimashoo.	Let's ask someone who can speak Japanese well.
Itsu ka anmari isogashiku nai toki ni ikimashoo.	Let's go there when we are not too busy.
Doko ka motto shizuka na tokoro e ikimashoo.	Let's go somewhere quieter.
Nani o mite mo kaitaku narimasu.[1]	Whatever I see, I [get to] want to buy.
Dare ga kite mo kyoo wa au koto ga dekimasen.	No matter who comes [Whoever may come], I can't meet him/her today.

---

[1] Note the construction: The interrogative plus the *-te* form plus *mo* = "-ever" plus the verb.

Itsu itte mo ano hito wa jimusho ni imasen deshita.	No matter when I went to his office, he wasn't there. [Whenever (I) went, he wasn't at his office.]
Doko e itte mo Eigo no dekiru hito ga imashita.	Wherever I went, there was someone who could speak English.

QUIZ 24

1. *Kaitai desu.*	a. Everything is supposed to have been done.
2. *Iku tsumori desu.*	b. I didn't buy anything.
3. *Kuru hazu desu.*	c. Let's drink something cold.
4. *Nani ka kaimashita ka?*	d. Nobody came.
5. *Kaitaku arimasen.*	e. I didn't intend to travel.
6. *Ryokoo suru tsumori desu.*	f. Anybody at all can enter.
7. *Doko ka de kikimashita.*	g. Let's ask someone who can speak Japanese well.
8. *Kita hazu desu.*	h. Did you buy something?
9. *Dare de mo hairemasu.*	i. It is supposed to come.
10. *Dare ka Nihongo no yoku dekiru hito ni kikimashoo.*	j. I intend to travel.

11. *Ryokoo suru tsu-*   k. I don't want to buy
    mori ja arimasen   it.
    deshita.

12. *Nani mo kaimasen*   l. I intend to go.
    deshita.

13. *Minna dekite iru*   m. I want to buy it.
    hazu desu.

14. *Dare mo kimasen*   n. I heard it some-
    deshita.   where.

15. *Nani ka tsumetai*   o. It is supposed to
    mono o nomi-   have come.
    mashoo.

ANSWERS

1—m; 2—l; 3—i; 4—h; 5—k; 6—j; 7—n; 8—o;
9—f; 10—g; 11—e; 12—b; 13—a; 14—d; 15—c.

E. WORD STUDY

kuraimakkusu	climax
kyasuto	cast
rabushiin	love scene
rokeishon	location
shiin	scene
shinario	scenario
sukuriin	screen
sutaa	star
sutajio	studio
taitoru	title

LESSON 30

DAI SANJUKKA

A. OF COURSE! IT'S A PITY! IT DOESN'T MATTER!

Mochiron desu.	Of course. Certainly.
Shoochi itashimashita.	Fine! [(I) have under-stood.]
Soo desu ka?	Indeed? Is that so?
Soo omoimasu.	I think so.
Soo omoimasen.	I don't think so.
Tanaka-san desu ka?	Are you Ms. Tanaka?
Hai, soo desu.	Yes, I am. [Am so.]
tabun	perhaps, probably
Tabun soo deshoo.	I suppose so. Probably it is so.
Tabun soo ja nai deshoo.	I suppose not. Probably it is not so.
Soo da to ii to omoimasu.	I hope so. [If (it) is so it would be good, that way (I) think.]
Soo ja nai to ii to omoimasu.	I hope not. [If (it) is not so it would be good, that way (I) think.]
Tashika ni soo desu.	Certainly. [Certainly (it) is so.]
Tashika ni soo ja arimasen.	Certainly not. [Certainly (it) is not so.]
Okinodoku desu.	It's a pity! It's a shame! She has my sympathy.
Sore wa baai ni yorimasu.	That depends [on the occasion].

Kamaimasen.   That's nothing. That's
                                not important. That
                                doesn't matter. [(I)
                                don't mind.]

Zenzen kamaimasen.   That doesn't matter at
                                all.

Gotsugoo ga   If you have no objec-
  yoroshi kereba.   tions. If it doesn't
                                inconvenience you.
                                [If (it) is convenient.]

Dochira de mo   I don't care. It's all the
  kekkoo desu.   same to me. [Either
                                will do.]

QUIZ 25

1. *Soo omoimasu.*   a. It's a pity.
2. *Mochiron desu.*   b. I suppose not.
3. *Tabun soo deshoo.*   c. I hope so.
4. *Shoochi itashi-*   d. If you have no
   mashita.   objections.
5. *Soo da to ii to*   e. I don't care. Either
   omoimasu.   will do.
6. *Tabun soo ja nai*   f. Certainly it is so.
   to omoimasu.
7. *Tashika ni soo*   g. I think so.
   desu.
8. *Okinodoku desu.*   h. Agreed!
9. *Gotsugoo ga*   i. Of course.
   yoroshikereba.
10. *Dochira de mo*   j. I suppose so.
    kekkoo desu.

ANSWERS
1—g; 2—i; 3—j; 4—h; 5—c; 6—b; 7—f; 8—a;
9—d; 10—e.

B. THE SAME

onaji	same
Onaji mono desu.	It's the same thing (*a tangible article*).
Onaji koto desu.	It's the same thing (*abstract*).
Kore wa onaji ja arimasen.	This isn't the same. These aren't the same.
dooji ni ⎫ onaji toki ni ⎭	at the same time
onaji shunkan ni	at the same moment
onaji machi ni	in the same town

C. ALREADY

moo	already
moo mukoo ni itte imasu.	He is already there. [(He) is already in the state of having gone there.]
Moo shite shimai-mashita.	He has already done that. [(He) has already done that and (it) is all finished.]
Moo dashite shimai-mashita ka?	Has he sent it already?
Moo sumasete shimai-mashita ka?	Have you finished already?

D. WORD STUDY

abunoomaru	abnormal
chaamingu	charming
derikeeto	delicate

ereganto	elegant
kurashikku	classic
modan	modern
noomaru	normal
riberaru	liberal
senchimentaru	sentimental
yuniiku	unique

LESSON 31

DAI SANJUU IKKA

A. I LIKE IT, IT'S GOOD

Suki desu.	I like it. [That's (my) favorite.]
Nihon ryoori ga suki desu.	I like Japanese cooking.
Kodomo ga suki desu.	I like children.
Hon o yomu koto ga suki desu.	I like reading books.
Oyogu koto ga suki desu.	I like swimming.
Kekkoo desu.	Good! It's good.
Kono wain wa kekkoo desu.	This wine is good.
Kono niku wa kekkoo desu.	This meat is good.
Kekkoo na otenki desu ne.	The weather is fine, isn't it?
Motto ikaga desu ka?	How about some more?
Moo kekkoo desu.	No, thanks, I'm fully satisfied.
Taihen kekkoo desu.	It's very good.

Subarashii desu.	It's wonderful.
Migoto desu.	It's admirable.
Kanzen desu.	It's perfect.
Taihen ki ni iri- **mashita.**	I'm very pleased with it. I like it very much.
Taihen ii hito desu.	He's very nice. [(He) is a very good person.]
Taihen kanji no ii **hito desu.**	He's very pleasant.
Doomo goshinsetsu **sama.**	You're very kind. That's very kind of you.

B. I Don't Like It, It's Bad

Suki ja arimasen.	I don't like it. It's not good. [That's not (my) favorite.]
Sakana wa suki ja **arimasen.**	I don't like fish. [Fish is not (my) favorite.]
Kirai desu.	I dislike it.
Sakana wa kirai desu.	I dislike fish.
Yamada-san wa kirai **desu.**[1]	I dislike Mr. Yamada.
Yoku nai desu.	It's not good.
Amari kekkoo ja **arimasen.**	It's not very good.
Warui desu.	It's bad.
Mazui desu.	It tastes bad.
Kanshin dekimasen.	It's not good. [I can't admire it.]
Hon o yomu koto wa **suki ja arimasen.**	I don't like reading books.
Hon o yomu koto wa **kirai desu.**	I dislike reading books.

[1] Note that this same sentence can also mean "Mr. Yamada dislikes it."

QUIZ 26

1. *Taihen kekkoo desu.*	a. He's very nice.
2. *Kanshin dekimasen.*	b. It's perfect.
3. *Subarashii desu.*	c. I'm very pleased with it.
4. *Kanzen desu.*	d. I dislike fish.
5. *Taihen ki ni irimashita.*	e. He's very pleasant.
6. *Sakana wa kirai desu.*	f. It tastes bad.
7. *Doomo goshinsetsu sama.*	g. You're very kind.
8. *Mazui desu.*	h. It's wonderful.
9. *Taihen kanji no ii hito desu.*	i. It's very good.
10. *Taihen ii hito desu.*	j. It's not good.

ANSWERS

1—i; 2—j; 3—h; 4—b; 5—c; 6—d; 7—g; 8—f; 9—e; 10—a.

REVIEW QUIZ 3

1. *San tasu ni wa* _____ (five) *desu.*
    a. *go*
    b. *roku*
    c. *hachi*

2. _____ (Last week) *kaerimashita.*
    a. *Sengetsu*
    b. *Senshuu*
    c. *Sakuban*

3. *Kyoo wa* _____ (Monday) *desu.*
   a. *Getsuyoobi*
   b. *Doyoobi*
   c. *Suiyoobi*

4. _____ (Must hurry) *narimasen.*
   a. *Ikanakereba*
   b. *Isoganakereba*
   c. *Oboenakereba*

5. *Koohii ga* _____ (want) *desu.*
   a. *hoshii*
   b. *suki*
   c. *yoku nai*

6. Ginkoo e _____ (am going).
   a. *haraimasu.*
   b. *kashimasu.*
   c. *ikimasu.*

7. _____ (Sugar) *wa ikaga desu ka?*
   a. *Osatoo*
   b. *Ocha*
   c. *Mizu*

8. *Okane o* _____ (a little) *kashite kudasai.*
   a. *sukoshi*
   b. *takusan*
   c. *nisen en*

9. *Okane o* _____ (much) *motte imasu.*
   a. *sukoshi*
   b. *takusan*
   c. *sukoshi mo*

10. _____ (More) *arimasu*.
    a. *Sukoshi*
    b. *Motto*
    c. *Moo sukoshi*

11. _____ (Enough) *arimasen*.
    a. *Nani mo*
    b. *Takusan*
    c. *Juubun*

12. _____ (Expensive) *desu*.
    a. *Yasui*
    b. *Takai*
    c. *Hikui*

13. *Sore wa kore* _____ (as) *oishiku arimasen*.
    a. *wa*
    b. *hodo*
    c. *mo*

14. _____ (All) *yonde shimaimashita*.
    a. *Hanbun*
    b. *Sukoshi*
    c. *Minna*

15. _____ (Anybody) *hairemasu*.
    a. *Dare de mo*
    b. *Dare ga*
    c. *Dare ka*

16. *Soo* _____ (don't think).
    a. *hurimasen.*
    b. *omoimasen.*
    c. *kaimasen.*

17. *Iku* _____ (intend to) *desu.*
   a. *hazu*
   b. *tsumori*
   c. *yoo*

18. _____ (Nothing) *kaimasen deshita.*
   a. *Dare mo*
   b. *Nani mo*
   c. *Dore mo*

19. *Dore de mo* _____ (same).
   a. *onaji desu.*
   b. *chigaimasu.*
   c. *hoshii desu.*

20. _____ (Already) *sumasete shimaimashita ka?*
   a. *Motto motto*
   b. *Motto*
   c. *Moo*

ANSWERS
1—a; 2—b; 3—a; 4—b; 5—a; 6—c; 7—a; 8—a;
9—b; 10—b; 11—c; 12—b; 13—b; 14—c; 15—a;
16—h; 17—b; 18—b; 19—a; 20—c.

C. WORD STUDY

bakkumiraa	rearview mirror
banpaa	bumper
bureeki	brake
enjin	engine
gasorin	gasoline
giya	gear
handoru	handle (of a tool), steering wheel

heddoraito	headlight
kuratchi	clutch
taiya	tire

D. *WARAIBANASHI*

Tanaka-san to Yamada-san ga resutoran e itte bifuteki o chuumon shimashita. Shibaraku tatte bifuteki ga kimashita. Hitokire wa ookikute hitotsu wa chiisakatta no desu. Tanaka-san wa sugu ookii hoo o torimashita. Sore o mite Yamada-san wa okorimashita. Soshite "Nan to reigi no nai hito daroo. Hito yori saki ni toru toki wa chiisai hoo o toru mon da" to iimashita.

Kore o kiite Tanaka-san wa: "Anata ga watashi dattara doo shimasu ka?" to tazunemashita.

"Mochiron chiisai hoo o torimasu yo!" to Yamada-san wa kotaemashita.

Tanaka-san wa: "Sore gorannasai, monku wa nai hazu ja arimasen ka? Chiisai hoo o anata ga, moratta n da kara," to iimashita.

A FUNNY STORY

Tanaka and Yamada went to a restaurant and ordered steak. A few minutes later the steaks arrived. One piece was large and one piece was small. Tanaka took the large piece. Yamada was furious and said to him: "What bad manners you have! Don't you know that since you were the first to help yourself you should have taken the smaller piece?"

Tanaka answered: "If you were in my place, which piece would you have taken?"

"The smaller one, of course," said Yamada.

"Well, then," Tanaka answered, "what are you complaining about? You got it, didn't you?"

NOTE

waraibanashi: "a story to laugh"

chuumon shimashita: ordered

shibaraku tatte: after a short while

okorimashita: got furious

soshite: and

Nan to . . . daroo: What a . . . !

reigi: manners

shiranai: (negative of *shiru*): don't know

. . . *mono da:* that's what one should do; that's an accepted way to do

dattara: if (you) were

torimasu yo: yo is an emphatic particle corresponding to an exclamation mark.

monku: complaint

nai hazu desu: there is supposed to be not; there isn't supposed to be

LESSON 32

DAI SANJUU NIKA

A. WHO? WHAT? WHEN? ETC.

dono	which . . . ?
Dono hon desu ka?	Which book is it?
Dono tegami desu ka?	Which letter is it?
dore	which one?
itsu	when?
dare	who?
nani, nan	what?
naze, dooshite	why?
doko	where?
ikura	how much?
doo, dooshite	how?

1. *Nani, Nan:* What?

Nani o shite imasu ka?	What are you doing?
Nani ga hoshii desu ka?	What do you want? What would you like?
Kore kara nani o shitai desu ka?	What do you want to do now?
Nani o sagashite imasu ka?	What are you looking for?

Nani is used instead of *nan* when the word that follows it is *desu, to* (with a verb *iu* [say], etc.), *no,* or a counter.

Onamae wa nan desu ka?	What's your name?
Kono machi no namae wa nan desu ka?	What's the name of this town?
Kono toori no namae wa nan desu ka?	What's the name of this street?
Nan to iimashoo ka?	What will we say?
Nan to osshaimashita ka?	What did she say *(extra polite)?*
Nan to iu machi desu ka?	What is the name of the town? [What is the town called?]
Nan no hon desu ka?	What book is it?
Kore wa nan no e desu ka?	What picture is this?
Kyoo wa nannichi desu ka?	What's today?
Nangatsu desu ka?	What month is it?
Nanji desu ka?	What time? [What hour is it?]

2. *Dore:* Which one?

Dore desu ka?	Which one is it?
Dore ga anata no hon desu ka?	Which is your book?
Watakushi no wa dore desu ka?	Which is mine?
Dore ga ii hoo desu ka?	Which is the better one?
Dore ga hoshii desu ka?	Which one do you want?
Dore ga tadashii desu ka?	Which one is right?

3. *itsu:* When?

Itsu desu ka?	When is it?
Itsu made desu ka?	Until when is (it)?
Itsu kimasu ka?	When are you coming?
Itsu oide ni narimasu ka?	When are you coming *(respect)*?
Itsu tachimasu ka?	When are you leaving?
Itsu otachi ni narimasu ka?	When are you leaving *(respect)*?

4. *Dare:* Who?

Dare desu ka?	{ Who is it? / Who are you?
Donata desu ka?	Who are you *(respect)*?
Dare ga sore o shitte imasu ka?	Who knows that?
Dare no desu ka?	Whose is it?
Dare no tame desu ka?	Who is it for? [Whose sake is it?]

Dare ni hanashite imasu ka?	Who are you talking to?
Dare no koto o hanashite imasu ka?	Who are you speaking about? [Whose matters are you speaking?]
Dare to kimasu ka?	Who are you coming with?
Dare ni aitai desu ka?	Who do you want to see?
Donata ni oai ni naritai desu ka?	Who do you want to see *(respect)?*
Dare o sagashite imasu ka?	Who are you looking for?
Donata o sagashite irasshaimasu ka?	Who are you looking for *(respect)?*

5. *Naze, dooshite:* Why?

Naze desu ka?	Why is it?
Dooshite desu ka?	Why is it?
Dooshite dame desu ka?	Why not? [Why is it no good?]
Naze sonna koto o iu n desu ka?	Why do you say that [such a thing]?
Dooshite sonna koto o shita n desu ka?	Why did he do such a thing?

6. *Doo, dooshite:* How?

Doo desu ka?	How is it?
Doo shimasu ka?	How do you do it?
Doo iu imi desu ka?	What do you mean?
Nihongo de kono kotoba wa doo kakimasu ka?	How do you write this word in Japanese?
Sore wa Eigo de doo iimasu ka?	How do you say that in English?

"Thanks" wa Nihongo de doo iimasu ka?	How do you say "thanks" in Japanese?
Doo shita n desu ka?	How did it happen?
Doo shitara ii n desu ka?	How does one go about it?
Doo sureba ii n desu ka?	How does one go about it?
Sore wa doo shite tsukurimasu ka?	How's it made? [Acting how do you make (it)?]
Sore wa dooshite tsukurimashita ka?	How did you make it?
Soko e wa doo ikimasu ka?	How do you go there?
Doo shimashoo ka?	What's to be done? What can one do? [How shall we do?]
Sono futatsu wa doo chigaimasu ka?	What is the difference between the two? [As for the two, how do they differ?]

QUIZ 27

1. *Dono hon desu ka?*   a. How is it?
2. *Nan to iimashita ka?*   b. What is the difference between the two?
3. *Nani o sagashite imasu ka?*   c. Why did he do such a thing?
4. *Dono tegami desu ka?*   d. Who are you looking for?
5. *Onamae wa nan desu ka?*   e. Why is it?
6. *Nani o shite imasu ka?*   f. How do you go there?

7. *Kyoo wa nannichi desu ka?*   g. Until when?

8. *Nani ga hoshii desu ka?*   h. Which one do you want?

9. *Nangatsu desu ka?*   i. What is the name of the street?

10. *Kono toori no namae wa nan desu ka?*   j. What do you want to do now?

11. *Kore kara nani o shitai desu ka?*   k. What time is it?

12. *Nanji desu ka?*   l. What do you want/ would you like?

13. *Sono futatsu wa doo chigaimasu ka?*   m. What month is it?

14. *Dooshite desu ka?*   n. Which letter?

15. *Dore ga hoshii desu ka?*   o. What is your name?

16. *Itsu made desu ka?*   p. What are you looking for?

17. *Donata o sagashite irasshaimasu ka?*   q. What's today?

18. *Dooshite sonna koto o shita n desu ka?*   r. What are you doing?

19. *Doo desu ka?*   s. Which book is it?

20. *Soko e wa doo ikimasu ka?*   t. What did you say?

ANSWERS

1—s; 2—t; 3—p; 4—n; 5—o; 6—r; 7—q; 8—l; 9—m; 10—i; 11—j; 12—k; 13—b; 14—e; 15—h; 16—g; 17—d; 18—c; 19—a; 20—f.

B. WORD STUDY

akademikku	academic
ekizochikku	exotic
gurotesuku	grotesque
nooburu	noble
pedanchikku	pedantic
romanchikku	romantic
senseeshonaru	sensational

C. HOW MUCH?

Nedan wa?	The price? How much is this?
Nedan wa ikura desu ka?	What's the price?
Ikura?	How much?
Ikura desu ka?	How much is it? How much do you want for it?
Zenbu de ikura desu ka?	How much for everything? How much does it all cost?
Hitotsu ikura desu ka?	How much each?

D. HOW MANY?

Ikutsu?	How many?
Ikutsu nokotte imasu ka?	How many are left?
Ikutsu motte imasu ka?	How many of them do you have?
Nannin desu ka?	How many persons?
Nanjikan?	How many hours?
Nando?	How many times?
Dono kurai desu ka?	How much time?

Dono kurai nagai desu ka?	How long?
Soko e iku ni wa dono kurai jikan ga kakarimasu ka?	How long [how much time] does it take to get there?

QUIZ 28

1. *Ikutsu arimasu ka?*	a. How many persons?
2. *Ikura desu ka?*	b. How much for everything?
3. *Ikutsu nokotte imasu ka?*	c. How long does it take to get there?
4. *Nedan wa ikura desu ka?*	d. How much each?
5. *Dono kurai nagai desu ka?*	e. What's the price?
6. *Zenbu de ikura desu ka?*	f. How much is it?
7. *Nannin desu ka?*	g. How many are left?
8. *Ikutsu motte imasu ka?*	h. How long is it?
9. *Hitotsu ikura desu ka?*	i. How many of them do you have?
10. *Soko e iku ni wa dono kurai jikan ga kakarimasu ka?*	j. How many are there?

ANSWERS
1—j; 2—f; 3—g; 4—e; 5—h; 6—b; 7—a; 8—i; 9—d; 10—c.

LESSON 33

DAI SANJUU SANKA

A. SOME, SOMEONE, SOMETHING[1]

ikura ka no	some *(an indeterminate amount of)*
ikutsu ka no	some *(an indeterminate number of)*
ikura ka no okane	some money
ikura ka no hiyoo	some expense
ikura ka no jikan	some time
Ikura ka no jikan ga kakarimasu.	It takes some time.
Ikura ka no okane ga irimasu.	We need some money.
Ikutsu ka no kotoba o shitte imasu.	I know some words.
nannin ka no	some *(an indeterminate number of persons)*
Nannin ka no hito ni kikimashita.	I have asked a number of people.
Nannin ka kite imasu.	Several people are here.
nani ka	something, anything *(not a specific thing)*
nani ka atarashii mono	something new, anything new
nani ka kaitai mono	something you want to buy, anything you want to buy
Nani ka kaitai mono ga arimasu ka?	Do you have anything you want to buy?

[1] See Lesson 29-F and Section 23 of the Summary of Japanese Grammar for more information.

Nani ka kikitai koto ga arimasu ka?	Do you have anything you want to ask?
Nani ka kudasai.	Give me something, please.
Nani ka kaku mono o kudasai.	Give me something to write with, please.
Nani ka ochimashita.	Something fell down.
Nani ka kaimashita.	She bought something.
Nani ka shirimasen.	I don't know what it is.
dare ka	someone
Dare ka sore no dekiru hito ga imasu ka?	Is there anyone who can do it?
Dare ka Eigo no yoku dekiru hito ga imasu ka?	Is there anyone who can speak English well?
aru hito	someone
Aru hito ga hoshii to itte imasu.	Someone (a certain person who shall be nameless) says that she wants to have it.
aru tokoro	someplace
Aru tokoro e iki-mashita.	He went someplace.
itsu ka	sometime
Itsu ka kite kudasai.	Please come sometime.
Itsu ka ikimashoo.	Let's go there some-time.
tokidoki	sometimes, occasion-ally
Sono hito ni tokidoki aimasu.	I see him sometimes.
Soko de tokidoki go-han o tabemasu.	I eat [my meal] there sometimes.

B. Once, Twice

-do, -kai	a time
ichido, ikkai	once, one time
nido, nikai	twice, two times
maido, maikai	every time, each time
kondo	this time, this coming time
dai ikkai	the first time
Dai ikkai wa sen kyuuhyaku kyuujuu deshita.	The first time was (in) 1990.
hajimete	for the first time
Hajimete ikimashita.	I went there for the first time.
tsugi	the next time, the next item, the next number, etc.
kono mae	last time
betsu no toki	another time, another occasion
mata	again
moo ichido	once more

C. Up to

made	up to
ima made	up to now
soko made	up to there
owari made	(up) to the end
eki made	up to the station
konban made	up to this evening
ashita made	up till tomorrow
Getsuyoobi made	up to Monday

D. I Need It, It's Necessary

Irimasu.	I need it.
Kore wa irimasen.	She doesn't need this one.
Nani ka irimasu ka?	Do you need anything?
Nani mo irimasen.	I don't need anything.
Zenzen irimasen.	I don't need it at all.
Zehi oai shinakereba narimasen.	It's absolutely necessary that I see you.
Ano hito ni hanasanakereba narimasen.	I have to tell him.
Hayaku uchi e kaette konakereba narimasen.	I must come home early.
Hontoo da to iu koto o mitomenakereba narimasen.	One must recognize the truth.

E. I Feel Like[1]

Hoshii desu.	I'd like to have it. I feel like having it. I want to have it.
Ikitaku arimasen.	I don't feel like going there. I don't want to go.
Ano hon ga hoshii.	I want that book.
Aisukuriimu ga hoshii desu.	I feel like having some ice cream.
Aisukuriimu ga tabetai desu.	I feel like eating some ice cream.
Kono eiga wa mitai desu ka?	Would you like to see this movie?

[1] See Lesson 29 for "I want to."

F. AT THE HOME OF

The choice of the particle *de* or *ni* depends on the verb that follows it.

... otaku de ⎫ ... otaku ni ⎬	at the home of (someone else)
uchi de ⎫ uchi ni ⎬	at my home
Sensei no otaku ni imashita.[1]	We were at the home of our teacher.
Yamada-san no otaku de aimashoo.[2]	I'll see you at the Yamadas' house.
Genkin wa uchi ni arimasen.	There is no cash at home.
Uchi de paatii o shimashita.	We had a party at my home.

QUIZ 29

1. *Ikura ka no okane.*   a. To the end.
2. *Ichido*   b. I need that.
3. *Owari made.*   c. Please come sometime.
4. *Irimasu.*   d. Some money.
5. *Itsu ka kite kudasai.*   e. Once.

ANSWERS
1—d; 2—e; 3—a; 4—b; 5—c.

[1] Notice that *ni* is used here because it appears in conjunction with a form of the verb *imasu*.
[2] Notice that *de* is used here because it appears in conjunction with a form of the verb *au*.

REVIEW QUIZ 4

1. *Kono machi no namae wa* _____ (what) *desu ka?*
    a. *dare*
    b. *nan*
    c. *doko*

2. *Ano kata wa* _____ (who) *desu ka?*
    a. *donata*
    b. *donna*
    c. *dotchi*

3. _____ (When) *kimasu ka?*
    a. *Ikutsu*
    b. *Itsu*
    c. *Ikura*

4. _____ (Why) *sonna koto o iu n desu ka?*
    a. *Donna*
    b. *Doo*
    c. *Dooshite*

5. *Dai* _____ (twelfth) *kai.*
    a. *juuni*
    b. *nijuu*
    c. *nijuuni*

6. *Kono booshi wa* _____ (two thousand) *en shi-mashita.*
    a. *niman*
    b. *nihyaku*
    c. *nisen*

7. *Ni-choome* _____ (seventeen) *banchi ni sunde imasu.*
    a. *shichijuu*
    b. *juushichi*
    c. *juuhachi*

8. _____ (Noon) *desu.*
    a. *Hiru*
    b. *Yoru*
    c. *Asa*

9. _____ (Six) *ji ni aimashoo.*
    a. *San*
    b. *Ku*
    c. *Roku*

10. *Sore o suru* _____ (time) *desu.*
    a. *hito*
    b. *jikan*
    c. *tokoro*

11. *Kyoo wa* _____ (Wednesday) *desu.*
    a. *Kayoobi*
    b. *Suiyoobi*
    c. *Getsuyoobi*

12. *Raishuu no* _____ (Tuesday) *ni demasu.*
    a. *Kayoobi*
    b. *Mokuyoobi*
    c. *Nichiyoobi*

13. *Kyoo wa* _____ (June) *no tsuitachi desu.*
    a. *Rokugatsu*
    b. *Shichigatsu*
    c. *Hachigatsu*

14. *Kore wa* _____ (doesn't need).
    a. *ikimasen.*
    b. *irimasen.*
    c. *arimasen.*

15. *Kono kotoba wa Nihongo de* _____ (how) *kaki-masu ka?*
    a. *dore*
    b. *doo*
    c. *dare*

16. *Watakushi wa Shigatsu* _____ (eleventh) *ni umaremashita.*
    a. *juuyokka*
    b. *nijuuninichi*
    c. *juuichinichi*

17. _____ (How many) *nokotte imasu ka?*
    a. *Ikutsu*
    b. *Kokonotsu*
    c. *Mittsu*

18. _____ (Intend to go) *desu.*
    a. *Iku hazu*
    b. *Iku tsumori*
    c. *Iku jikan*

19. *Ashita* _____ (I must go).
    a. *ikanakereba narimasen.*
    b. *ikanakute mo ii desu.*
    c. *itte mo ii desu.*

20. *Yamada-san wa sono koto o* _____ (is supposed to know).
    a. *shitte imasen deshita.*
    b. *shitte iru hazu desu.*
    c. *shiritai deshoo.*

ANSWERS
1—b; 2—a; 3—b; 4—c; 5—a; 6—c; 7—b; 8—a; 9—c; 10—b; 11—b; 12—a; 13—a; 14—b; 15—b; 16—c; 17—a; 18—b; 19—a; 20—b.

LESSON 34

DAI SANJUU YONKA

A. ON THE ROAD

Chotto ukagaimasu ga, kono machi no namae wa nan deshoo ka?	Excuse me, but what is the name of this town?
Tookyoo made dono kurai arimasu ka?	How far is it to [as far as] Tokyo?
Koko kara Tookyoo made nan kiro arimasu ka?	How many kilometers from here to Tokyo?
Koko kara jukkiro desu.	It's ten kilometers from here.
Koko kara nijukkiro desu.	That's twenty kilometers from here.
Koko kara Tookyoo made doo ikimasu ka?	How do I get to Tokyo from here?
Kono michi o ikimasu.	Follow this road.
Kono banchi e doo iku no ka oshiete kudasai.	Can you tell me how I can get to this address?
Koko e doo iku no ka oshiete kudasai.	Can you tell me how I can get to this place?
Kono toori no namae wa nan to iimasu ka?	What is the name of this street?
... wa doko desu ka?	Where is ... ?
Ginza Doori wa doko desu ka?[1]	Where is Ginza Doori?

---

[1] *doko desu ka?* is the same as *doko ni arimasu ka?*

Koko kara tooi desu ka?	Is it far from here?
Koko kara chikai desu ka?	Is it near here?
Migi e toori mittsu mukoo desu.	It's the third block to the right.
Kono michi o ikimasu.	Go this way.
Massugu ikimasu.	Go straight ahead.
Kado made itte hidari e magarimasu.	Go to the corner and turn left.
Migi ni magarimasu.	Turn right.
Gareeji wa doko ni arimasu ka?	Where is the garage?
Keisatsusho wa doko desu ka?	Where is the police station?
Shiyakusho wa doko desu ka?	Where is City Hall?

B. BUS, TRAIN, SUBWAY, TAXI

Kono basu wa doko kara kimasu ka?	Where does this bus come from?
Shinjuku kara kimasu.	It comes from Shinjuku.
Basutei wa doko desu ka?	Where is the bus stop?
Chuushingai ni iku basu wa dore desu ka?	Which bus goes to the center of town?
Dono eki de orimasu ka?	What station do I get off at?
Doko de orimasu ka?	Where do I get off?
Chikatetsu no eki wa doko desu ka?	Where's the subway station?

Densha no eki wa doko ni arimasu ka?	Where is the train station?
Tookyoo yuki no densha ni wa doko kara norimasu ka?	Where do I get the train for Tokyo?
Niban sen desu.	On track two.
Densha wa ima demashita.	The train just left.
Tsugi no densha wa nanji ni demasu ka?	What time does the next train leave?
Kyooto yuki no oofukukippu o kudasai.	May I have a round-trip ticket for Kyoto?
Ikura desu ka?	How much is that?
Nisen gohyaku gojuu en desu.	Two thousand five hundred and fifty yen.
Jikan wa dono kurai kakarimasu ka?	How long does it take to get there?
Kujikan to chotto desu.	A little over nine hours.

C. WRITING AND MAILING LETTERS AND FAXES

Tegami o kakitai n desu ga . . .	I'd like to write a letter, but (would you mind if I did?)
Enpitsu o motte imasu ka?	Do you have a pencil?
Pen o motte imasu ka?	Do you have a pen?
Waapuro o motte imasu ka?	Do you have a word processor?

Fuutoo o motte imasu ka?	Do you have an envelope?
Kitte o motte imasu ka?	Do you have a postage stamp?
Kitte wa doko de kaemasu ka?	Where can I buy a postage stamp?
Kookuubin no kitte o motte imasu ka?	Do you have an airmail stamp?
Yuubinkyoku wa doko desu ka?	Where is the post office?
Kono tegami o dashitai n desu ga ...	I'd like to mail this letter.
Kitte wa nanmai irimasu ka?	How many stamps do I need on this letter?
Posuto wa doko ni arimasu ka?	Where is the mailbox?
Kado ni arimasu.	At the corner.
Fakkusu o okuritai n desu ga ... Doko de okuremasu ka?	I'd like to send a fax. Where can I send it?
Kono jimusho de okuremasu.	You can send it in (from) this office.
Soko e tsuku no ni dono kurai kakarimasu ka?	How long will it take to get there?

D. TELEPHONING

Koko ni denwa ga arimasu ka?	Is there a phone here?
Doko de denwa ga kakeraremasu ka?	Where can I phone?
Denwa wa doko ni arimasu ka?	Where is the telephone?

Denwa bokkusu wa doko ni arimasu ka?	Where is the phone booth?
Tabakoya ni arimasu.	In the cigar store [tobacco shop].
Denwa o kashite kudasai.	May I use your phone? [Please lend me your phone.]
Doozo otsukai kudasai.	Go ahead! [Please use (it).]
Chookyori denwa o onegai shimasu.	May I have long distance, please?
Tookyoo e no tsuuwa wa ikura desu ka?	How much is a call to Tokyo?
Goo roku kyuu rei no ichi ichi ichi ni ban o onegai shimasu.	5690-1112, please.
Chotto omachi kudasai.	One moment, please.
Ohanashichuu desu.	The line's busy.
Moshi moshi, chigau bangoo ni kakarimashita.	[Hello, hello,] Operator, you gave me the wrong number.
Ohenji ga gozaimasen.	There is no answer *(extra polite)*.
Yamada-san o onegai shimasu.	May I speak to Mr. Yamada, please?
Watakushi desu.	Speaking.
Kochira wa Taitasu desu.	This is Titus speaking. [This side (it) is Titus.]

E. WORD STUDY

anaunsaa	announcer
antena	antenna

daiyaru	dial
nyuusu	news
purojuusaa	producer
puroguramu	program
rajio	radio
saikuru	cycle
suitchi	switch
terebi	television

LESSON 35

DAI SANJUU GOKA

A. WHAT'S YOUR NAME?

Onamae wa nan to osshaimasu ka?	What is your name?
Yamada Yoshio to mooshimasu.[1]	My name is Yoshio Yamada.
Ano hito no namae wa nan to iimasu ka?	What is his name?
Ano hito no namae wa Tanaka Makoto desu.	His name is Makoto Tanaka.
Ano hito no namae wa nan to iimasu ka?	What is her name?
Ano hito wa Satoo Michiko to iimasu.	Her name is Michiko Sato.
Ano hitotachi no namae wa nan to iimasu ka?	What are their names?

[1] *moosu* = call, say (humble verb).

Ano otoko no hito no namae wa Shimada Yukio de, ano onna no hito no namae wa Takahashi Noriko desu.	His name is Yukio Shimada and hers is Noriko Takahashi.
Ano hito no namae wa nan to iimasu ka?	What's his first name?
Ano hito no namae wa Nobuo desu.	His first name is Nobuo.
Ano hito no myooji wa nan to iimasu ka?	What is his last name?
Ano hito no myooji wa Yasuda to iimasu.	His last name is Yasuda.

B. WHERE ARE YOU FROM? HOW OLD ARE YOU?

Okuni wa dochira desu ka?	Where are you from?
Tookyoo desu.	I'm from Tokyo.
Anata wa doko de umaremashita ka?	Where were you born?
Nagoya de umaremashita.	I was born in Nagoya.
Otoshi wa ikutsu desu ka?	How old are you?
Hatachi[1] desu.	I'm twenty.
Kugatsu de nijuu ichi ni narimasu.	I'll be twenty-one in September.

[1] *hatachi* = twenty years old.

Watashi wa sen kyuuhyaku nanajuu nen no Hachigatsu juuku nichi ni umaremashita.	I was born August 19, 1970.
Anata no otanjoobi wa itsu desu ka?	When is your birthday?
Watashi no tan-joobi wa nishuukan saki no Ichigatsu nijuu sannichi desu.	My birthday is in two weeks—January twenty-third.
Otoko no kyoodai wa nannin arimasu ka?	How many brothers do you have?
Ani ga hitori to otooto ga hitori imasu.	I have one older brother and one younger brother.
Ani wa nijuu go sai desu.	My older brother is twenty-five.
Sono ani wa daigaku ni itte imasu.	He attends the university.
Otooto wa juushichi desu.	My younger brother is seventeen.
Otooto wa kookoo no sannensei desu.	My younger brother is in the third year of senior high school.
Oneesan ya imooto san wa nannin desu ka?	How many older and younger sisters do you have?
Imooto ga hitori aru dake desu.	I have just one younger sister.
Imooto wa juugo desu.	She's fifteen.
Imooto wa chuugakkoo no sannensei desu.	She is in the third year of junior high school.

C. Professions

Donna shigoto o shiteirasshaimasu ka?	What do you do?
Otoosan no oshigoto wa nan desu ka?	What does your father do?
Okaasan no oshigoto wa nan desu ka?	What does your mother do?
Chichi wa bengoshi desu.	He's [Father is] a lawyer.
Chichi wa kenchikuka desu.	He's an architect.
Kyooshi desu.	He's a teacher.
Daigaku kyooju desu.	He's a university professor.
Okaasan no oshigoto wa nan desu ka?	What does your mother do?
Isha desu.	She's a doctor.
Kaishain desu.	She's a company employee.
Orimonogaisha o yatte imasu.	She's in the textile business.
Hyakushoo desu.	She's a farmer.
Koomuin desu.	She's a government employee.
Jidoosha koojoo de hataraite imasu.	He works in an automobile factory.

D. Family Matters

Koko ni goshinseki ga oari desu ka?	Do you have any relatives here?
Gokazoku wa minna koko ni sunde irasshaimasu ka?	Does your whole family live here?

Sofubo no hoka wa kazoku wa minna koko ni sunde imasu.	All my family except my grandparents.
Sofubo wa Nagoya ni sunde imasu.	They live in Nagoya.
Anata wa Taketomi-san no goshinseki desu ka?	Are you related to Mr. Taketomi?
Watashi no oji desu.	He's my uncle.
Ano hito wa watashi no itoko desu.	He's my cousin.
Anata wa Sakata-san no goshinseki desu ka?	Are you related to Ms. Sakata?
Watashi no oba desu.	She's my aunt.
Watashi no itoko desu.	She's my cousin.

REVIEW QUIZ 5

1. _____ (This) *machi no namae wa nan to iimasu ka?*
    a. *Koko*
    b. *Kore*
    c. *Kono*

2. *Koko kara Tookyoo made* _____ (how) *ikimasu ka?*
    a. *doko*
    b. *doo*
    c. *dore*

3. *Kono toori no namae wa* _____ (what) *to iimasu ka?*
   a. *dore*
   b. *naze*
   c. *nan*

4. *Ginza Doori wa* _____ (where) *desu ka?*
   a. *doko*
   b. *nan*
   c. *dore*

5. _____ (Post office) *wa doko desu ka?*
   a. *Yuubinkyoku*
   b. *Shiyakusho*
   c. *Basutei*

6. *Kado made itte* _____ (left) *e magarimasu.*
   a. *hidari*
   b. *migi*
   c. *higashi*

7. _____ (How much) *desu ka?*
   a. *Ikutsu*
   b. *Ikura*
   c. *Itsu*

8. *Tegami o* _____ (would like to write) *n desu ga.*
   a. *dashitai*
   b. *kakitai*
   c. *mitai*

9. _____ (Postage stamp) *wa doko de kaemasu ka?*
   a. *kitte*
   b. *zasshi*
   c. *shinbun*

10. _____ (Corner) *ni arimasu.*
    a. *Kado*
    b. *Tonari*
    c. *Asoko*

11. _____ (Here) *ni denwa ga arimasu ka?*
    a. *Koko*
    b. *Soko*
    c. *Asoko*

12. _____ (Wrong) *bangoo ni kakarimashita.*
    a. *Chigau*
    b. *Hoshii*
    c. *Byooin no*

13. *Ano hito no* _____ (first name) *wa nan to iimasu ka?*
    a. *namae*
    b. *myooji*
    c. *jimusho*

14. *Anata wa doko de* _____ (was born) *ka?*
    a. *kaimashita*
    b. *umaremashita*
    c. *aimashita*

15. *Otooto wa* _____ (seventeen) *desu.*
    a. *juushichi*
    b. *juuichi*
    c. *juuhachi*

16. *Chichi wa* _____ (lawyer) *desu.*
    a. *hyakushoo*
    b. *bengoshi*
    c. *isha*

17. _____ (Government employee) *desu.*
    a. *Koomuin*
    b. *Kyooshi*
    c. *Kaishain*

18. *Anata wa Taketomi-san no* _____ (relative)
    desu ka?
    a. *goshinseki*
    b. *tomodachi*
    c. *bengoshi*

19. _____ (Birthday) *wa itsu desu ka?*
    a. *Goryokoo*
    b. *Tanjoobi*
    c. *Gokekkon*

20. *Koko kara* _____ (far) *desu ka?*
    a. *tooi*
    b. *chikai*
    c. *nan kiro*

21. *Niban* _____ (track) *desu.*
    a. *sen*
    b. *me*
    c. *resshu*

22. _____ (Next) *densha wa nanji ni demasu ka?*
    a. *Tsugi no*
    b. *Asa no*
    c. *Gogo no*

23. _____ (Envelope) *o motte imasu ka?*
    a. *Fuutoo*
    b. *Enpitsu*
    c. *Kitte*

24. _____ (Line's busy) *desu*.
    a. *Ohanashichuu*
    b. *Chigau bangoo*
    c. *Tashika*

25. *Sofubo* _____ (except) *kazoku wa minna koko ni sunde imasu.*
    a. *no hoka*
    b. *to issho ni*
    c. *to*

ANSWERS
1—c; 2—b; 3—c; 4—a; 5—a; 6—a; 7—b; 8—b; 9—a; 10—a; 11—a; 12—a; 13—a; 14—b; 15—a; 16—b; 17—a; 18—a; 19—b; 20—a; 21—a; 22—a; 23—a; 24—a; 25—a.

LESSON 36

DAI SANJUU ROKKA

A. *KAIMONO:* SHOPPING

Study the notes at the end of this section for greater comprehension.

1. **Ikura desu ka?**
    How much is it?

2. **Sen en desu.**
    One thousand yen.

3. **Chotto takasugimasu ga, hoka ni arimasen ka?**
    It's [a little] too expensive. Don't you have anything else?

4. **Onaji shurui no desu ka?**
   Of the same kind?

5. **Onaji shurui no ka nita no ga hoshii n desu ga.**
   I want the same kind or something similar.

6. **Koo yuu no ga gozaimasu.**
   We have this (kind).

7. **Moo hoka ni wa arimasen ka?**
   Don't you have anything else (to show me)?

8. **Motto oyasui no desu ka?**
   Less expensive [one]? [Cheaper one?]

9. **Moshi attara.**
   If possible. [If there is.]

10. **Kore wa ikaga desu ka?**
    Would you like this? [How about this one?]

11. **Sore wa nedan ni yorimasu ne.**
    That depends on the price. [(I think it is all right) depending on the price.]

12. **Kore wa hassen en desu.**
    This is eight thousand yen.

13. **Kore wa doo desu ka? Mae no yori yasui n desu ka, takai n desu ka?**
    How about this? Is it cheaper or more expensive (than the former one)?

14. **Motto takai desu.**
    More expensive.

15. **Hoka ni arimasen ka nee?**
    Don't you have anything else?

16. **Ima wa gozaimasen ga, atarashii kata no ga chikajika kuru hazu desu ga ...**
    Not at the moment, but I'm expecting some new styles soon. [... new style ones are supposed to come soon.]

17. **Itsu goro desu ka?**
    When? [About when?]

18. **Moo jiki da to omoimasu ga. Konshuu matsu goro otachiyori kudasai mase.**
    Any day now. Drop in toward the end of the week. [I think it'll be very soon ...]

19. **Ja soo shimasu. Tokoro de kore wa ikura desu ka?**
    I'll do that. By the way, how much is this?

20. **Issoku sanbyaku en desu.**
    Three hundred yen a pair.

21. **Ichi daasu kudasai.**
    Let me have a dozen. [Give me a dozen, please.]

22. **Omochi ni narimasu ka?**
    Will you take (them with you)?

23. **Iie, haitatsu shite kudasai.**
    No. Please deliver them.

24. **Gojuusho wa onaji desu ne?**
    At the same address? [The address is the same, isn't it?]

25. **Onaji desu.**
It's still the same.

26. **Maido arigatoo gozaimasu.**
Thank you very much. [Thank you (for your patronage) each time (you come).]

27. **Sayonara.**
Good-bye.

28. **Sayonara.**
Good-bye.

NOTE

Title: *Kaimono* = Shopping

4. *Shurui no:* same as *shurui no mono* = one(s) of the same kind. See also #13 for similar construction.

5. *Nita no ga* = one (that) resembles (it).

6. *Gozaimasu:* an extra-polite form of *arimasu* which would be used by the shopkeeper to the customer.

8. *Oyasui:* an extra-polite form of *yasui* or *yasui desu* containing the "honorific" prefix o-. Nearly all adjectives can take this prefix "honoring" the person to whom or about whom you are speaking. However, an adjective that itself begins with *o* cannot add the honorific prefix *o*. For instance, *omoshiroi* [It is interesting] cannot become *oomoshiroi.*

10. *Ikaga* is extra-polite for *doo.*

11. *Ni yorimasu* = depending on.

13. *Mae no:* same as *mae no mono* = one(s) of the previous time.

16. *Chikajika* = very recently.
Kuru hazu desu ga: When the particle *ga* is used to terminate a clause, it signifies "but" or "and,"

but does not have quite the same force. It serves to make the sentence less sharp or less pointed, and is commonly used in extra-polite speech.

Otachiyori kudasai (respect): same as *tachiyotte kudasai*.

Note the construction: *O* plus the pre-*masu* form plus *kudasai*.

For example: *okaki kudasai = kaite kudasai; otabe kudasai = tabete kudasai.*

19. *Ja:* same as *de wa* = well, then.
    Tokoro de = by the way.

20. *Soku* = a counter for socks, stockings, shoes.

22. *Omochi ni narimasu ka* (respect): same as *mochimasu ka* or *motte ikimasu ka*. Notice the construction: *o* plus the pre-*masu* form plus *ni narimasu*. This method for the construction of the respect form of a verb can be used for almost any plain verb (i.e., a verb that is not already respect). Further examples: *okaki ni narimasu = kakimasu; otabe ni narimasu = tabemasu; okai ni narimashita = kaimashita.*

24. *Gojuusho* (respect): same as *juusho*. *Gojuusho* and all other respect words of expressions introduced here cannot be used for things or actions pertaining to the speaker or persons identified with the speaker.

26. *Maido arigatoo gozaimasu:* The usual expression used by shopkeepers.

QUIZ 30

1. _____ (How much) *desu ka?*
   a. *Ikura*
   b. *Ikaga*
   c. *Ikutsu*

2. *Onaji* _____ (kind) *no desu ka?*
   a. *shurui*
   b. *nedan*
   c. *tokoro*

3. *Onaji shurui no* _____ (or) *nita no ga hoshii n
   desu ga . . .*
   a. *ga*
   b. *ka*
   c. *to*

4. _____ (This type) *ga gozaimasu ga . . .*
   a. *Doo yuu no*
   b. *Soo yuu no*
   c. *Koo yuu no*

5. _____ (Less) *oyasui no desu ka?*
   a. *Sukoshi*
   b. *Motto*
   c. *Taihen*

6. _____ (That) *wa nedan ni yorimasu ne.*
   a. *Sore*
   b. *Kore*
   c. *Dore*

7. *Ima wa gozaimasen* _____ (but) *atarashii kata
   no ga chikajika kuru hazu desu ga . . .*
   a. *kara*
   b. *ga*
   c. *noni*

8. _____ (Around when) *desu ka?*
   a. *Itsu*
   b. *Nanji gurai*
   c. *Itsu goro*

9. _____ (One dozen) *kudasai.*
   a. *Ichi mai*
   b. *Ichi daasu*
   c. *Issatsu*

10. _____ (Deliver) *shite kudasai.*
   a. *Haitatsu*
   b. *Benkyoo*
   c. *Kekkon*

ANSWERS
1—a; 2—a; 3—b; 4—c; 5—b; 6—a; 7—b; 8—c;
9—b; 10—a.

B. WORD STUDY

baketsu	bucket
booru	bowl
fooku	fork
furaipan	frying pan
gasu	gas
mikisaa	mixer
napukin	napkin
naifu	knife
supuun	spoon
toosutaa	toaster

LESSON 37

DAI SANJUU NANA KA

A. *ASAGOHAN:* BREAKFAST

Study the notes at the end of this section for greater comprehension.

1. Mr. Y:[1] **Onaka ga suitadaroo.**
   Mr. Y: You must be hungry.

2. Mrs. Y: **Ee, nani ka itadakitai wa.**
   Mrs. Y: Yes, (I) would like to have something.

3. Mr. Y: **Kono hoteru ni wa ii resutoran ga aru to yuu kara soko e itte miyoo.**
   Mr. Y: They say there is a good restaurant in this hotel. Let's go there.

4. Mrs. Y: **Sore ga ii wa. Soo shimashoo.**
   Mrs. Y: That's a good idea. Let's do that.

5. Mr. Y: **Chotto sumimasen!**
   Mr. Y: Hello! [Excuse me.]

6. W: **Oyobi de gozaimasu ka?**
   W: Yes? [(You) called, (sir)?]

7. Mr. Y: **Asagohan o tabetai n desu ga ...**
   Mr. Y: We'd like some breakfast.

8. Mrs. Y: **Nani ga itadakemasu no?**
   Mrs. Y: What can we have?

9. W: **Onomimono wa koohii koocha hotto chokoreeto. Nan ni itashimashoo ka?**
   W: Coffee, black tea, or hot chocolate. What would you like to have? [What shall I make it to be?]

10. Mrs. Y: **Hoka no mono wa?**
    Mrs. Y: What else?

[1] *Mr. Y* stands for "Mr. Yamada," *Mrs. Y* for "Mrs. Yamada," *W* for "Waiter."

11. W: **Rooru pan ni toosuto, sore kara hotto keeki mo dekimasu.**
    W: Rolls, toast, and hotcakes, too.

12. Mrs. Y: **Bataa wa tsukanai n desu ka?**
    Mrs. Y: No butter?

13. W: **Mochiron tsukimasu. Hoka ni jamu mo otsuke shimasu.**
    W: Of course, butter and jelly. [Of course, (we) will serve (it). (We) will serve jelly also.]

14. Mrs. Y: **Dewa watakushi wa koohii to toosuto dake ni shimasu.**
    Mrs. Y: I'd like to have some coffee and toast.

15. Mr. Y: **Kochira mo sore to onaji ni shite sono hoka ni hanjuku tamago o tsukete kudasai.**
    Mr. Y: The same for me, and a soft-boiled egg as well.

16. W: **Kashikomarimashita. Hoka ni nani ka?**
    W: Certainly, sir. Would you like anything else?

17. Mr. Y: **Iya, sore de takusan.**
    Mr. Y: No, that'll be all.

18. Mrs. Y: **Napukin o motte kite kudasaimasu ka?**
    Mrs. Y: May I have a napkin, please?

19. Mr. Y: **Sore kara fooku mo. Koko ni wa fooku ga nai yoo dakara.**
    Mr. Y: Would you also get a fork, please? I don't have one. [(It) seems (it) is not here.]

20. Mrs. Y: **Osatoo mo onegai shimasu.**
    Mrs. Y: And some sugar, too, please.

21. W: **Omatase itashimashita.**
    W: Here you are, madam. [Sorry to have kept you waiting.]

22. Mrs. Y: **Kono koohii wa sukkari tsumetaku natte iru wa. Atsui no to torikaete kudasaimasu ka?**
    Mrs. Y: My coffee is cold. Please bring me another cup.

23. W: **Kashikomarimashita.**
    W: Gladly.

24. Mr. Y: **Denpyoo o motte kite kudasai.**
    Mr. Y: May I have the check?

25. W: **Omatase itashimashita.**
    W: Here you are, sir. [Sorry to have kept you waiting.]

26. Mr. Y: **Ja kore de totte kudasai. Otsuri wa ii desu.**
    Mr. Y: Here, keep the change.

27. W: **Maido arigatoo gozaimasu.**
    W: Thank you very much, sir.

28. Mr. Y: **Ja sayonara.**
    Mr. Y: Good-bye.

NOTE

Title: *Asagohan* = Breakfast

1. The conversation here is first carried on between husband and wife; later it is continued between

the couple and the waiter. Notice how freely the plain forms instead of the usual *-masu* or *-desu* forms of verbs and adjectives are used in such a conversation.

Onaka ga suitadaroo (from *onaka ga suku* = get hungry [The stomach gets empty]. *-daroo* [must be, probably]) is the plain form of *-deshoo*. *-daroo* at the end of a sentence is used exclusively by men in casual conversation.

2. *Itadakitai* (extra polite, humble)[1] (from *itadaku*) = want to eat, drink, receive.

Wa: a particle used exclusively by women in casual conversation. It appears at the end of a sentence and adds a feminine touch.

8. *No:* another particle used almost exclusively by women which takes the place of *no desu* or *n desu* at the end of a sentence. With a rising intonation, it is, like the particle *ka,* a spoken question mark.

12. *Tsukanai* (from *tsuku*) = does not go with; is not served with.

13. *Otsuke shimasu: otsuke* comes from *tsukeru* = serve something with. It is a transitive verb to be paired with *tsuku* (see #12, above). The construction employed here, that is, *o* plus the pre-*masu* form plus *suru,* is the one used in respectful speech when the speaker discusses doing something for the person with whom or about whom he/she is talking.

14. *Ni shimasu* = one makes (his/her choice or decision) to be; one decides on (taking).

15. *Kochira* = this side, this way; sometimes used in place of *watakushi* [I]. Similarly, *sochira* or

---

[1] *Humble,* as opposed to *respect,* is a word form that demotes the status of the speaker. Usually it is the speaker who humbles him- or herself.

sochira sama can be used for "you," "he," "she," or "they."

18. *-kudasaimasu ka:* one type of a request form. It is softer than *-kudasai*.

20. *Onegai shimasu:* an idiom used when the speaker requests someone to do something.

22. *Tsumetaku natte iru* = is cold, is chilled [is in the state of having become cold].

26. *Ja:* a variant of *de wa* = Well, then, if that is the case, when used at the beginning of a sentence. *Kore de totte kudasai* = Using this (money), please take (what I owe you). *Otsuri wa ii desu* = Keep the change. [As for the change (it) will be all right (for you to keep it).]

B. A SAMPLE MENU

KONDATE	MENU
Suimono	Clear Soup
sayori	snipe fish
warabi	brackens
namayuba	fresh bean curd
Sashimi	Sashimi
maguro	tuna
Sunomono	Salad
sazae	turbo
udo	udo (Japanese asparagus)
karashisumiso	dressed with vinegar, mustard, and bean paste
Yasai Nimono	Cooked Vegetables
kuwai	arrowhead bulbs
sayaendoo	snow peas
takenoko	bamboo shoots
udo	udo

Yakimono	Fish
koi-teriyaki	broiled carp
tsukeawase	served with fancy relish
Kobachi	Small Bowl
tsukushi-	omelet with horsetails
tamago-toji	(vegetable)
Gohan	Rice
satoimo-gohan	rice cooked with taro
	(root vegetable)
Misoshiru	Soybean Paste Soup
toofu	tofu
negi	green onions
Tsukemono	Pickles
takuan	pickled white radish
narazuke	pickles seasoned with sake
kabura	turnips

REVIEW QUIZ 6

1. *Onaka ga* _____ (must be hungry).
    a. *tsuitadaroo.*
    b. *suitadaroo.*
    c. *kaitadaroo.*

2. _____ (Something) *itadakitai wa.*
    a. *Nani mo*
    b. *Nani ka*
    c. *Nan de mo*

3. *Kono hoteru ni wa ii resutoran ga* _____ (there is).
    a. *arimasu.*
    b. *imasu.*
    c. *shimasu.*

4. *Kono koohii wa* _____ (cold) *natte iru wa.*
   a. *waruku*
   b. *samuku*
   c. *tsumetaku*

5. *Kochira mo sore to* _____ (the same) *ni shite kudasai.*
   a. *nita*
   b. *onaji*
   c. *chigau*

6. _____ (Sugar) *o motte kite kudasaimasu ka?*
   a. *Osatoo*
   b. *Ocha*
   c. *Tamago*

7. *Sore kara fooku* _____ (also).
   a. *moo.*
   b. *to.*
   c. *mo.*

8. _____ (Check) *o motte kite kudasai.*
   a. *Denpyoo*
   b. *Kippu*
   c. *Tanjoobi*

9. *Fooku ga* _____ (missing) *yoo da.*
   a. *nai*
   b. *inai*
   c. *ikanai*

10. _____ (Change) *wa ii desu.*
    a. *Denpyoo*
    b. *Okane*
    c. *Otsuri*

ANSWERS
1—b; 2—b; 3—a; 4—c; 5—b; 6—a; 7—c; 8—a;
9—a; 10—c.

LESSON 38

DAI SANJUU HACHI KA

A. IN, ON, UNDER

1. *Ni, de, e, no:* In, into

Sore wa jisho ni arimasu.	That's in the dictionary.
Poketto ni iremashita.	He put it in his pocket.
Ano hito no heya ni arimasu.	You'll find it in his room.
Hikidashi ni irete kudasai.	Put it into the drawer, please.
Me ni nani ka hairimashita.	I have something in my eye. [Something got into my eyes.]
Tookyoo de kaimashita.	I bought it in Tokyo.
Tookyoo no hakubutsukan de mimashita.	I saw it in the museum in Tokyo.

2. *No naka ni (. . . de, . . . e, . . . no, . . . o):* Inside

Sono kaban no naka o mite kudasai.	Please look in that briefcase. [Please look in the within of that briefcase.]

Gakkoo no naka no shokudoo de gohan o tabemashita.	We ate [had our meal] in the dining room of [in the within of] the school.
Yamada-san to issho ni tatemono no naka c hairima-shita.	Together with Mr. Yamada, we entered the inside of the building.
Kusuriya wa sono tatemono no naka ni arimasu.	The drugstore is in [inside] that building.

3. *No ue ni (. . . de, . . . no, . . . e):* On

Kono tegami o, sono hito no tsukue no ue ni oite kudasai.	Please put this letter on his desk.
Oka no ue de asonde imasu.	They are playing on the hill.
Fuutoo no ue ni kaite kudasai.	Please write it on the envelope.

4. *No shita ni (. . . de, . . . no, . . . e):* Under

Isu no shita ni ari-masu.	It's under the chair.
Sono hon wa hoka no hon no shita ni ari-masu.	You'll find the book under the others.
Beddo no shita ni oki-mashita.	She put it under the bed.
Hashi no shita de hiroimashita.	I picked it up under the bridge.

5. *Naka:* Place inside

Naka wa samui desu.	It is cold inside.
Naka o minaide kudasai.	Please do not look inside.

6. *Ue:* Top, surface

Ue ni oite kudasai.	Put it on top.
Ue o mite kudasai.	Look on the top.

7. *Shita:* Bottom, place under, place below

Sore o shita ni oite kudasai.	Please put that underneath.
Kono shita o mite kudasai.	Please look under here.

B. IF, WHEN

1. *Moshi*[1] . . . *-ba; -nara:* If

Notice that the *-(r)eba* ending form of a verb, the *-kereba* ending form of an *i-* adjective, and the *nara* form of a copula express the idea "if (something) happens," or "if (something) is the case."[2]

These forms are called the "provisional" and are used *only* for a present or future hypothetical condition.

moshi dekireba	if I can
moshi juubun okane ga areba	if I have enough money

---

[1] *Moshi* is optional.

[2] Use *-eba* with consonant verbs; use *-reba* with vowel verbs. For further discussion of the formation of *-ba* form, see Section 36 of the Summary of Japanese Grammar.

Soko e ikeba minna ni aemasu.	If you go there, you can meet everybody.
Samukereba sugu kaerimasu.	If it is cold, I will come back right away.
Yasukereba kau tsumori desu.	If it is inexpensive, I intend to buy it.
Tenisu ga joozu nara ii n desu ga . . .	I hope she is good at tennis. [If she is good at tennis, it is good . . .]
Sashimi nara nan demo kekkoo desu.	If it is raw fish, anything is fine.

2. *-Tara:* If, when

Notice that the *-tara* form is made by adding *-ra* to the *-ta* form. It is used to express a condition of the past, present, or future. The *-tara* form is called the "conditional."

Ashita ame ga futtara ikimasen.	If it rains tomorrow, I won't go.
Ashita atsukattara ikimasen.	If it's hot tomorrow, I won't go.
Okane ga nakattara kaemasen.	If you don't have the money, you can't buy it.
Anmari takai to ittara yasuku shimashita.	When I said it was too expensive, he lowered the price [he made it cheap].
Tabetakattara tabete mo ii desu.	If you want to eat it, you can [eat it].
Takakattara honmono desu.	If it is expensive, it is [a] genuine [thing].

Sono kusuri o nondara sugu yoku narimashita.	When I took [drank] that medicine, I got well right away.

3. *To:* If, when, whenever

Notice that *to* is used only when what follows it is a natural consequence of what is stated in the clause that precedes it. *To* is always preceded by the present form of a verb, an adjective, or the copula; it cannot be used when the terminal clause ends in *-te kudasai*.

Kono michi o mas- sugu iku to bijutsu- kan no mae ni demasu.	If you follow [go] this road straight ahead, you will come to the front of the Fine Arts Museum.
Basu de iku to goji- kan kakarimasu.	If you go by bus, it takes five hours.
Wakaranai koto ga aru to Yamada-san ni kikimasu.	When there are things that I don't under- stand, I ask Mr. Yamada.
Ame ga furu to kuru hito ga sukunaku narimasu.	When it rains, fewer people come [per- sons who come get fewer].
Mainichi kaku to joozu ni narimasu.	When you write it ev- ery day, you become more skillful [in it].

C. WITHOUT

1. *Nashi ni:* Without

okane nashi ni	without money
nani mo nashi ni	without anything

machigai nashi ni	without fail
konnan nashi ni	without difficulty
Konnan nashi ni dekimasu.	You can do it without any difficulty.

2. *-Nai de:* Without

Asagohan o tabenai de dekakemashita.	I went out without having breakfast.
Benkyoo shinai de shiken o ukemashita.	Without studying, I took a test.

QUIZ 31

1. *Sore o shita ni oite kudasai.*
2. *Poketto ni iremashita.*
3. *Sore wa jisho ni arimasu.*
4. *Fuutoo no ue ni kaite kudasai.*
5. *Oka no ue de asonde imasu.*
6. *Ue o mite kudasai.*

7. *yasukereba*
8. *moshi juubun okane ga areba*
9. *anmari takai to ittara*
10. *machigai nashi ni*
11. *konnan nashi ni*

a. It's in the dictionary.
b. Please put that underneath.
c. He put it in his pocket.
d. They are playing on the hill.
e. Write it on the envelope, please.
f. You will find the book under the others.
g. Put it on top, please.
h. Look on the top, please.
i. if it is cold
j. if it is inexpensive
k. if I have enough money

12. *okane nashi ni*
13. *samukereba*
14. *Ue ni oite kudasai*
15. *Sono hon wa hoka no hon no shita ni arimasu.*

l. when I said it was too expensive
m. without money
n. without fail
o. without difficulty

ANSWERS
1—b; 2—c; 3—a; 4—e; 5—d; 6—h; 7—j; 8—k; 9—l; 10—n; 11—o; 12—m; 13—i; 14—g; 15—f.

REVIEW QUIZ 7

1. _____ (That one) *ga hoshii desu.*
   a. *Asoko*
   b. *Are*
   c. *Anna*

2. _____ (This) *wa ikaga desu ka?*
   a. *Kore*
   b. *Kono*
   c. *Koko*

3. *Nihongo de* _____ (how) *iimasu ka?*
   a. *dore*
   b. *donna*
   c. *doo*

4. *Soko e itta* _____ (never).
   a. *tsumori desu.*
   b. *koto ga arimasen.*
   c. *hazu desu.*

5. _____ (Nothing) *kaimasen deshita.*
   a. *Nan de mo*
   b. *Nani ka*
   c. *Nani mo*

6. *Kono hon wa* _____ (her) *desu.*
   a. *dono hito no*
   b. *sono otoko no hito no*
   c. *ano hito no*

7. *Watashi no* _____ (aunt) *desu.*
   a. *oba*
   b. *oji*
   c. *itoko*

8. _____ (One week) *kakarimasu.*
   a. *Ikkagetsu*
   b. *Isshuukan*
   c. *Ichinen*

9. _____ (Next) *basu de ikimashoo.*
   a. *Ashita no*
   b. *Tsugi no*
   c. *Asatte no*

10. *Doomo* _____ (thanks).
    a. *wakarimasen.*
    b. *arigatoo gozaimasu.*
    c. *dekimasen.*

11. *Ni san* _____ (days) *shitara denwa o kakete kudasai.*
    a. *jikan*
    b. *nichi*
    c. *nen*

12. *Kono kata o* _____ (know) *ka?*
    a. *gozonji desu*
    b. *sagashite imasu*
    c. *goshookai itashimasu*

13. *Iie, soo* _____ (don't think).
    a. *ikimasen.*
    b. *omoimasen.*
    c. *kimasen.*

14. *Kyooto de* _____ (bought).
    a. *tsukurimashita.*
    b. *kikimashita.*
    c. *kaimashita.*

15. *Sono tegami wa* _____ (wrote) *ka?*
    a. *mimashita*
    b. *kakimashita*
    c. *uketorimashita*

16. *Watakushi wa* _____ (morning) *wa koohii o nomimasu.*
    a. *hiru*
    b. *yoru*
    c. *asa*

17. *Eki de tomodachi ni* _____ (met).
    a. *hanashimashita.*
    b. *aimashita.*
    c. *kikimashita.*

18. *Anata no denwa bangoo o* _____ (give me).
    a. *shitte imasu.*
    b. *kudasai.*
    c. *agemashoo.*

19. *Sore wa taihen* _____ (good) *desu.*
    a. *kekkoo*
    b. *omoshiroi*
    c. *yasui*

20. _____ (Soon) *kimasu*.
   a. *Sugu*
   b. *Ashita*
   c. *Ato de*

ANSWERS

1—b; 2—a; 3—c; 4—b; 5—c; 6—c; 7—a; 8—b;
9—b; 10—b; 11—b; 12—a; 13—b; 14—c; 15—b;
16—c; 17—b; 18—b; 19—a; 20—a.

D. *SHAKUYA SAGASHI:* HOUSE HUNTING

Study the notes at the end of this section for greater
comprehension.

1. **Kashiya ga aru soo desu ga.**
   I hear you have a house to rent.

2. **Dochira deshoo ka? Futatsu aru n desu ga.**
   Which one? We have two.

3. **Shinbun no kookoku o mite shitta no desu ga.**
   It's the one advertised in the paper.

4. **Hai, wakarimashita.**
   Oh, that one.

5. **Donna ie ka sukoshi setsumei shite moraemasen ka?**
   Can you describe them?

6. **Ookii hoo wa go-eru-dii-kee desu.**
   The larger of the two is 5LDK.

7. **Chiisai hoo wa doo desu ka?**
   How about the smaller one?

8. **Yon-eru-dii-kee desu.**
   (It) is 4LDK.

9. **Ookii hoo wa gareeji ga tsuite imasu ka?**
   Does the larger house have a garage?

10. **Hai, tsuite imasu.**
    Yes, it does.

11. **Niwa ga arimasu ka?**
    Is there a garden there?

12. **Hai, gozaimasu. Nihonshiki no rippa na niwa desu.**
    Yes, there is. It's a fine, Japanese-style garden.

13. **Chiisai hoo wa?**
    How about the smaller house?

14. **Niwa to iu hodo no niwa wa gozaimasen ga miharashi no ii takadai ni gozaimasu.**
    There isn't any garden to speak of, but the house is situated on top of a hill and has a nice view. [(It)'s not much of a garden that there is . . .]

15. **Shizuka na tokoro desu ka?**
    Is it in a quiet neighborhood?

16. **Hai, oodoori kara hanarete imasu kara taihen shizuka desu.**
    Yes, it is away from big streets and it's very quiet there.

17. **Yachin wa dono kurai desu ka?**
    What's the rent?

18. **Ookii hoo wa tsuki nijuuman en desu.**
    The rent for the larger house is two hundred thousand yen per month.

19. **Chiisai hoo wa?**
    And the smaller house?

20. **Tsuki juugoman en desu.**
    One hundred and fifty thousand yen per month.

21. **Kagu zoosaku wa doo nan desu ka?**
    What about furniture and other equipment?

22. **Mina tsuite orimasu. Tatami mo harikaeta bakari desu.**
    (It)'s well furnished. The floor mats have been completely repaired.

23. **Reizooko nado wa nai deshoo ne?**
    I suppose a refrigerator is not included?

24. **Iie, saishinshiki no reizooko ga tsuite orimasu.**
    There is a late-model refrigerator. [There is a refrigerator of the latest style.]

25. **Ichinen no keiyaku de karitai to omotte iru n desu ga, sore de ii desu ka?**
    I would like to get a lease for a year. Do you think that's possible [agreeable]?

26. **Sono ten wa yanushi to gosoodan itadakitai to omoimasu.**
    You'd have to see the owner for that.

27. **Shikikin wa iru n desu ka?**
    Do I have to pay a security deposit? [Is a security deposit necessary?]

28. **Hai, sankagetsubun itadaku koto ni natte ori-masu.**
Yes, we ask three months' rent (for it).

29. **Hoka ni wa?**
Nothing else?

30. **Hoshoonin ga irimasu.**
You have to have references.

31. **Tsuide ni okiki shimasu ga denwa wa tsuite imasu ka?**
Is there a telephone already installed?

32. **Ainiku tsuite orimasen.**
No, there isn't. [Sorry, but it isn't installed.]

33. **Aa soo desu ka.**
I see.

34. **Chikatetsu ya JR no eki ni mo chikakute tai-hen benri na tokoro desu.**
The house is located not too far from the sub-way and the JR-line station. So it's quite con-venient.

35. **Aa soo desu ka. Soko kara Marunouchi made wa dono kurai kakarimasu ka?**
I see. How much time does it take from there to Marunouchi?

36. **Yaku nijuppun gurai desu.**
I would say about twenty minutes.

37. **Basu mo chikaku o tootte imasu ka?**
Is there any bus line running nearby?

38. **Hai, Tookyoo-eki yuki ga kado hitotsu saki o tootte imasu.**
Yes, there is one a block away. The bus goes to Tokyo Station.

39. **Sono uchi wa ima itte miraremasu ka?**
May we see the house now?

40. **Sumimasen ga gozen-chuu shika ome ni ka-kerarenai n desu ga.**
I'm sorry, but it is open for inspection only in the morning.

41. **Aa soo desu ka. Sore ja ashita no asa kimasu. Iroiro osewasama deshita.**
Very well. I'll come tomorrow morning. Thanks a lot.

42. **Doo itashimashite. Kochira koso shitsurei itashimashita.**
Not at all. Glad to be able to help you.

NOTE
Title: *Shakuya Sagashi* = Searching (for) a House to Rent
1. *Aru soo desu* = I understood that there is.
2. *Dochira* = which (of the two).
3. *Kookoku* = advertisement.
5. *Setsumei shite moraemasen ka* = Can't I have you explain the details for me?
6. *Go-eru-dii-kee* = 5LDK (5 rooms, L = living room, DK = dining kitchen).
9. *Tsuite imasu* = are attached; are equipped.
14. *Niwa to iu hodo no niwa* = a garden (worthy of) calling it a garden; (there isn't any) garden to speak of.

Miharashi = view.

Takadai = top of a hill (within a city area).

16. *Hanarete imasu* = is away from.
17. *Yachin* = house rent.
18. *Tsuki* = per month.
21. *Kagu zoosaku* = furniture and other equip-ment(s).
22. *Tatami* = Japanese-style floor mat.
   Harikaeta bakari desu = We have just replaced the mat covers with new ones (the *-ta* form of a verb plus *bakari desu* = just finished doing . . .).
23. *Reizooko nado* = a refrigerator and things like that.
24. *Iie* = no. Notice that this is used where "yes" would be used in English, for the thought is, "No, what you have mentioned is not correct." *Sai-shinshiki no reizooko* = latest-model refrigerator.
   Orimasu: a synonym for *imasu*, but more formal.
25. *Keiyaku* = contract; lease.
26. *Yanushi* = landlord.
   Gosoodan itadakitai = I would like to have you consult.
27. *Shikikin* = key money, security deposit.
28. *Sankagetsubun* = the equivalent of three months' (rent). (*-bun* = the portion for.)
   Koto ni natte orimasu = It is arranged that, it is fixed that (we receive).
30. *Hoshoonin* = reference (i.e., one who guarantees).
34. *Chikatetsu* = subway.
35. *Marunouchi* = the heart of the business section in Tokyo.
38. *Tookyoo-eki yuki* = bound for Tokyo: *yuki* = bound for, when used after a place-name.
39. *Miraremasu* = can see. The same form—made by adding *-(r)areru* to the base—is used for both the passive voice and respect expressions.

40. *Ome ni kakerarenai* = can't show (you); *kake-rarenai:* a negative form of *kakerareru*, which is a potential form made from *kakeru* by adding *-rareru* to the base.
41. *Osewasama deshita* = thanks: a common way of expressing thanks for services rendered.

QUIZ 32

1. _____ (Quiet) *na tokoro desu ka?*
   a. *Rippa*
   b. *Shizuka*
   c. *Benri*

2. *Oodoori kara* _____ (away from) *imasu.*
   a. *hanarete*
   b. *hanashite*
   c. *tooi*

3. _____ (Rent) *wa dono kurai desu ka?*
   a. *Yachin*
   b. *Nedan*
   c. *Shikikin*

4. *Sankagetsubun* _____ (receive) *koto ni natte orimasu.*
   a. *harau*
   b. *itadaku*
   c. *tazuneru*

5. _____ (Furniture) *wa tsuite imasu ka?*
   a. *Tatami*
   b. *Reizooko*
   c. *Kagu zoosaku*

6. *Yaku* _____ (twenty minutes) *gurai desu.*
    a. *nijuppun*
    b. *juunifun*
    c. *nijuufun*

7. _____ (Garden) *ga arimasu ka?*
    a. *Heya*
    b. *Niwa*
    c. *Takadai*

8. *Gozenchuu* _____ (only) *ome ni kake-raremasen.*
    a. *demo*
    b. *hoka*
    c. *shika*

9. _____ (Tomorrow) *no asa kimasu.*
    a. *Kinoo*
    b. *Ashita*
    c. *Asatte*

10. *Iroiro* _____ (thanks for your service) *deshita.*
    a. *omachidoosama*
    b. *ohanashichuu*
    c. *osewasama*

ANSWERS
1—b; 2—a; 3—a; 4—b; 5—c; 6—a; 7—b; 8—c;
9—b; 10—c.

LESSON 39

DAI SANJUU KYUU KA

A. *KURU:* TO COME

Kimasu.	I (you, he, she, we, they) come.
Kite kudasai.	Please come!
Koko e kite kudasai.	Come here, please.
Watakushi to issho ni kite kudasai.	Come with me, please.
Mata kite kudasai.	Come again, please.
Uchi made kite kudasai.	Come to the house, please.
Itsu ka yoru kite kudasai.	Come some night, please.
Konaide kudasai.	Please don't come.
Doko kara kimasu ka?	Where are you coming from?
Tookyoo kara kimasu.	I am coming from Tokyo.
Gekijoo kara kimasu.	I am coming from the theater.
Sugu kimasu.	I am coming right away.

-ta bakari desu = to have just completed an action

Amerika kara kita bakari desu.	I have just come from the United States.
Sono tegami wa ima kita bakari desu.	That letter has just arrived.

-te kuru = to have just started to, to have started doing something and continued up to the present

Ame ga futte kima-shita.	The rain has started to fall.
Nihongo ga wakatte kimashita.	I have started to understand Japanese. [Japanese has begun to be clear to me.]
Nihongo o rokkagetsu benkyoo shite ki-mashita.	I have been studying Japanese for six months.
Nihongo no hon bakari yonde ki-mashita.	I have been reading nothing but books in Japanese.

B. *IU (YUU):* TO SAY

Iimasu.	I (you, he, she, we, they) say.

to iu = to say that . . .

Ikanai to iimashita.	I said that I wouldn't go. [(I) said, "(I) will not go."]
Ikanai ka to ii-mashita.	I said, "Aren't you going?" He said, "Aren't you going?"

to ka iu = to say something to the effect that, to say something like

Ikanai ka to ka ii-mashita.	He said something like, "Aren't you going?" (but I am not exactly sure what he said).

Hitori de itta to ka iimashita.	He said something to the effect that he went alone.
Iinikui desu.	It's hard to say.
Itte kudasai.	Say (it)! Tell (it), please.
Moo ichido itte kudasai.	Say it again, please.
Nihongo de itte kudasai.	Say it in Japanese, please.
Yukkuri itte kudasai.	Say it slowly, please.
Iwanaide kudasai.	Don't say that, please.
Sono hito ni itte kudasai.	Tell (it) to him, please.

yoo ni iu = to tell someone to

Kuru yoo ni itte kudasai.	Tell him to come, please.
Konai yoo ni itte kudasai.	Please tell him not to come.
Kau yoo ni itte kudasai.	Please tell him to buy (it).
Kawanai yoo ni itte kudasai.	Please tell him not to buy (it).
Sono hito ni iwanaide kudasai.	Don't tell him, please.
Sono hito ni nani mo iwanaide kudasai.	Don't tell him anything, please.
Dare ni mo iwanaide kudasai.	Please don't tell that to anybody.
Nan to iimashita ka?	What did you say?
Nan to osshaimashita ka?	What did you say *(respect)?*
Nani mo iimasen deshita.	She hasn't said anything.

QUIZ 33

1. *Gekijoo kara kimasu.*	a. Come with me, please.
2. *Hitori de itta to ka iimashita.*	b. Where are you coming from?
3. *Sugu kimasu.*	c. Come some night, please.
4. *Doko kara kimasu ka?*	d. I'm coming right away.
5. *Itte kudasai.*	e. I'm coming from the theater.
6. *Nihongo de itte kudasai.*	f. Say it in Japanese, please.
7. *Ame ga futte kimashita.*	g. I have just come from the United States.
8. *Itsu ka yoru kite kudasai.*	h. The rain has started to fall.
9. *Watakushi to issho ni kite kudasai.*	i. He said something to the effect that he went alone.
10. *Amerika kara kita bakari desu.*	j. Tell me, please.

ANSWERS

1—e; 2—i; 3—d; 4—b; 5—j; 6—f; 7—h; 8—c; 9—a; 10—g.

C. *SURU:* TO DO

Shimasu.	I (you, he, she, we, they) do.
Shite imasu.	I'm doing it.
Nani o shite imasu ka?	What are you doing?

Doo shimasu ka?	How do you do that?
Nani o shite imashita ka?	What have you been doing?
Shinaide kudasai.	Please don't do it!
Moo shinaide kudasai.	Please don't do it anymore.
Shinakereba narimasen.	You must do it.
Shite wa ikemasen.	You mustn't do it.
Moo shite wa ikemasen.	You mustn't do it anymore.
Shite shimaimashita.	It's done. [(I)'ve finished doing (it).]
Nani mo shite imasen.	I'm not doing anything.
Nani mo shinaide kudasai.	Don't do anything, please.
Moo ichido shite kudasai.	Please do it once more.
Hayaku shite kudasai.	Do it quickly, please!
Chuui shite kudasai.	Pay attention, please!
Benkyoo shite kudasai.	Please study it.
Ima shita bakari desu.	I've just done it now.
Moo oai shimashita.	I've already met her *(respect)*.
Doo shimashoo ka?	What's to be done? What shall we do? What can be done? [How shall we do?]
Dare ga shimashita ka?	Who did that?
Doo shitara ii ka wakarimasen.	I don't know what to do.
Ookiku shimashita.	We enlarged (it).
Iku koto ni shimashita.	We've decided to go. [(We)'ve acted on (our) going.]

QUIZ 34

1. *Doo shimasu ka?*
2. *Shinaide kudasai.*
3. *Shite shimaimashita.*
4. *Doo shimashoo ka?*
5. *Chuui shite kudasai.*
6. *Ookiku shimashita.*
7. *Moo ichido shite kudasai.*
8. *Dare ga shimashita ka?*
9. *Ima shita bakari desu.*
10. *Iku koto ni shimashita.*
11. *Shinakereba ikemasen.*
12. *Shite wa ikemasen.*
13. *Nani o shite imasu ka?*
14. *Hayaku shite kudasai.*
15. *Nani o shite imashita ka?*

a. You mustn't do it.
b. Do it quickly, please.
c. What are you doing?
d. How do you do that?
e. Please don't do it.
f. It's done.
g. You must do it.
h. What's to be done?
i. What have you been doing?
j. Do it once more, please.
k. Pay attention, please.
l. We've decided to go.
m. I've just done it now.
n. We made it large.
o. Who did that?

ANSWERS

1—d; 2—e; 3—f; 4—h; 5—k; 6—n; 7—j; 8—o; 9—m; 10—l; 11—g; 12—a; 13—c; 14—b; 15—i.

REVIEW QUIZ 8

1. *Sugu* _____ (I'm coming).
   a. *kite imasu.*
   b. *kimasu.*
   c. *kimashita.*

2. _____ (Hard to say) *desu.*
   a. *Inikui*
   b. *Ikinikui*
   c. *Iinikui*

3. *Nani o* _____ (do) *imasu ka?*
   a. *shitte*
   b. *shite*
   c. *shiite*

4. *Doo* _____ (do) *ii ka wakarimasen.*
   a. *ittara*
   b. *mitara*
   c. *shitara*

5. *Ano hito wa rippa na uchi o* _____ (have).
   a. *tsukutte imasu.*
   b. *motte imasu.*
   c. *sagashite imasu.*

6. _____ (Don't take) *kudasai.*
   a. *Toranaide*
   b. *Minaide*
   c. *Nomanaide*

7. *Sugu* _____ (stop) *kudasai.*
   a. *tomatte*
   b. *tatte*
   c. *tabete*

8. *Ashita wa ii otenki ni nareba ii to* _____
   (think).
   a. *iimasu.*
   b. *omoimasu.*
   c. *kakimashita.*

9. *Watashi wa* _____ (did not see).
   a. *ma ni aimasen deshita.*
   b. *mairimasen deshita.*
   c. *mimasen deshita.*

10. *Moo ichido* _____ (see) *kudasai.*
    a. *mite*
    b. *nite*
    c. *shite*

11. *Ano hito no banchi wa* _____ (do not know).
    a. *arimasen.*
    b. *shirimasen.*
    c. *chigaimasu.*

12. *Sono koto wa mae kara yoku* _____ (know).
    a. *shite imasu.*
    b. *shitte orimasu.*
    c. *benkyoo shite orimasu.*

13. *Ima denwa de* _____ (is talking).
    a. *kotaete imasu.*
    b. *kiite imasu.*
    c. *hanashite imasu.*

14. *Ima sugu iku* _____ (can).
    a. *tsumori desu.*
    b. *koto ga dekimasu.*
    c. *hazu desu.*

15. *Ano hito wa watakushi no iu koto ga yoku*
    _____ (understands).
    a. *dekimasu.*
    b. *wakarimasu.*
    c. *kikoemasu.*

16. *Booshi o* _____ (please buy).
    a. *totte kudasai.*
    b. *katte kudasai.*
    c. *motte kudasai.*

17. *Kono machi ni* _____ (person I know) *wa dare
    mo orimasen.*
    a. *yonde iru hito*
    b. *shite iru hito*
    c. *shitte iru hito*

18. *Moo sukoshi* _____ (want) *desu.*
    a. *hoshikatta*
    h. *hoshiku nai*
    c. *hoshii*

19. *Ikutsu* _____ (left) *imasu ka?*
    a. *nokotte*
    b. *katte*
    c. *motte*

20. *Itsu* _____ (must you go) *ka?*
    a. *ikanakute mo ii desu*
    b. *ikanakereba narimasen*
    c. *itte wa ikemasen*

ANSWERS
1—b; 2—c; 3—b; 4—c; 5—b; 6—a; 7—a; 8—b;
9—c; 10—a; 11—b; 12—b; 13—c; 14—b; 15—b;
16—b; 17—c; 18—c; 19—a; 20—b.

D. I'M A STRANGER HERE

Gomen kudasai.
Hello. [Pardon.]

Aa Sumisu-san desu ka. Omachi shite orimashita.
Oh, Ms. Smith. I've been waiting for you.

Kyoo wa doo mo oisogashii tokoro o arigatoo goza-imasu.
I certainly appreciate your taking time out for me.
[Thank you (for taking the time for me) when you are so busy.]

Doo itashimashite. Oyasui goyoo desu. De wa sugu dekakemashoo.
Don't mention it. It is an easy task. Shall we get going?

Watakushi wa mada migi mo hidari mo wakari-masen kara yoroshiku onegai itashimasu.
I'm a total stranger here. [(I) can't even tell right from left, and would appreciate (your) taking me around.]

Hai, kashikomarimashita. Yuubinkyoku ni goyoo ga aru to osshaimashita ne.
Surely. You said you wanted to go to the post office, didn't you?

E, soo na n desu.
Yes, that's right.

De wa kono michi o ikimashoo.
Then let's take this street.

Kono michi no namae wa nan to yuu n desu ka?
What's the name of this street?

Shoowa Doori to iimasu. Omo na mise wa taitei koko ni arimasu.
It's Showa Street. Most of the important stores are here.

Nakanaka nigiyaka na tokoro desu ne.
It's quite busy here, isn't it?

E, itsu mo koo desu.
Yes, it is always crowded here, day and night.

Aa, ano ookii tatemono wa nan desu ka?
Oh, yes. What's that big building over there?

Aa, are desu ka?
You mean that one?

Ee.
Yes (that one).

Are wa depaato desu.
Oh, a department store.

Hoo, asoko ni wa Amerika no shokuryoohin nado mo arimasu ka?
[Oh, I see.] Do they sell any American food?

Ikura ka arimasu.
Not much but some.

Sore kara ima no depaato no tonari no tatemono wa nan desu ka?
What's that building next to the department store? [And then . . .]

Shiyakusho desu. Sugu ushiro ni keisatsusho ga arimasu.
That is City Hall. The police station is right in back of it.

Hoo, kore wa zuibun ookii kusuriya desu ne.
Isn't that a big drugstore! [Oh I see . . .]

Ee, kore wa Amerikan Faamashii to itte Nippon no kusuri mo gaikoku no kusuri mo utte imasu.
Yes, this is called (the) American Pharmacy and carries both Japanese and foreign drugs.

Soo desu ka? Kono machi ni wa ii byooin ga arimasu ka?
Is that right? Is there a good hospital in this city?

Hai, ikutsu mo arimasu ga, ma, Daigaku Byooin ga ichiban ii deshoo.
Yes, there are quite a few of them, but—well—perhaps the best is the University Hospital.

Aa soo desu ka.
Oh, I see.

Daigaku Byooin ni wa Eigo no yoku dekiru isha ga takusan imasu.
There are many doctors there who speak English.

Soo desu ka? Doko ni aru n desu ka?
Is that right? Where is it?

Daigaku no koonai desu ga, koko o hashitte iru basu de iku to nijuppun gurai desu.
It's on the university campus. If you take the bus from here, you can get there in twenty minutes.

Kore wa rippa na hoteru desu ne.
This is a fine hotel, isn't it?

Soo desu nee. Gaikokujin wa taitei koko ni tomarimasu.
Yes. Foreigners usually stay here.

Haa? Sore kara eki wa doko desu ka?
I see. Then where is the railroad station?

**Tsugi no kado o migi ni magatte kado hitotsu saki
desu.**
You turn right at the next corner. It's one block from
there.

Aa densha no jikokuhyoo ga hoshii n desu ga ...
[Oh, (I remember).] I wanted to get a timetable.

**E! Sore nara eki made ikanakute mo te ni hairi-
masu. Sono kado no hon'ya de utte imasu.**
[Yes,] if that's the case, you don't have to go to the station. You can buy [get hold of] (one) at the bookstore
on the corner.

Densha no jikokuhyoo wa kau n desu ka?
So you have to pay for it, do you?

**Ee, soo na n desu. Kono kuni de wa jikokuhyoo wa
kawanakereba narimasen.**
That's right. In this country you have to buy train
timetables.

Soo desu ka. Sore wa shirimasen deshita.
Oh, I see. I didn't know that.

**Yuubinkyoku wa sugu soko desu ga, jikokuhyoo o
kau no wa ima ni shimasu ka, soretomo ato ni shimasu ka?**
The post office is right there, but do you want to buy
the timetable now or [otherwise] later?

**Soo desu nee. Ato ni shimasu. Saki ni kakitome o
dashite shimaitai desu kara.**
Let me see. I'll buy it later. I would like to send registered mail first.

Aa soo desu ka. Sore ja sugu ikimashoo.
Oh, I see. Then let's go right away.

Onegai itashimasu.
That'll be fine.

Kore ga yuubinkyoku desu.
This is the post office.

Zuibun konde imasu ne.
It's quite crowded, isn't it?

Kakitome no madoguchi wa hidari no hoo desu.
The registered mail window [window for registered mail] is to the left.

Aa wakarimashita. Asoko desu ne.
Oh, yes. I see it. That's it, isn't it?

Soo desu. Watakushi[1] wa koko no benchi de omachi shimasu.
Right. I'll be waiting for you at the bench here.

Soo desu ka. De wa onegai itashimasu.
Fine! I would appreciate that.

Goyukkuri doozo.
Don't hurry.

QUIZ 35

1. _____ (Don't mention it.)
   a. *Gomen kudasai.*
   b. *Doo itashimashite.*
   c. *Kashiko-marimashita.*

[1] Note the use of the formal *watakushi*.

2. _____ (The post office) *ni ikimashoo.*
   a. *Yuubinkyoku*
   b. *Shiyakusho*
   c. *Jimusho*

3. *Migi mo hidari mo* _____ (can't tell).
   a. *miemasen.*
   b. *wakarimasen.*
   c. *kakimasen.*

4. *Kono machi ni wa* _____ (hospital) *ga arimasu ka?*
   a. *byooin*
   b. *byooki*
   c. *biyooin*

5. *Kono* _____ (street) *no namae wa nan to iimasu ka?*
   a. *machi*
   b. *michi*
   c. *uchi*

6. *Ano ookii* _____ (building) *wa nan desu ka?*
   a. *tabemono*
   b. *uchi*
   c. *tatemono*

7. *Depaato no* _____ (next) *ni Shiyakusho ga arimasu.*
   a. *tonari*
   b. *ushiro*
   c. *mae*

8. *Gaikokujin wa taitei kono hoteru ni* _____ (stay).
   a. *sumimasu.*
   b. *yasumimasu.*
   c. *tomarimasu.*

9. _____ (Registered mail) *o dashite shimaitai desu.*
   a. *Denwa*
   b. *Densha*
   c. *Kakitome*

10. _____ (The station) *wa doko desu ka?*
    a. *Eki*
    b. *Densha*
    c. *Shiyakusho*

ANSWERS
1—b; 2—a; 3—b; 4—a; 5—b; 6—c; 7—a; 8—c; 9—c; 10—a.

LESSON 40

DAI YONJUKKA

A. THE MOST COMMON VERB FORMS

1. Plain forms:

	I EAT (VOWEL VERB)	I FINISH (CONSONANT VERB)	I COME (IRREGULAR VERBS)	I DO
PRESENT AFFIRMATIVE (DICT. FORM)	*taberu*	*owaru*	*kuru*	*suru*
-ta FORM (PAST)	*tabeta*	*owatta*	*kita*	*shita*
-te FORM (TENTATIVE)	*tabeyoo*	*owaroo*	*koyoo*	*shiyoo*

Verbs ending in *-eru* or *-iru,* with some exceptions, take all the forms listed above for *taberu.* For example:

hareru	the sky clears
atsumeru	gather (something)
hajimeru	start (something)
ochiru	fall

All other verbs, except *kuru* [come] and *suru* [do], which are irregular, are declined like *owaru.* For construction of the *-ta* forms, see Lesson 12 and Section 17 of the Summary of Japanese Grammar. For example:

agaru	rise
arau	wash
atsumaru	gather
hakaru	measure

2. Polite forms:

tabemasu	I eat, I'll eat
tabemashita	I ate
tabemashoo.	I think I'll eat
owarimasu	I finish, I'll finish
owarimashita	I finished
owarimashoo	I think I will finish ...
kimasu	I come
kimashita	I came
kimashoo.	I think I'll come
shimasu	I do, I'll do
shimashita	I did
shimashoo	I think I'll do

3. future:

tabemasu	owarimasu	kimasu	shimasu
tabemashoo	owarimashoo	kimashoo	shimashoo
taberu	owaru	kuru	suru
deshoo	*deshoo*	*deshoo*	*deshoo*

Notice that the forms used to express the future vary. If the event under discussion is definite, you use *-masu,* the same form used for the present. If it is not definite, you use *-mashoo* or *-(r)u deshoo.* Use *-mashoo* when whether or not the event will take place depends on the speaker. Usually, the event will take place for the sake of the nonspeaker. Use *-(r)u deshoo* when it does not depend on you. Compare these forms:

Tabemasu.
> I shall eat it.
> I will eat it.
> I eat it.
> [Eating takes place definitely, in the present or the future.]

Tabemashoo.
> I think I'll eat it.
> Let's eat it.
> [(It)'s not definite but (I) think (I)'ll eat; (the choice) is up to me (us).]

Taberu deshoo.
> I think he will eat it.
> [(It)'s not definite, but he will probably eat it; it's not up to me.]

Denwa o kakemashoo.	Let's phone.
Kawaku deshoo.	It'll dry, I think.
Juppun de kawaki-masu.	It will dry in ten minutes (definitely).
Koko ni oitara nakunaru deshoo.	If you leave it here, it will get lost (I think).
Sugu naoru deshoo.	He'll get well soon.
Tanaka-san ni tano-mimashoo.	Let's ask Ms. Tanaka to do it.
Yamada-san ga tetsudau deshoo.	Mr. Yamada will probably help you.
Sonna ni hataraitara tsukareru deshoo.	If you work so hard, you will probably get tired.
Tsuzukemashoo.	Let's continue it.

4. Past:

tabe-mashita	*owari-mashita*	*ki-mashita*	*shi-mashita*
(from *taberu*)	(from *owaru*)	(from *kuru*)	(from *suru*)

The *-mashita* form expresses an action or state that is already completed, and in most cases is equivalent to the past and present perfect tenses in English. For example:

Tsutsumimashita.	I wrapped it up.
Ugokashimashita.	I moved it.
Ugokimashita.	It moved.
Urimashita.	I sold it.
Utaimashita.	I sang it.
Wakemashita.	I divided it.
Waraimashita.	I laughed.

Warimashita.	I broke it.
Watashimashita.	I handed it.
Yaburimashita.	I tore it.

5. I used to ...

Tabeta mono deshita. *Tabeta mono desu.*	I used to eat.
Owaraseta mono deshita. *Owaraseta mono desu.*	I used to finish.
Kita mono deshita. *Kita mono desu.*	I used to come.
Shita mono deshita. *Shita mono desu.*	I used to do.

Use the *-ta* form plus *mono deshita* (or *desu*) when referring to an action or state that used to take place but no longer does. For example:

Bikkuri shita mono deshita.	I used to be surprised.
Te de hakonda mono deshita.	I used to carry it by hand.
Maitoshi hikkoshita mono deshita.	I used to move every year.

6. I have ...
(EXPERIENCE)

Tabeta koto ga arimasu.	I have eaten it.
Yonda koto ga arimasu.	I have read it.
Kita koto ga arimasu.	I have come.
Shita koto ga arimasu.	I have done (it).

Most of the ideas expressed in English by the present perfect ("have" plus the past participle) are expressed in Japanese by the use of the *-mashita* form.

However, when you mean that you have had the experience of doing something one or more times in the past, you use the *-ta* form plus *koto ga arimasu,* as seen above. Other examples:

Eigo ni yakushita koto ga arimasu.	I [have] once translated it into English.
Eigo ni yakushima-shita.	I [have] translated it into English.
Tabako wa mae ni yameta koto ga ari-masu.	I have once before stopped [discontinued] smoking.
Sono koto ni tsuite shirabeta koto ga arimasu.	I have [once] made an investigation concerning that matter.

7. I had . . .

Kaite arimashita.	I had written it. [(It) had been written.]
Yonde arimashita.	I had read it. [(It) had been read.]
Kite imashita.	I had come.
Shite arimashita.	I had done it. [(It) had been done.]

In most cases the ideas expressed in English by the past perfect ("had" plus the past participle) can be expressed in Japanese by *-te arimashita* for transitive verbs and *-ta imashita* for intransitive verbs. Note that in the case of transitive verbs, however, the object of the verb in Japanese becomes the subject in English. For example:

Kudamono wa katte arimashita.	I had purchased the fruit (when he arrived). [The fruit had been purchased . . .]

Hana wa moo chitte imashita.	The flowers had already fallen off (the trees when we went there).
Puroguramu wa moo hajimatte imashita.	The program had already started (when we arrived there).
Zaseki wa totte ari-mashita.	She had already taken the seats (for us when we arrived).

8. Commands and requests:

Each verb has a form called the "plain imperative," which is very brusque and is used almost exclusively in conversations between men. To form the plain imperative, add *-ro* to the base for vowel verbs and *-e* to the base for consonant verbs.

Tabero!	Eat!
Dete ike!	Leave!
Damare!	Shut up!
Koi![1]	Come!
Hayaku shiro![2]	Do it quickly!

Another command expression is the pre-*masu* form plus *nasai.* An adult will usually use this form when ordering a child to do something.

Soko e ikinasai.	Go there.
Heya o katazukenasai.	Tidy up the room.
Sugu nenasai.	Go to bed right away.

---

[1] Irregular: from *kuru.*
[2] Irregular: from *suru.*

Notice that an ordinary polite request ends in -*te kuda-sai* for the affirmative. An adult will usually use this form when ordering a child to do something.

Yomanaide kudasai.	Please don't read.
Tabenaide kudasai.	Please don't eat.

To form an even more polite expression of request, prefix the pre-*masu* form of the verb with *o-* and add *kudasai* or *ni natte kudasai* for the affirmative. Form the negative as in the paragraph above.

Otori kudasai.	Take it, please.
Otori ni natte kudasai.	Take it, please *(re-spect)*.
Otori ni naranaide kudasai.	Please do not take it *(respect)*.
Tetsudatte kudasai.	Please help me! [Give a hand, please.]
Moo sukoshi motte kite kudasai.	Bring me some more, please.
Watakushi no tokoro e motte kite kudasai.	Bring it to me. [Bring it to my place, please.]
Tomatte kudasai!	Stop, please!
Sugu tomatte kudasai!	Stop right here, please!
Sono hito o tomete kudasai!	Stop him, please!
Koshikakete kudasai.⎤ *Okoshikake kudasai.*⎦	Sit down./Have a seat, please.
Shinjite kudasai.	Please believe me!
Kiite kudasai.	Please listen.
Watakushi no iu koto o kiite kudasai.	Listen to me. [Listen to what I say, please.]

Kore o kiite kudasai.	Listen to this, please.
Chuui shite kiite kudasai.	Listen carefully, please.
Ano hito no iu koto o kiite kudasai.	Listen to him, please.
Ano hito no iu koto o ki-kanaide kudasai.	Please don't listen to him.
Haitte kudasai.	Please come in! Please enter!
Ohairi kudasai.	Come in. Enter, please.
Sono hito no tokoro e okutte kudasai.	Send it to him, please.
Watakushi no tokoro e okutte kudasai.	Send them (it) to me, please.
Sono hito no tokoro e ikuraka okutte kudasai.	Send him some, please.
Watakushi no tokoro e ikuraka okutte kudasai.	Send me some, please.
Tameshite kudasai.	Please try. [Please check!]
Tamesanaide kudasai.	Please don't try!
Tabete mite kudasai.	Please try eating it.
Yonde mite kudasai.	Please try reading it.
Kao o aratte kudasai.	Please wash yourself [wash your face]!
Tatte kudasai.	Please stand up! Please get up!
Otachi kudasai.	Please stand up. Kindly rise.
Yonde kudasai.	Please read that!
Watakushi o soko e tsurete itte kudasai.	Please take me there!
Moo hitotsu otori kudasai.	Please take another one. [Please take one more.]

Densha de itte kudasai.	Please take the train. [Please go by train.]
Densha de oide kudasai.	Please take the train. [Please go by train.] *(respect)*
Takushii de itte kudasai.	Take a taxi, please.
Mite kudasai.	Please look!
Goran ni natte kudasai.	Please look *(respect)!*
Moo ichido mite kudasai.	Please look again!
Koko o mite kudasai.	Please look here!
Watashi o mite kudasai.	Please look at me!
Kore o mite kudasai.	Please look at this!
Minaide kudasai.	Please don't look.
Goran ni naranaide kudasai.	Please don't look *(respect).*
Kaeshite kudasai.	Please return it to me.
Okaeshi ni natte kudasai.	Please return it to me *(respect).*
Soko o agatte kudasai.	Go up there, please.
Misete kudasai.	Please show me!
Misenaide kudasai.	Please don't show it!
Wasurenaide kudasai.	Please don't forget.
Dete itte kudasai.	Please leave!
Sugu dete itte kudasai.	Please leave quickly! Please go right away!
Dete ikanaide kudasai.	Please don't leave!
Kore o asoko e motte itte kudasai.	Carry this over there, please.
Totte kudasai.	Take it, please.
Otori kudasai.	Please take it.
Toranaide kudasai.	Please don't take it.
Otori ni naranaide kudasai.	Please don't take it *(respect).*
Uchi e kaette kudasai.	Please go home!

Hayaku uchi e kaette kuda-sai.	Please go home early!
Moo ichido itte kudasai.	Please say it again.
Moo ichido osshatte kudasai.	Please say it again *(respect).*
Ite kudasai.	Please stay.
Koko ni ite kudasai.	Please stay here.
Shizuka ni shite kudasai.	Please be quiet.
Ugokanaide kudasai.	Please be still. Please don't move.
Tsuite kite kudasai.	Please follow. Please follow me.
Ano hito ni tsuite itte kuda-sai.	Please follow him.
Sawaranaide kudasai.	Please don't touch!
Koohii o tsuide kudasai.	Please pour me some coffee.

B. *KYUUYUU TO NO SAIKAI:*
   MEETING AN OLD FRIEND

Study the notes at the end of this section for greater comprehension.

1. Y: **Zuibun hisashiburi desu ne? Ogenki desu ka?**
   Y: Well! (Long time no see!) How are you?

2. S: **Okage sama de. Otaku wa?**
   S: Fine, thanks. (And) you and your family?

3. Y: **Arigatoo. Minna genki desu. Nagai goryokoo de otsukare deshoo.**
   Y: Thanks, we're all well. (You're) not too tired from your trip?

4. S: **Iya. Betsu ni.**
   S: Not at all.

5. Y: **A! Kanai o goshookai shimashoo.**
   Y: [Oh, yes.] I'd like you to meet my wife.

6. S: **Doozo.**
   S: I'd be very happy to.

7. Y: **Kochira wa Satoo-san.**
   Y: This is (my friend) Sato.

8. S: **Hajimemashite. Doozo yoroshiku.**
   S: I am very happy to know you.

9. Mrs. Y: **Kochira koso.**
   Mrs. Y: Glad to know you.

10. S: **Yaa. Hisashiburi de yukai desu ne.**
    S: Yes, indeed. It's really good to see you again.

11. Y: **Yaa. Mattaku dookan desu. Tokorode Satoo-san anata wa chitto mo kawarimasen ne.**
    Y: Yes, indeed. By the way, you haven't changed a bit.

12. S: **Iyaa. Sono ten ja anata mo sukoshi mo kawatte imasen yo.**
    S: Neither have you. [No, in that respect you haven't changed a bit.]

13. Mrs. Y: **Okusama wa Amerika no goseikatsu o otanoshimi desu ka?**
    Mrs. Y: How does your wife like the United States?

14. S: **Ee. Hijoo ni tanoshinde orimasu.**
    S: [Yes.] She likes it a lot.

15. Mrs. Y: **Achira wa Tookyoo to wa daibu chi-
    gau no deshoo ne?**
    Mrs. Y: It must be very different from Tokyo.

16. S: **Tashika ni chigau tokoro wa arimasu ne.**
    S: There certainly are lots of very curious things
    in the United States!

17. Mrs. Y: **Tatoeba doo iu tokoro nan desu no?**
    Mrs. Y: For example?

18. S: **Tatoeba desu ne, soo, kusuriya de shokuji o
    suru nado to itte mo chotto gosoozoo ni nare-
    nai deshoo?**
    S: For example [so, (here is a good one)], it cer-
    tainly wouldn't occur to you to have a meal in a
    pharmacy.

19. Y: **Joodan deshoo.**
    Y: You're joking!

20. S: **Iya. Majime na hanashi desu yo.**
    S: Not at all. I'm very serious.

21. Mrs. Y: **Maa! Kusuriya de oshokuji o nasaru!**
    Mrs. Y: (Imagine) eating [having a meal] in a
    pharmacy!

22. S: **Soo na n desu yo. Bifuteki datte aru n desu
    yo, okusan.**
    S: Yes, you can even have a steak.

23. Y: **Kusuriya ni?**
    Y: In a pharmacy?

24. S: **Soo na n desu. Dezaato ni wa oishii aisu-
    kuriimu ga arimasu shi ne.**
    S: Yes, in a pharmacy—with excellent ice cream
    for dessert.

25. Mrs. Y: **Demo kusuri no nioi ga oki ni nari-
    masen?**
    Mrs. Y: But the smell of the pharmacy—doesn't
    that bother you?

26. S: **Nioi nanka shimasen yo.**
    S: There isn't any smell.

27. Y: **Hee? Kusuri o utte ite mo desu ka?**
    Y: Really? Even when they sell drugs?

28. S: **Ee. Sore ga shinai n desu yo. Amerika no
    Doraggu Sutoa wa.**
    S: No [yes, (what you said is right)] there isn't
    any in American "drugstores."

29. Y: **Hoo . . . a, wakatta. Iwayuru Nihon de yuu
    kusuriya to chigau n desu ne.**
    Y: [Hmm . . .] Oh! That's the trick! It's a differ-
    ent place from the kind of place we call phar-
    macy in Japan, isn't it?

30. Y: **Dakara yakkyoku ja nai to iu wake na n
    desu ne.**
    Y: Therefore it's no longer a pharmacy.

31. S: **E. Doraggu sutoa de wa omocha to ka, kitte to ka, tabako to ka okashi no yoo na mono made mo utteru n desu.**
S: You also find many other things in a drugstore: toys, stamps, cigarettes, candy . . .

32. Y: **Hoo . . . ! Kawatte iru n desu ne?**
Y: Hmm! That's really very funny.

33. S: **Mada sono ue ni hon mo aru, bunboogu mo aru, daidokoro yoohin mo aru, keshoohin mo aru, maa, nani mo ka mo aru to itta katachi desu yo.**
S: . . . books, stationery, cooking utensils, cosmetics, and what have you.

34. Y: **Hmm! Ma, yorozuya to iu wake desu ne.**
Y: Hmm? [So to speak] it's a general store, then?

35. S: **Ee, demo kusuri wa chan to utteru n desu yo.**
S: Yes, but it's (still) a pharmacy!

NOTE
Title: *Kyuuyuu to no Saikai* = Meeting an Old Friend
  1. *Hisashiburi desu* = It has been a long time since (I saw you last).
  2. *Otaku wa* = your family, you.
  3. *Goryokoo de* = on account of a trip.
     Otsukare deshoo = You must be tired.
  4. *Iya* (same as *iie*) = no.
     Betsu ni = (not) especially.
  7. *Satoo-san:* Note the use of *san* in spite of Sato's being Yamada's old friend. Adding a *san* is a common practice regardless of the extent of the friendship. The first name is not usually mentioned in a situation like this.

11. *Mattaku dookan desu* = I'm in complete agreement with you. [The] same here.
    Tokorode = by the way.
    Satoo-san: Notice the use of the surname of the person with whom you are speaking.
    Kawarimasen = (you) don't change.

12. *Kawatte imasen* = You haven't changed. [You are not in the state of having changed.]

13. *Tanoshimu* = enjoy; *otanoshimi desu: o* plus the pre-*masu* form plus *desu*, a respect expression.

17. *Tatoeba* = for instance.

18. *Desu ne* = a meaningless expression similar to the American phrase "you know."
    Gosoozoo ni narenai = You cannot imagine *(respect); nareru* = potential form derived from the consonant verb *naru*.

22. *Datte* (same as *de mo*) = even (used in everyday speech).

24. *Shi:* adds the feeling of "and it's in addition to what I've said."

25. *Oki ni narimasen* (when spoken with a rising intonation) = Doesn't it bother you? (a respect form of *ki ni naru* [something bothers]).

26. *Nanka* = and things like that (used in everyday speech); *nanka* is usually mutually exclusive with the particles *ga, wa,* and *o*.

27. *Utte ite mo desu ka* = Is it so even when they are selling medicines?

28. Notice the inverted word order used in informal conversation.

29. *Wakatta* = I've got it. [(It) has become clear.]

30. *Yakkyoku* = pharmacy.

31. ... *to ka* ... *to ka* ... *to ka* (comparable to ... *ya* ... *ya* ... *ya*) = and ... and ... and (with the implication that the listing is incomplete).

32. *Kawatte iru* = is different.

33. *Sono ue ni* = on top of that.
    Nani mo ka mo = and what have you; everything.
34. *To iu wake desu* = it amounts to saying; it means.
    Yorozuya = ten-thousand-variety shop; general
    store.

QUIZ 36

1. _____ (Long time no see) *desu ne.*
   a. *Omoshiroi*
   b. *Atatakai*
   c. *Hisashiburi*

2. _____ (Fine, thanks) *sama de.*
   a. *Oki no doku*
   b. *Okage*
   c. *Omachidoo*

3. *Nagai goryokoo de* _____ (tired) *deshoo.*
   a. *omoshirokatta*
   b. *otanoshimi*
   c. *otsukare*

4. _____ (Wife) *o goshookai shimashoo.*
   a. *Kanai*
   b. *Kodomo*
   c. *Tomodachi*

5. *Hisashiburi de* _____ (pleasure) *desu ne.*
   a. *arigatai*
   b. *yukai*
   c. *saiwai*

6. _____ (Not at all) *kawarimasen ne.*
   a. *Anmari*
   b. *Sukoshi shika*
   c. *Chitto mo*

7. _____ (Serious) *na hanashi desu.*
   a. *Majime*
   b. *Kantan*
   c. *Hen*

8. _____ (Delicious) *aisukuriimu ga arimasu.*
   a. *Oishii*
   b. *Takai*
   c. *Yasui*

9. _____ (Bother) *ni narimasen ka?*
   a. *Oki*
   b. *Okaki*
   c. *Oyomi*

10. _____ (On top of that) *hon mo bunboogu mo arimasu.*
    a. *Sono kawari ni*
    b. *Sono ue ni*
    c. *Sono mise ni*

ANSWERS
1—c; 2—b; 3—c; 4—a; 5—b; 6—c; 7—a; 8—a; 9—a; 10—b.

C. THE MOST COMMON VERBS AND VERB PHRASES

1. *Miru:* To see

PLAIN	POLITE[1]	
miru	*mimasu*	I see
mita	*mimashita*	I saw
mite	*mite*	I see (saw) and . . .
miyoo	*mimashoo*	let's see
minai	*mimasen*	I don't see
Mimashoo.		Let's see. Let's take a look.
Mimasen.		I don't see.
Nan de mo mi-masu.		I see every-thing.

Notice that *miru* means "to see" only in the sense of perceiving by the eye. Study the following:

Nikko o mita koto ga arimasu ka?	Have you ever seen the Nikko (Shrine)?
Yamada-san ni atta[2] koto ga arimasu ka?	Have you ever seen Mr. Yamada?
Ima atta bakari desu.	I've just seen him.
Watashi wa eiga o mimasen.	I don't go to the mov-ies. [I don't see movies.]
Anata no iu koto ga wakarimasen.[3]	I don't see what you mean.

---

[1] In the verb forms that follow, the plain form is given in the first column, the polite form in the second column.

[2] *au* = see (meet).

[3] *wakaru* = see (understand).

*Donata ni oai ni nari-
masu ka?*   Who do you see?

*Ima atte itadakemasu
ka?*   Can you see me now
(humble)? [Can (I)
have (you) see me
now?]

*Itsu ka yoru asobi ni
kite kudasai.*[1]   Please come to see us
some night.

2. *Shitte iru:* To know
   Shiru: To learn, to get to know

shitte iru	*shitte imasu*	I know
shitte ita	*shitte imashita*	I knew
shitte ite	*shitte ite*	I know (knew) and . . .
shiranai	*shirimasen*	I don't know
shiru	*shirimasu*	I learn
shitta	*shirimashita*	I learned
shitte	*shitte*	I learn (learned) and . . .
shiroo	*shirimashoo*	let's learn
shiranai	*shirimasen*	I don't know

Shitte imasu.   I know it. [I'm in the
state of having
learned it.]

Shirimasen.   I don't know. [I
haven't learned.]

Yoku shitte imasu.   I know it well.
Nani mo shirimasen.   He doesn't know anything.

[1] *asobi ni kuru* = come to see (visit).

Sono koto ni tsuite wa nani mo shirimasen.	I don't know anything about it.
Koko ni iru koto o shitte imasu.	I know that he is here. [I know the fact that he is here.]
Sore o shitte imasu ka?	Do you know that?
Doko ni iru ka shitte imasu ka?	Do you know where she is?
Sono koto ni tsuite wa kore ijoo shirimasen.	She doesn't know any more [than this] about it.
Sono koto ni tsuite wa anata ga shitte iru yoo ni wa shirimasen.	She doesn't know any more about it than you do [know].
Sono koto wa shinbun de shirimashita.	I learned (of) it through the newspaper.

3. *Motsu:* To hold

motsu	*mochimasu*	I hold
motta	*mochimashita*	I held
motte	*motte*	I hold (held) and . . .
motoo	*mochimashoo*	I think I'll hold, let's hold
motanai	*mochimasen*	I don't hold

Kore o chotto motte kudasai.	Hold this for me a moment, please.
Te ni booshi o motte imasu.	He's holding a hat in his hand.
Ima wa motte imasu.	I have it now.
Shikkari motte kudasai.	Hold firm, please.

Notice that the ideas expressed by the English word "have" and "possess" are expressed in Japanese by using the *-te* form of the verb *motsu* [to hold] plus *imasu*. See also Lesson 14. Compare the following:

Okane wa ikura motte imasu ka?	How much money do you have?
Nisen en motte imasu.	I have two thousand yen.
Sore wa omosugimasu kara hitori de motsu koto wa dekimasen.	It's too heavy [and] so I can't hold it alone.

Notice also that the ideas expressed in English by "take (to)," "bring," and "carry around," are expressed in Japanese by using the *-te* form of the verb *motsu* together with the verb *iku* [go], *kuru* [come], *aruku* [walk]. Compare the following:

Kasa o motte itte kudasai.	Please take your umbrella (with you).
Kasa o motte kite kudasai.	Please bring over (your) umbrella.
Ano hito wa itsu mo kasa o motte arukimasu.	He always carries his umbrella around.

4. *Dekiru:* To be able

dekiru	*dekimasu*	I can
dekita	*dekimashita*	I could
dekite	*dekite*	I can (could) and . . .
dekinai	*dekimasen*	I can't

Suru koto ga dekimasu.	I can do it.
Kuru koto ga dekimasu ka?	Can you come?
Sono shitsumon ni wa kotaeru koto ga deki-masen.	I can't answer the question.
Soko e iku koto ga de-kimasen.	I can't go there.
Itsu deru koto ga deki-masu ka?	When can we leave?
Tetsudatte itadakemasuka?	Can you help me?

The idea "to be able to (do something)" or "can (do something)" can be expressed in several ways. The most common is by the use of a dictionary form plus *koto ga dekiru*, demonstrated above. Another way is to use a derived potential verb as follows:

    a. For consonant verbs:
       Drop the final *-u* of the dictionary form and add *-eru*. The resulting form is a vowel verb that means "capable of doing something."

CONSONANT VERB		DERIVED POTENTIAL VERB	
iku	go	*ikeru*	can go
kau	buy	*kaeru*	can buy
hanasu	speak	*hanaseru*	can speak

Ashita ikemasu ka?	Can you go tomorrow?
Shirokiya de kaemasu ka?	Can you buy it at Shi-rokiya's (department store)?

    b. For vowel verbs:
       Drop the final *-eru* or *-iru* and add *-rareru* in its place.

VOWEL VERB	DERIVED POTENTIAL VERB	
taberu	*taberareru*	can eat
miru	*mirareru*	can see
okiru	*okirareru*	can get up

Kore wa nama de tabe-raremasu ka? — Can we eat this raw?

Nara e iku to furui tatemono ga takusan miraremasu. — If you go to the city of Nara, you can see many ancient buildings.

c. For irregular verbs:

IRREGULAR VERB	DERIVED POTENTIAL VERB	
kuru	*korareru*	can come
suru	*dekiru*	can do

Koko e sugu koraremasu ka? — Can you come here right away?

Konnan nashi ni dekimasu. — You can do it without any difficulty.

5. *Wakaru:* To understand

wakaru	*wakarimasu*	I understand
wakatta	*wakarimashita*	I understood
wakatte	*wakatte*	I understand (understood) and ...
wakaranai	*wakarimasen*	I don't understand

Ano hito wa kore ga wakarimasen. — He doesn't understand this.

Yoku wakarimasu. — I understand very well.

Watashi no iu koto ga wakarimasu ka?	Do you understand me [what (I) say]?
Watashi no iu koto ga wakarimasen ka?	Don't you understand me?
Wakarimasu ka?	Do you understand?
Nihongo ga wakarimasu ka?	Do you understand Japanese?
Eigo ga wakarimasu ka?	Do you understand English?
Ano hito ga anata ni itte iru koto ga minna wakarimasu ka?	Do you understand everything he's saying to you?
Wakarimasen.	I don't understand.
Wakarimashita ka?	Did you understand?
Watashi no iu koto ga wakatte moraemasen.	I can't make myself understood. [(I) can't have what (I) say understood.]
Ano hito wa shoobai no koto wa sukoshi mo wakarimasen.	He doesn't understand [not a bit] about business.
Zenzen wakarimasen. *Kaimoku wakarimasen.* *Sukoshi mo wakarimasen.*	I don't understand it at all. I don't understand anything about it. It's a mystery to me. I'm completely in the dark.

6. *Oku:* To put, to place

oku	okimasu	I put
oita	okimashita	I put (*past*)
oite	oite	I put and . . .
okoo	okimashoo	I think I'll put, let's put
okanai	okimasen	I don't put

Soko ni oite kudasai. — Put it there, please.
Doko ni okimashita ka? — Where did you put it?
Ano hito wa jibun de mono o oita tokoro o sugu wasuremasu. — He never knows where he puts (his) things. [He forgets right away the place where he has put (his) things himself.]

You use *oku* when you are talking about "putting" or "placing" a thing someplace. To express the thought of "putting on" wearing apparel, you may use several different words. For example:

kaburu — to put on one's head; to put a thing over one's head

Booshi o kabutte kudasai. — Put your hat on, please.
kiru — to wear on the body
Nihon no kimono o kimashita. — She wore a Japanese kimono.
haku — to wear on the foot or leg

Kuroi kutsu o haite ikimashita. — He was wearing black shoes (when) he went.

When *oku* follows another verb using the *-te* form, it implies that the action of the verb preceding *oku* takes place in anticipation of some future situation. For example:

Sono koto wa Yamada-san ni denwa de shirasete okimashita.[1] — I [have] notified Mr. Yamada in advance over the telephone.

---

[1] The statement implies, "I have the intention of explaining it in detail when I see him, but for now . . ."

Konshuu wa Doyoobi ni kaimono ga dekinai node Suiyoobi ni kaimono o shite okimashita.

Since I can't do any shopping on Saturday, I did the shopping on Wednesday.

7. *Kuru:* To come

kuru	*kimasu*	I come
kita	*kimashita*	I came
kite	*kite*	I come and . . .
koyoo	*kimashoo*	I think I'll come, let's come
konai	*kimasen*	I don't come

Hitori de kimashita.

I came alone. I came by myself.

Hitori de kuru deshoo.

I think she is coming alone.

Moo kite imasu.

He is already here. [He is in the state of having come already.]

Sanji made ni konakattara saki ni ikimashoo.

If he doesn't come by three, let's go ahead of him.

8. *Matsu:* To wait

matsu	*machimasu*	I wait
matta	*machimashita*	I waited
matte	*matte*	I wait (waited) and . . .
matoo	*machimashoo*	I think I'll wait, let's wait
matanai	*machimasen*	I don't wait

Koko de matte kudasai.	Wait here, please.
Watashi o matte kudasai.	Wait for me, please.
Sukoshi matte kudasai.	Wait a little, please.
Chotto matte kudasai.	Wait a minute, please.
Matanaide kudasai.	Don't wait, please.
Sono hito o matte imasu.	I'm waiting for her.
Hoka no hitotachi o matte iru no desu.	She is waiting for the others.
Dare o matte iru no desu ka?	Who are you waiting for?
Naze matte iru no desu ka?	Why are you waiting?
Matasete[1] sumimasen deshita. *Omachidoo sama deshita.*	I'm sorry I kept you waiting. [I caused you to wait; I'm sorry.]

9. *Kiku:* To ask

Asoko de kiite kudasai.	Ask over there, please.
Asoko de sono hito no koto o kiite kudasai.	Ask about him over there, please.
Nani o kiite iru no desu ka?	What's she asking?
Michi ga wakaranaku nattara hito ni kiite kudasai.	Please ask the way if you get lost.
Sono hito ni jikan o kiite kudasai.	Ask him the time, please.
Kiite kite kudasai.	Please go and ask him. [Please ask and come back (to this place).]

[1] *matsu* plus *-aseru* (causative ending) = *mataseru:* cause someone to wait, make (have, let) someone wait.

Dare ka watashi no koto o kiitara sugu kaette kuru to itte kudasai.		If someone asks for me [please tell him that], I'll be back in a moment.
Doko ni aru ka kiki-mashita.		She asked where it is.
Denwa o kakete kiite kudasai.		Call her on the phone [and ask], please.

10. *-Tai:* To want to (do something)

Ikitai.	*Ikitai desu.*	I want to go.
Ikitakatta.	*Ikitakatta desu.*	I wanted to go.
Ikitakute ...	*Ikitakute ...*	I want (wanted) to go and ...
Ikitai daroo.	*Ikitai deshoo.*	I suppose he wants to go.
Ikitaku nai.	*Ikitaku nai desu.*	I don't want to go.

Kaitai desu.	I want to buy it.
Nani mo kaitaku arimasen.	I don't want to buy anything.
Dekiru no desu ga shitaku nai no desu.	He can do it, but he doesn't want to.
Kaeritai no desu ka?	Does she want to return?
Watashitachi to issho ni ikitai[1] desu ka?	Do you want to come with us?

[1] Notice the use of *iku* (going away from where we are now).

Notice that the expression *-tai desu* is used when you want to do something. When you want to have or get something you use *hoshii desu*. For example:

Hoshii desu.	I want it.
Hoshiku nai desu. ⎫ *Hoshiku arimasen.* ⎭	I don't want it.
Nani mo hoshiku ari- *masen.*	I don't want anything.
Sukoshi hoshii desu.	I want some.
Nani ga hoshii desu ka?	What do you want?

For *-tai desu* and *hoshii desu*, see Lesson 29 and Lesson 33 also.

11. *-(A)nakereba narimasen:* To have to

PLAIN PRESENT NEGATIVE →		*-BA* FORM →	HAVE TO
ikanai	don't go	*ikanake-* *reba*	*ikanakereba* *narimasen*
tabenai	don't eat	*tabenake-* *reba*	*tabenakereba* *narimasen*
konai	don't come	*konake-* *reba*	*konakereba* *narimasen*
shinai	don't do	*shinake* *reba*	*shinakereba* *narimasen*

See Lesson 27 and Lesson 33, and Section 28 of the Summary of Japanese Grammar also.

Ikanakereba nari- *masen.*	I must go.
Konakereba narimasen.	He should (has to) come.
Koko ni inakereba na- *rimasen.*	She should (has to) be here.

Sono hitotachi wa soko ni inakereba nari-masen.	They have to be there.
Soko e ikanakereba narimasen ka?	Do you have to go there?
Watashi wa nani o shinakereba naranai no desu ka?	What do I have to do?
Ikura okaeshi shi-nakereba naranai no desu ka?	How much do I owe you?
Nani mo harawanakute ii desu.	You don't owe me anything. [You need not pay anything.]
Kyoo wa konakute mo ii desu.	You don't have to come today.

Notice that the idea of "don't have to" or "need not" is expressed by a sequence quite different from that for "have to" or "need to":

PLAIN PRESENT NEGATIVE	→	-TE FORM	→	DON'T HAVE TO
ikanai	don't go	*ikanakute*		*ikanakute mo[1] ii desu*
tabenai	don't eat	*tabenakute*		*tabenakute mo ii desu*
konai	don't come	*konakute*		*konakute mo ii desu*
shinai	don't do	*shinakute*		*shinakute mo ii desu*

[1] The use of *mo* is optional.

12. *Suki desu:* To love, to like (something)

Anata wa ano hito ga suki desu ka?	Do you like him (her)?
Sore wa suki ja arimasen.	I don't like it.
Moo hitotsu no hoo ga suki desu.	I like the other better.
-koto ga suki desu	to love, to like to do (something)
Sanpo suru koto ga suki desu.	I love to [take a] walk.
Gaikokugo o narau koto ga suki desu.	I like to learn foreign languages.
Kuruma de ryokoo suru koto ga suki desu.	I like to travel by car.

For *suki desu,* see also Lesson 31.

13. *-(R)areru:*

    a. For the passive (to be, to get plus a past participle)
    b. For the potential (to be able to)
    c. Respect

CONSONANT VERB		$\rightarrow$	PASSIVE, POLITE (RESPECT)
kaku	write		*kakareru*
yomu	read		*yomareru*
VOWEL VERB			
tomeru	stop		tomerareru
okiru	get up		okirareru
IRREGULAR VERB			
kuru	come		korareru
suru	do		sareru

For potential verbs, see Section C-4 of Lesson 40.

(1) Passive:

Keikan ni tomerare-mashita.	I was stopped by a policeman.
Watakushi wa Yamada-san ni Tanaka-san to machigaerare-mashita.	I was mistaken by Mr. Yamada for Ms. Tanaka.
Iriguchi de namae o kikaremashita.	I was asked my name at the entrance. [At the entrance, I was asked to state my name.]
Ame ni furaremashita.	We were caught in the rain. [We underwent the falling of the rain.]

Notice that the agent of the action is designated by the particle *-ni,* and the person who is affected by the action of the verb is marked with *wa* or *ga.*

(2) Potential:

Ano hito wa gorufu ga suki de yamerare-masen.	He likes golf and can't stop (playing) it.
Okane ga nai node tsuzukeraremasen.	As I do not have (enough) money, I can't continue it.
Kippu no nai hito wa toosemasen.	We can't admit [pass] persons who have no tickets.

Toshokan ga shimatte iru node shiraberare-masen.
The library is closed, so I can't check it.

Kore wa anmari hidoku kowareta node moo naosemasen.
This has been damaged so badly that we can't repair it any longer.

(3) Respect:

Note that all of the following sentences are spoken very politely.

Sensei wa itsu kaette koraremasu ka?
When is the teacher coming back?

Yamada-sensei[1] wa Kyooto ni ryokoo saremashita.
Mr. Yamada, the teacher, traveled to Kyoto.

Yoshino-san wa sakunen nakuna-raremashita.
Mr. Yoshino died last year.

Tanaka-san wa sono tanomi o kotowarare mashita.
Mr. Tanaka refused that request.

Satoo-san wa sugu Shigeta-san ni denwa o kakeraremashita.
Mr. Sato phoned Ms. Shigeta right away.

14. *-(S)aseru:* To make (have, let, allow, force) one to (do something)—causative

CONSONANT VERB		→	CAUSATIVE
iku	go		*ikaseru*
tobu	fly		*tobaseru*

[1] *sensei:* teacher, sir [one who was born earlier]. *Yamada-sensei:* Mr. Yamada (said with great respect).

VOWEL VERB

taberu	eat	*tabesaseru*
oshieru	teach	*oshiesaseru*

IRREGULAR VERB

kuru	come	*kosaseru*
suru	do	*saseru*

Kodomo ni erabase-mashita.	I had the child choose them.
Musume ni nimotsu o hakobasemashita.	I had my daughter carry the baggage.
Kyoo wa sanji ni uchi e kaerasete kudasai.	Please let me go home at three o'clock.
Sono tegami o watakushi ni yomasete kudasai.	Please let me read that letter.
Kono kusuri o yojikan oki ni nomasete kudasai.	Please have him take this medicine every four hours.

QUIZ 37

1. *Misete kudasai.*	a. Please look at this.
2. *Ohairi kudasai.*	b. Please look here.
3. *Wasurenaide kudasai.*	c. Please take the train.
4. *Moo ichido itte kudasai.*	d. Please take another one.
5. *Matte kudasai.*	e. Please take it.
6. *Otori kudasai.*	f. Please wait.
7. *Densha de itte kudasai.*	g. Please don't forget.
8. *Moo hitotsu otori kudasai.*	h. Say it again, please.
9. *Koko o mite kudasai.*	i. Come in, please.

10. *Kore o mite kuda-sai.*   j. Show me, please.

ANSWERS

1—j; 2—i; 3—g; 4—h; 5—f; 6—e; 7—c, 8—d; 9—b; 10—a.

D. PUBLIC NOTICES AND SIGNS

Kooji	Public Notice	公示
Danshi	Gentlemen	男子
Fujin	Ladies	婦人
Danshi(yoo) tearaijo	Men's Room	男子 (用) 手洗所
Fujin(yoo) tearaijo	Ladics' Room	婦人 (用) 手洗所
Tearaijo	Restroom	手洗所
Kin'en, Tabako goenryo ku-dasai	No Smoking	禁煙、煙草 ご遠慮下さい。
Eigyoochuu	Open	営業中
(Honjitsu) heiten	Closed (Today)	(本日) 閉店
(Honjitsu) kyuugyoo	Closed (Today)	(本日) 休業
Iriguchi	Entrance	入口
Deguchi	Exit	出口
Hijooguchi	Emergency Exit	非常口
Erebeetaa	Elevator	エレベーター
Ikkai	First Floor	一階
Osu	Push	押す
Mawasu	Turn	廻す
Beru o narashi-te kudasai	Please Ring	ベルを鳴らして 下さい。

Tachiiri kinshi	Keep Out!	立入禁止
Tsuukoo kinshi	No Thorough-fare!	通行禁止
Ohairi kudasai	Come In	お入り下さい。
Nokku muyoo	No need to knock	ノック無用
Nokku o shinaide ohairi kudasai	Enter Without Knocking	ノックをしないで お入り下さい。
Nokku o shite kudasai	Knock	ノックをして下さい。
Nokku o shite kara ohairi kudasai	Knock Before Entering	ノックをしてから お入り下さい。
Kaisoo ni tsuki kyuugyoo	Closed for Repairs	改装につき休業
Shinsoo kaiten	Under New Management	新装開店
Nyuujoo okoto-wari	No Admittance	入場お断り
Kinjitsu kaiten	Will Open Shortly	近日開店
Shuuya eigyoo	Open All Night	終夜営業
Tsuba o hakanaide kudasai	No Spitting	つばを 吐かないで 下さい。
Tsuba o haku bekarazu		つばを吐く べからず。
Hakimono o nugutte kudasai	Wipe Your Shoes	履物を拭って下さい。
Inu o kusari kara hanasanaide kudasai	Leash Your Dog	犬をくさりから 放さないで下さい。

Hokoosha oko- towari	Pedestrians Keep Out	歩行者お断り
Kujoo soodanjo *Kujoo shoribu*	Complaint Department	苦情相談所 苦情処理部
Madoguchi de omooshikomi kudasai	Apply at the Window	窓口でお申し込み 下さい。
Ryoogaejo	Money Ex- changed	両替所
Urimono	For Sale	売物
Chintai itashimasu	For Rent	賃貸いたします。
Kashi apaato kagu nashi	Unfurnished Apartment for Rent	貸アパート家具なし
Kashi apaato kagu tsuki	Furnished Apartment for Rent	貸アパート家具付
Waribiki hanbai *Tokka hanbai*	Reduction	割引販売 特価販売
Uridashi	Sale	売り出し
Keitaihin azukarijo	Check Room, Cloakroom	携帯品預り所
Yoomuinshitsu	Janitor's Room	用務員室
Ukai	Detour	迂回
Koojichuu	Under Con- struction	工事中
Kaabu kiken	Dangerous Curve	カーブ危険
Chuusha kinshi	No Parking	駐車禁止

Ippoo kootsuu	One-Way Street	一方通行
Senro o yoko-giranaide kudasai		線路を横切らないで下さい。
Senro no oodan kinshi	Don't Cross Tracks	線路の横断禁止
Fumikiri	Railroad Crossing	踏切
Tetsudoo	Railroad	鉄道
Gaado	Underpass/Overpass	ガード
Tomare	Stop!	止まれ！
Chuui	Caution!	注意！
Oodanhodoo	Pedestrian Crossing	横断歩道
Koosaten	Crossroads	交差点
Basu teiryuu-jo	Bus Stop	バス停留所
Harigami kin-shi	Post No Bills	貼紙禁止
Jisoku sanjuk-kiro ika	Speed Limit 30 K.P.H.	時速30キロ以下
Jokoo	Go Slow	徐行
Gakkoo kuiki jokoo	School—Go Slow	学校区域徐行
Kiken, Abunai	Danger!	危険！危ない！
Penki nuri-tate	Fresh Paint	ペンキ塗りたて
Mado kara kao ya te o dasanaide kudasai	Don't Lean Out of the Window!	窓から顔や手を出さないで下さい。
Keihooki	Alarm Signal	警報機
Kooatsusen chuui	High Voltage	高圧線注意

Chikatetsu iriguchi	Subway Entrance	地下鉄入口
Keitaihin ichiji azukarijo	Baggage Room, Check Room	携帯品一時預り所
Machiaishitsu	Waiting Room	待合室
Ittoo	First Class	一等
Nitoo	Second Class	二等
Santoo	Third Class	三等
Toochaku	Arrival	到着
Hassha	Departure (Trains, Buses)	発車
Purattohoomu, Hoomu	Platform	プラットホーム、ホーム
Annaijo	Information	案内所
Kippu uriba	Box Office	切符売場
Yuubinkyoku	Post Office	郵便局
Posuto	Mailbox	ポスト
Nyuujooken uriba ⎫ *Kippu uriba* ⎭	Ticket Office	入場券売場 切符売場
Kasaihoochiki	Fire Alarm Box	火災報知機
Kooritsu tosho-kan	Public Library	公立図書館
Keisatsusho	Police Station	警察署
Gasorin sutando	Gas Station	ガソリンスタンド
Shoten	Bookstore	書店
Shiyakusho	City Hall	市役所
Rihatsuten	Barber Shop	理髪店
Biyooin	Beauty Shop	美容院
Ishi	Physician	医師
Iin	Physician's Office	医院
Shika	Dentistry	歯科
Kutsu shuuri	Shoe Repairing	靴修理

Machinee	Matinee	マチネー
Yakan kooen hachiji sanjuppun kaien	Evening Performance at 8:30	夜間公演 8時30分開演
Seisoo chakuyoo	Formal Dress	正装着用
Heifuku chakuyoo	Informal Dress	平服着用
Renzoku kooen	Continuous Performance	連続公演
Bangumi henkoo	Change of Program	番組変更
Kissaten	Coffee Shop	喫茶店

FINAL REVIEW QUIZ

1. ______ (Fine) *desu ka?*
   a. *Ikura*
   b. *Ogenki*
   c. *Itsu*

2. *Yukkuri* ______ (speak) *kudasai*.
   a. *hanashite*
   b. *kaite*
   c. *tabete*

3. *Tabako ga* ______ (have) *ka?*
   a. *hoshii desu*
   b. *kaitai desu*
   c. *arimasu*

4. *Menyuu o* ______ (show me) *kudasai*.
   a. *misete*
   b. *totte*
   c. *motte kite*

5. *Koohii o ippai* _____ (give me).
   a. *nomimashita.*
   b. *kudasai.*
   c. *agemashita.*

6. _____ (Breakfast) *wa hachiji ni tabemashita.*
   a. *Yuuhan*
   b. *Asagohan*
   c. *Hirugohan*

7. *Supuun o* _____ (bring).
   a. *motte itte kudasai.*
   b. *motte kite kudasai.*
   c. *motte kudasai.*

8. _____ (Station) *wa doko ni arimasu ka?*
   a. *Denwa*
   b. *Eki*
   c. *Yuubinkyoku*

9. _____ (Which way) *desu ka?*
   a. *Sochira*
   b. *Kochira*
   c. *Dochira*

10. *Taihen* _____ (near) *desu.*
    a. *tooi*
    b. *chikai*
    c. *ookii*

11. *Okane o* _____ (does he have) *ka?*
    a. *hoshii desu*
    b. *uketorimashita*
    c. *motte imasu*

12. *Watakushi no tegami ga* _____ (are there) *ka?*
    a. *arimasen*
    b. *arimasu*
    c. *arimashita*

13. _____ (Do you understand) *ka?*
    a. *Shitte imasu*
    b. *Wakarimasu*
    c. *Kiite imasu*

14. *Hajimete* _____ (glad to know you).
    a. *ome ni kakarimasu.*
    b. *ryokoo shimashita.*
    c. *sore o kikimashita.*

15. *Sukoshi hoshii desu ka* _____ (want a lot) *desu ka?*
    a. *sukoshi mo hoshiku nai*
    b. *takusan hoshii*
    c. *anmari hoshiku nai*

16. *Yamada-san ni* _____ (must see).
    a. *hanasanakereba narimasen.*
    b. *awanakereba narimasen.*
    c. *kikanakereba narimasen.*

17. *Sore wa Nihongo de doo* _____ (does one say) *ka?*
    a. *kikimasu*
    b. *iimasu*
    c. *kakimasu*

18. *Denwa wa san rei roku no* _____ (3307) *ban desu.*
    a. *sanjuu san shichi*
    b. *san san rei nana*
    c. *sansen sanbyaku shichi*

19. _____ (What time) *desu ka?*
    a. *Nan' yoobi*
    b. *Nannichi*
    c. *Nanji*

20. _____ (Tomorrow morning) *kite kudasai.*
    a. *Ashita no yoru*
    b. *Ashita no asa*
    c. *Ashita no gogo*

21. *Itta keredomo* _____ (couldn't meet).
    a. *atta koto ga arimasen deshita.*
    b. *au koto ga dekimasen deshita.*
    c. *au tsumori ja arimasen deshita.*

22. _____ (I want to go) *desu.*
    a. *Ikitai*
    b. *Hoshii*
    c. *Iku koto ga suki*

23. *Tanaka-san wa ima Tookyoo ni inai* _____
    (I hear).
    a. *soo desu.*
    b. *to omoimasu.*
    c. *no deshoo.*

24. _____ (Check) *o motte kite kudasai.*
    a. *Otsuri*
    b. *Ocha*
    c. *Denpyoo*

25. *Kyooto e* _____ (I have been to).
    a. *iku koto ga dekimasen.*
    b. *itta koto ga arimasu.*
    c. *iku koto ga suki desu.*

ANSWERS
1—b; 2—a; 3—c; 4—a; 5—b; 6—b; 7—b; 8—b;
9—c; 10—b; 11—c; 12—b; 13—b; 14—a; 15—b;
16—b; 17—b; 18—b; 19—c; 20—b; 21—b; 22—a;
23—a; 24—c; 25—b.

SUMMARY OF JAPANESE GRAMMAR

1. THE ALPHABET AND ROMANIZATION

The sounds of Japanese have been transcribed into the Roman alphabet, and all letters of the English language except "l," "q," and "x" are employed. Generally speaking, the *r* sound is close to "l." Note that *c* is used only in the combination *ch*.

There are two major systems of romanization: the Hepburn System and the Japanese National System. The Hepburn System has a longer history and wider acceptance than the Japanese National System. The National System is more logical and reflects the phonological structure of the language better.

A slightly modified form of the Hepburn System is used here to present Japanese words and sentences. The system has been modified as follows:

a. So-called "long vowels" are written as double vowels instead of with a macron (ˉ) over the vowel symbol (i.e., *Tookyoo* instead of *Tōkyō; kuukl* instead of *kūki*).

b. The syllabic *n* is written as an *n* at all times instead of as an *m* when it precedes *p, b,* or *m.*

The following table illustrates the various ways in which consonants and vowels are combined in the Hepburn System to produce the sounds of Japanese.

Chart I aligns *vertically* the five vowel sounds, and shows *horizontally* the basic (mostly voiceless) consonants with which they can be used to create the basic syllables of Japanese. Chart II shows the sounds (mostly the voiced counterparts) into which these consonants can change. The same relationship that exists between Charts I and II exists also between Charts III and IV.

A blank occurring in the charts (at the junction of a vertical and horizontal column) denotes that that combination of consonant and vowel is *never* used.

TABLE I
SYLLABLES OF THE MODIFIED HEPBURN SYSTEM IN MODERN JAPANESE[1,2]

			0	1	2	3	4	5	6	7	8	9	10
CHART I	V	1	a	ka	sa	ta	na	ha[3] (fa)	ma	ya	ra	wa	n
	O	2	i	ki	shi	chi (ti)	ni	hi (fi)	mi		ri		
	W	3	u	ku	su	tsu (tu)	nu	hu	mu	yu	ru		
	E	4	e	ke	se	te (tse)	ne	he (fe)	me		re		
	L	5	o	ko	so	to	no	ho (fo)	mo	yo	ro		
	S												

[1] The *o* in column 9 and the *o* in column 0 are pronounced the same, but are represented by different *hiragana;* see "The Writing System." The *o* in column 9 is used only for the particle *o*.

[2] The syllables in parentheses appear in borrowed words.

[3] Notice that in vertical column 5, the *h* of Chart I is converted to either *b* or *p* in Chart II.

		0	1	2	3	4	5	6	7	8	9	10
CHART	1		ga	za	da		ba	pa				(va)
II	2		gi	ji	(di)		bi	pi				(vi)
	3		gu	zu	(du)		bu	pu				(vu)
	4		ge	ze	de		be	pe				(ve)
	5		go	zo	do		bo	po				(vo)

		0	1	2	3	4	5	6	7	8	9
CHART	1		kya	sha	cha	nya	hya	mya		rya	
III	3		kyu	shu	chu	nyu	hyu	myu		ryu	
	5		kyo	sho	cho	nyo	hyo	myo		ryo	
				(she)	(che)						

		0	1	2	3	4	5	6	7	8	9
CHART	1		gya	ja			bya	pya			
IV	3		gyu	ju			byu	pyu			
	4			(je)							
	5		gyo	jo			byo	pyo			

CHART		-kk-	-ss-	-tt-		-pp-				
V			-ssh-	-tch-						
				-tts-						
		-(gg)-	-(zz)-	-(dd)-						
				-(dj)-						

The differences between the Hepburn and National Systems are limited to the syllables listed below:

HEPBURN SYSTEM	JAPANESE NATIONAL SYSTEM	HEPBURN SYSTEM	JAPANESE NATIONAL SYSTEM
shi	*si*	*chu*	*tyu*
chi	*ti*	*cho*	*tyo*
tsu	*tu*	*ja*	*zya*
fu	*hu*	*ju*	*zyu*
ji	*zi*	*jo*	*zyo*
sha	*sya*		
shu	*syu*		
sho	*syo*		
cha	*tya*		

TABLE II
SYLLABLES OF THE NATIONAL SYSTEM
IN MODERN JAPANESE

Syllables in italics are spelled differently in the Hepburn system. See the list of syllables on page 292 for a comparison.

			0	1	2	3	4	5	6	7	8	9	10
CHART	V	1	a	ka	sa	ta	na	ha	ma	ya	ra	wa	n
I	O	2	i	ki	*si*	*ti*	ni	hi	mi		ri		
	W	3	u	ku	su	*tu*	nu	*hu*	mu	yu	ru		
	E	4	e	ke	se	te	ne	he	me		re		
	L												
	S	5	o	ko	so	to	no	ho	mo	yo	ro		

CHART	1	ga	za	da		ba	pa			va	
II	2	gi	zi	zi		bi	pi			vi	
	3	gu	zu	zu		bu	pu			vu	
	4	ge	ze	de		be	pe			ve	
	5	go	zo	do		bo	po			vo	

CHART	1	kya	sya	tya	nya	hya	mya		rya			
III	3	kyu	syu	tyu	nyu	hyu	myu		ryu			
	5	kyo	syo	tyo	nyo	hyo	myo		ryo			

CHART	1	gya	zya			hya	pya					
IV	3	gyu	zyu			byu	pyu					
	5	gyo	zyo			byo	pyo					

CHART		-kk-	-ss-	-tt-			-pp-					
V												

2. SIMPLE VOWELS

a   like the "a" in "father," but short and crisp.

i   like the "e" in "keep," but short and crisp.

u   like the "u" in "put," but without rounding the lips.

e   like the "ay" in "may," but without the final *y* sound.

o   like the "o" in "go," but without the final *u* sound.

Remember that *i* and *u* differ from the other vowels in that they tend to become "voiceless" or whispered (1) when they are surrounded by the voiceless consonants *ch, f, h, k, p, s, sh, t, ts*, or (2) when they are preceded by a voiceless consonant and followed by a silence or pause (as at the end of a sentence). This is especially true when the syllable is not accented. In the following examples, the vowel with a circle underneath is a devoiced vowel:

arimasу̥   there is
kу̥tte   postage stamp

3.   VOWEL CLUSTERS

a. Double vowels:

All simple vowels can appear as double[1] or "long" vowels. A double vowel is always pronounced twice as long as a simple vowel:

aa   pronounced twice as long as a single *a: haato* [heart]

ii   pronounced twice as long as a single *i: riiru* [reel]

uu   pronounced twice as long as a single *u: suugaku* [math]

ee   pronounced twice as long as a single *e: teeburu* [table]

oo   pronounced twice as long as a single *o: Tookyoo* [Tokyo]

---

[1] Double vowels can be indicated by writing the single vowel with a macron over it: e.g., *ā* (for *aa*).

b. Other vowel clusters:

All simple vowels can also appear in combination with one or more other simple vowels to form "vowel clusters." In such combinations, each of the vowels has equal weight and is pronounced so that it retains the sound it has as a simple vowel. Vowel clusters should *not* be pronounced like diphthongs, which combine two vowels to make a new sound. For example:

au   *a* and *u* are both pronounced and given equal clarity and length.

ai   *a* and *i* are both pronounced and given equal clarity and length.

4. CONSONANTS AND SEMI-VOWELS

a. The letters *b, d, j, k, m, p, s, ts, v,* and *y* in Japanese sound almost like the same letters in English. Pronounce the other sounds as follows:

ch   as in "cheese."

f   by forcing the air out from between the lips; similar to English "wh."

g   at the beginning of a word, somewhat like the "g" in the English word "go"; in the middle of a word, it resembles the "ng" in "singer."

h   like the "h" in "high," when it precedes *a, e, o;* like the "h" in "hue," when it comes before *i* or *y.*

n   as in "name" (but with the tip of the tongue touching the back of the teeth) when it precedes *a, e, o, u;* as in "onion" when it precedes *i* or *y.*

r   by placing the tip of the tongue near the back of
        the upper teeth and quickly bringing it down;
        it sometimes sounds like the "r" in a British
        version of "very" ("veddy").

sh   somewhat like the English "sh" in "sheep."

t   as in the English "to," but with the tip of the
        tongue touching the back of the upper teeth.

w   like the "w" in "want," but without rounding or
        protruding the lips; occurs only before *a*.

z   at the beginning of a word, like the *ds* in "beds";
        in the middle of a word, like the *z* in "zero"
        (but some Japanese speakers do not make this
        distinction; they use the two sounds inter-
        changeably).

b. When a word begins with *ch, h, k, s, t*, or *ts*, and it
joins with another word (which then *precedes* it) to
make a new compound word, the initial letter or
letters may undergo a change:

ch   may become *j*, as it does in the change from *chie*
        [wisdom] to *warujie* [guile, wiles].

f   and *h* may become *p* or *b*, as *h* does in the change
        from *hanashi* [story] to *mukashibanashi* [a
        story of the past].

k   may become *g*, as it does in the change from *ken*
        (a counter for houses) to *sangen* [three houses].

s   may become *z*, as it does in the change from *sen*
        [one thousand] to *sanzen* [three thousand].

sh   may become *j*, as it does in the change from
        shika [deer] to *ojika* [male deer].

t   may become *d*, as it does in the change from *to*
        [door, windows] to *amado* [storm window,
        Japanese rain window].

ts   may become *z*, as it does in the change from
        tsuki [month] to *tsukizuki* [monthly].

5. DOUBLE CONSONANTS

When a double *p, t, k,* or *s* (*d, z,* or *g* in borrowed words) appears in a word, then the initial consonant of the cluster has one syllable length. This same lengthening takes place when *tch, tts,* or *ssh* (*dj* in borrowed words) appears in a word:

kippu	ticket
mattaku	indeed
nikki	diary
itchi	agreement

6. THE SYLLABIC *N*

The syllabic *n* differs from the ordinary *n* in several ways:

a. It always forms a full syllable by itself (that is, it is always held as long as one full syllable). It *never* joins with a vowel or another consonant to form a syllable. If a vowel follows the syllabic *n*, there is always a syllable boundary between the *n* and the vowel. For example, the word *gen'in* [cause] has four syllables—*ge-n-i-n*—since each of the syllabic *n*'s has the value of a full syllable.

b. The syllabic *n* seldom appears at the beginning of a word.

c. Its sound changes, depending on what follows it:

(1) Before *n, ch, t,* and *d,* it is pronounced like the English "n" in "pen," but the sound is held longer:

*ko*n*na*	this sort of
*ha*n*choo*	group leader
*cha*n*to*	properly
*ko*n*do*	this time

(2) Before *m, p,* or *b,* it is pronounced like the English "m" but the sound is held longer:

SPELLING	PRONUNCIATION	MEANING
*sa*n*mai*	*sammai*	three sheets
*shi*n*pai*	*shimpai*	worry, anxiety
*ka*n*ban*	*kamban*	signboard

(3) Before a vowel or a semi-vowel *(w, y),* the syllabic *n* is pronounced somewhat like the English "ng" in "singer," but without finishing the *g* sound, and the preceding vowel is often somewhat nasalized. Notice that an apostrophe is used when a vowel or *y* follows the syllabic *n.*

*ge*n'*an*	original plan
*ta*n'*i*	unit
*ho*n'*ya*	bookstore
*shi*n*wa*	mythology

(4) When the syllabic *n* precedes *k, g,* or *s,* or when it appears at the end of a word (that is, when it is followed by a pause), it is pronounced as in (3) above:

*so*n*kei*	respect
*sa*n*gen*	three houses
*so*n	loss
*ka*n*sei*	completion

7. CONTRACTIONS

a. The particle *de* [at, by means of] sometimes combines with the particle *wa* [as for] thus: *de* plus *wa = ja*.

Nihon ja yasui desu.   It is cheap in Japan (but not here).

b. The *-te* form of the copula *de* (from *desu*) also can combine with the particle *wa* thus: *de* plus *wa = ja*.

Nihonjin ja arimasen.   She is not Japanese.

c. The *-te* form of a verb sometimes combines with the particle *wa* thus: *-te* plus *wa = cha*, or *-de* plus *wa = ja*.

Itcha ikemasen.   You mustn't go.
Yonja ikemasen.   You mustn't read it.

8. ACCENT

Word accent in Japanese is indicated by lowering the pitch of the voice *after* the accented syllable.

Some words have an accent in Japanese, some do not. Accentless words are spoken with the voice pitch held even on all syllables of the word except the first; here the pitch is slightly lower. This is true regardless of the length of the word.

Certain words lose their accent when they are placed next to an accented word. Hence the accents are sometimes marked and sometimes not marked within the same sentence.

The inclusion or omission of accent is further determined by various subsidiary rules, not all of which are thoroughly understood at the present time. The student can learn much about the refinements of accentuation through listening to native Japanese speakers.

9. INTONATION

a. In a declarative sentence:
There is a marked drop in the pitch of the voice on the last voiced syllable.

b. In a direct question:
There may be a rising intonation on the last voiced syllable. This rise in pitch is optional when the sentence ends with the question particle *ka* or contains a question phrase such as *doko e* [where to]. When neither a question particle nor question word is used, the rising intonation is used.

c. Suspension:
The last voiced syllable is spoken in approximately the same level tone as what precedes it.

10. NOUNS

a. Most nouns in a sentence are accompanied by one or two noun-particles[1] (i.e., *wa, ga, o, mo, no, ni, de, kara*) or by some form of the copula *desu* [it is]. Nouns are not declined.

Nihon ni wa yama ga takusan arimasu.	There are many mountains in Japan.
Fujisan wa takai yama desu.	Fuji is a high mountain.

[1] See the material on page 309 for particles used with nouns.

b. There are certain nouns, usually having to do with time, degree, or quantity, which may or may not appear with a particle. Such nouns may have the functions not only of nouns but also of adverbs, and may be used to modify predicates or entire clauses.

Kinoo ikimashita.	I went there yesterday.
Kinoo wa ikimasen deshita.	I didn't go there yesterday.

Here is a list of some more of these nouns:

maiasa	every morning
mainichi	every day
ima	present time, now
moto	former time, previously
sukoshi	a small amount, a little, some
takusan	a large amount, a great deal, plentifully, in a large quantity
hotondo	nearly all, almost completely
mada	as yet, still
zenzen	whole, completely (used with a negative predicate)
nakanaka	quite, considerably

c. Some nouns frequently take on a special function, i.e., they are used to relate or tie one part of a sentence to another, assuming a role comparable in the English language to that of a preposition, adverb, or conjunction. When so used, these nouns are always modified by a clause. They are sometimes classified as particles rather than as nouns. The list that follows contains some of the most widely used functional nouns:

NOUN	NOUN MEANING	FUNCTIONAL WORD MEANING
aida	duration, space; interval	during; as long as; while
ato	site; place behind; time following; condition following	after, subsequent to (usually preceded by the *-ta* form of a verb and followed by *de*)
baai	occasion; situation	in the event that, in case; when; should (something) happen
dake	height; extent	as much as
hazu	notch (of an arrow)	it (something) is "in the cards," it is expected that, it is supposed that (when followed by *desu*); it is not reasonable to expect that, it is hardly possible that (when followed by *wa* or *ga arimasen*)
hodo	approximate degree	to the extent of; not as . . . as . . . (usually followed by a negative predicate):
A wa B hodo yoku arimasen.		A is not as good as B.
Sono sake wa nomeba nomu hodo motto nomitaku narimasu.		The more you drink that sake, the more you want to drink; the more . . . the more . . . (when preceded by a single verb in the present tense or a verb in the provisional

		form together with the same verb in the present)
hoo	side, direction, alternative direction	the use of this word denotes that a comparison is being made:
Kono hoo ga yasui desu.		This is cheaper.
Kusuri o nonda hoo ga ii desu.		It would be better (for you) to take some medicine.
ijoo (wa)	the above-mentioned	now that, since, inasmuch as, because of
kagiri	limits, bounds; maximum degree	as far as, so long as, as much as, provided that
kekka	result, outcome, consequence	with the result that, as a result of, because of
kiri	limit	nothing happened after:
Nippon e itta kiri tayori ga arimasen.		There is no news from him since he went to Japan.
koto	fact; thing (abstract)	the act of doing . . . ; the act of having done . . . (makes a noun equivalent out of inflected words; used in many idiomatic expressions):
Hanasu koto wa dekimasen.		Talking is not permitted [possible]. I can't talk.
Hanashita koto wa arimasen.		I've never talked (with him). [The experience of having talked with him does not exist.]
mae	the front; prior time, former time	before, prior to [usually followed by *ni*], ago

mama	will (wish)	as it is (without doing anything further, without taking additional action); as it stands; exactly as; according to
mono	thing (tangible); person	the thing which; the one who; it's because (when it is used at the end of a sentence, usually in talk by a woman—a use similar to *kara* or *node*); that's the thing to do, you should, it is expected that (when preceded by a verb in the present form and followed by *desu*); used to do (when preceded by the *-ta* form of a verb and followed by *desu*)
nochi	the time after	after (used either with or without *ni* following it); subsequent to having done . . . (when it is preceded by the *-ta* form of a verb)
tabi	occasion, time	every time that
tame	sake	for the sake of; for the purpose of; because of
toki	time	(at the time) when
tokoro	place	just when, in the act of (when followed by *ni* or *de*); even if, no matter who, no matter what (when followed by *de*);

		to be on the point of (when preceded by the present form of a verb and followed by *desu*); to have just finished doing . . . (when preceded by the *-ta* form of a verb and followed by *desu*)
toori	the way, avenue	exactly as
tsumori	idea in mind	intend to, plan to (when preceded by the present tense of a verb and followed by *desu*); (my) notion [recollection] about it is that (something) was the case (when preceded by the *-ta* form of a verb and followed by *desu*)
uchi	the inside [the within]	while, during the time when
ue	top, surface, place over	on top of doing, having done (something), upon doing . . . , besides (doing) . . . ; upon finishing, after (doing something), (when followed by *de*)
wake	reason, meaning, logic	that's the background of it, that's the story of it, that's what it is (when followed by *desu*); it is

hardly believable that (something) should happen (or should have happened) (when followed by *ga arimasen*).

d. Some nouns are converted into verbs when they are used with *suru*. The resultant combination means "do the action of (something)." For instance:

shookai	introduction
shookai suru	to introduce
ryokoo	travel
ryokoo suru	to travel

e. The pre-*masu* form can function as a noun:

yomu	to read
yomi	reading; pronunciation
tsuru	to fish
tsuri	fishing

f. The stem of an adjective (i.e., the plain present affirmative minus the final *i*) can function as a noun:

akai red   *aka* the color red

The stem of an adjective can also function as a noun when *sa* or *mi* is added:

akai red	*akasa* redness
fukai deep	{ *fukasa* depth (as a measure) / *fukami* depth (of thought) }

g. Particles[1] used with nouns:

Following is a list of particles used with nouns, and many of their functions:

ga marks an emphatic grammatical subject (see *mo*, below).

wa marks a sentence topic that may be either the subject or object of the sentence, or a modifier. Some of the modifiers in b above can be used with *wa* also.

no links a noun to another noun. It is most frequently used for the possessive ("of").

ni links a noun or noun equivalent (such as the pre-*masu* form of a verb) to a verb, adjective, or copula.

o marks the thing acted on (see *mo*, below).

mo can be used instead of *ga* or *o* (see above) but carries the additional meaning of "that thing/person also."

e links a noun to a verb and marks the direction toward which an action is performed.

to does one of two things: (i) it links nouns together in a complete list (see *ya*, below) or (ii) it marks the partner with whom the action is being performed.

ya links nouns together in an incomplete list (see *to*, above).

yori marks a noun or noun equivalent as the standard against which a comparison is made.

kara marks a starting point in time or space.

made marks the ending point in time or space.

---

[1] Note that Japanese has many of these so-called "particles," which show the grammatical relationship of one word to another within a sentence; see also Lesson 11. Mastery of these particles is a key to rapid learning of Japanese. See "Particles Used with Verbs," Section 18 of the Summary of Japanese Grammar.

de marks the means, way, place, or manner in which an action is performed.

bakari has one of two functions: (i) it can be used in place of (or sometimes together with) *ga* or *o* to carry the additional meaning of "nothing else," or (ii) if it follows a number, it signifies that the number is only approximate.

dake can be used in place of or together with *ga* or *o* to carry the additional meaning of "that was the limit."

hodo can be used (i) to mark a thing against which a comparison is made and which is about the same in degree or extent as the thing compared, or (ii) to mark a number that is only approximate.

kurai (or *gurai*) marks the approximate quantity, quality, or degree, and can often be used interchangeably with *hodo* (see above).

ka (i) shows that a statement is a question, or (ii) has the meaning of "either . . . or."

11. COUNTERS

Counters form a subclass of nouns often used adverbially to mean "to the extent of." There are several types:

a. Unit counters:

   (1) Unit counters name specifically what is being counted. The following unit counters are used with primary numbers—*ichi, ni, san* [one, two, three], etc.—and are suffixed to these numbers. Where an exception to the general rule occurs, it is shown.

COUNTER	MEANING	EXCEPTIONS
-jikan	hours	*yojikan* = four hours
-ji	o'clock	*yoji* = four o'clock
-fun (or *-pun*)	minutes	See also Section 4-b of the Grammar Summary for change of sound
-byoo	seconds	
-nichi	days	See also Lesson 25 for variations
-shuukan	weeks	
-kagetsu	months	
-gatsu	name of the month	
-nen	years	*yonen* = four years
-en	yen (Japanese currency)	
-sento	cent (U.S. currency)	
-doru	dollar (U.S. currency)	
-shiringu	shillings (British currency)	
-pondo	pounds (unit of weight or of British currency)	
-meetoru	meters	
-kiro	kilometers, kilograms	

-kiroguramu	kilograms
-kiromeetoru	kilometers
-mairu	miles
-inchi	inches
-do	times
-peeji	pages; page number
-gyoo	lines; line number
-wari	one-tenth
-paasento	percent
-kai	story (of a building)

(2) The following unit counters are used with secondary numbers (*hito-*, *futa-*, *mi-*, etc.). They are usually used to count amounts less than four.

-ban	nights
-heya	room
-ma	room

b. Class counters:

(1) Class counters are used in a general rather than a specific sense. The following class counters are used with primary numerals (*ichi, ni, san . . .*):

COUNTER	MEANING	EXCEPTIONS
-hiki (or *-biki*, or *-piki*)	animals, fish, insects	*ippiki, sanbiki, roppiki, jippiki*
-too	large animals (such as horses, cows)	—
-wa (or *-ba*, or *-pa*)	birds	*sanba, roppa, jippa*

-satsu	bound volumes (of books and magazines)	
-mai	flat, thin things (such as sheets, newspapers, handkerchiefs)	
-hon (or *-pon*, or *-bon*)	thin, long things (such as pencils, tubes, sticks, matches, cigarettes)	*ippon, sanbon, roppon, jippon*
-ken (or *-gen*)	houses	*sangen*
-tsuu	documents, letters, telegrams	
-dai	vehicles (such as cars, wagons), machines (such as typewriters, sewing machines)	
-ki	planes and other aircraft	
-chaku	suits of clothes	
-soku (or *-zoku*)	pairs of things worn on the feet or legs (such as shoes, socks, stockings)	*sanzoku*

| *-ko* | lumps (such as apples, stones, candy) |
| *-hai* (or *-pai,* or *-bai*) | something in containers (such as water, coffee) |

(2) The following class counters are used with secondary numerals (*hito-, futa-, mi-,* etc.):

-fukuro	bagful (of)
-hako	boxful (of)
-kumi	set, group, couple (of people)
-soroi	set, group
-iro	kind, variety
-kire	slices
-tsumami	pinch

12. PRONOUNS

All of the Japanese words that correspond to English pronouns are nouns. They take the same particles as other nouns and are modified by the same type of words, phrases, and clauses that are used to modify other nouns. Note that in Japanese there are more varieties of words that correspond to personal pronouns than there are in English.

A list of Japanese equivalents of personal pronouns and instructions for using them follows:

a. I, we:

SINGULAR	PLURAL	MEANING AND USAGE
watakushi	*watakushitachi*	I, we (formal)
watashi	*watashitachi*	I, we (slightly less formal than *watakushi* and used most widely)
boku	*bokutachi*	I, we (used by males only: informal)
ore	*oretachi*	I, we (used by males, but not in refined speech)

b. You:

Avoid using any definite word for "you" as long as the sentence meaning is clear without it. If you cannot avoid using such a word, use the name (usually the surname) of the person you are addressing and add -*san* with the appropriate particle. If you are speaking to a small child, use the child's given name with -*kun* (for male) or -*chan* (for female). If you are speaking to a teacher, a doctor, etc., use *sensei* either preceded by or without the surname of the person you are addressing. If you must employ the pronoun instead of the name, use *anata* [you (sing.)], *anatagata* [you (pl.)], *minasan* [you (pl.)], or *minasama* [you (pl., very formal)]. Many of the sentence examples in this course contain *anata* or *anatagata*, but it is well to remember that these should be replaced in actual conversation by the name of the person to whom you are speaking, whenever possible.

c. He, she, they:

SINGULAR	PLURAL	MEANING AND USAGE
ano kata	*ano katagata*	he, she, they *(respect)*
ano hito	*ano hitotachi*	he, she, they *(respect)*
ano otoko no kata	*ano otoko no katagata*	he, they (respect: used only when it is necessary to indicate specifically "he [that man]" or "they [those men]")
ano otoko no hito	*ano otoko no hitotachi*	he, they (neutral: same as above)
ano onna no kata	*ano onna no katagata*	she, they (*respect:* used only when there is need to indicate specifically "she" or "they" [those women])
ano onna no hito	*ano onna no hitotachi*	she, they (neutral: same as above)

kare	*karera*	he, they (less common and less accepted in writing)
kanojo	*kanojora*	

d. Possessives:

There are no possessive pronouns as such in Japanese. To form the possessive, combine a noun (used for the person referred to) with *no* [things of], as in the following examples:

watashi no	my, mine
anato no (or the name of the person) plus *no*	your, yours
ano hito no	his, hers
watashitachi no	our, ours
anatagata no ⎱ *minasan no* ⎰	your, yours *(pl.)*
ano hitotachi no	their, theirs

13. PRENOUNS

"Prenouns"—words such as *kono* [this] or *konna* [this kind of] precede a noun and modify its meaning. No particle is used to separate the prenoun and noun. Prenouns do not change their forms.

kono	this
sono	that
ano	that over there
dono	which?
konna	this kind of
sonna	that kind of
anna	that kind of
donna	what kind of?

14. *Ko-So-A-Do* Words

Some Japanese nouns and prenouns come in sets of four words that are usually pronounced alike, except for the first syllable. These sets of words are called "ko-so-a-do words" because the first syllable is always one of the following four: *ko-*, *so-*, *a-*, or *do-*. Note that the word in such a group that begins with *do* is always a question word.

a. *Ko-so-a-do* nouns:[1]

kore	this one
sore	that one
are	that one over there
dore	which one?
koko	this place
soko	that place
asoko[2]	that place over there
doko	which place? where?
kochira, kotchi	this way, this one (of two)
sochira, sotchi	that way, that one (of two)
achira, atchi	that way, that one (of two)
dochira, dotchi	which way, which (of two)?

b. *Ko-so-a-do* prenouns:

kono	this
sono	that
ano	that over there
dono	which?
konna	this sort of
sonna	that sort of (for something not far removed in feeling or time)

[1] See Lesson 17.
[2] An irregular form.

anna	that sort of (for something more remote in feeling or time)
donna	what sort of?

15. ADJECTIVES

a. *I*- adjectives:

I- adjectives can end in *-ai, ii, ui,* or *-oi,* but never in *-ei.*

akai	(is) red
utsukushii	(is) beautiful
samui	(is) cold
kuroi	(is) black

I- adjectives are conjugated as follows:

(1) Plain forms:

PRESENT	*takai*	it is high
PAST	*takakatta*	it was high
TENTATIVE PRESENT	*takai daroo*	it is probably high
TENTATIVE PAST	*takakatta daroo*	it was probably high

(2) Polite forms:

PRESENT	*takai desu*	it is high
PAST	*takakatta desu*	it was high
TENTATIVE PRESENT	*takai deshoo*	it is probably high
TENTATIVE PAST	*takakatta deshoo*	it was probably high

(3) Other forms:

-*TE* FORM	*takakute*	it is (was) high, and . . .
-*KU* FORM	*takaku*	it is (was) high, and . . . highly
-*BA* FORM	*takakereba*	if it is high
-*TARA* FORM	*takakattara*	if (when) it is (was) high

b. *Na-* adjectives:

(1) Plain forms:

PRESENT	*shizuka da*	it is quiet
PAST	*shizuka datta*	it was quiet
TENTATIVE PRESENT	*shizuka daroo*	it is probably quiet
TENTATIVE PAST	*shizuka datta daroo*	it was probably quiet

(2) Polite forms:

PRESENT	*shizuka desu*	it is quiet
PAST	*shizuka deshita*	it was quiet
TENTATIVE PRESENT	*shizuka deshoo*	it is probably quiet
TENTATIVE PAST	*shizuka datta deshoo*	it was probably quiet

(3) Other forms:

-*TE* FORMS	*shizuka de*	it is (was) quiet and . . .

| -*NI* FORMS | *shizuka ni* | quietly |
| -*TARA* FORMS | *shizuka dattara* | if (when) it is (was) quiet and . . . |

16. COMPARISONS

There are several ways to show comparison:

a. Use *no hoo* [the side of] to show what is being compared:

Kyooto no hoo ga suki desu.	I like Kyoto better.
Tookyoo no hoo ga samui desu.	Tokyo is colder [in climate].
Kuruma de iku hoo ga ii desu.	It is better to go by car.

Notice that when a verb comes before *hoo*, *no* is omitted.

b. Use *yori* [than] to mark the standard against which a comparison is made:

| *Kyooto yori samui desu.* | It is colder than Kyoto. |
| *Kore wa sore yori ta-kai desu.* | This is more expensive than that. |

c. Use both *no hoo* and *yori* in the same sentence to show that a comparison is being made:

| *Tookyoo no hoo ga Kyooto yori samui desu.* | Tokyo is colder than Kyoto. |

Yomu hoo ga hanasu   Reading is more diffi-
  yori muzukashii desu.   cult than speaking.

d. Use *zutto* [by far the more] either with or without
   no hoo or *yori:*

Sono densha no hoo ga
  kono densha yori   That train is much
  zutto hayai desu.   faster (than this
Sono densha ga zutto   train).
  hayai desu.
Kore wa zutto yasashii   This is much easier.
  desu.

e. Use *motto* [still more] either with or without *no
   hoo* or *yori:*

Sore wa motto takai
  desu.   That is still more ex-
Sore wa kore yori   pensive (than this
  motto takai desu.   one).
Motto yukkuri hana-   Please speak more
  shite kudasai.   slowly.

f. Use *ichiban* [number one, most of all] or *mottomo*
   [the most] when comparing more than two things.
   (*Mottomo* is more formal than *ichiban*.)

Ano hito ga ichiban
  se ga takai desu.
Ano hito ga mottomo   He is the tallest.
  se ga takai desu.
Ichiban ii no o kudasai.   Give me the best kind,
                                please.

g. Use *dochira* or *dotchi* [which of the two], or *dore* [which of more than two] when asking a question involving a comparison:

Nagoya to Kyooto de wa dochira ga chikai desu ka?	Which is nearer— Nagoya or Kyoto?
Nagoya to Kyooto to Hiroshima de wa dore ga ichiban tooi desu ka?	Which is the farthest— Nagoya, Kyoto, or Hiroshima?

h. Use *hodo* (to show approximate degree) and a negative predicate when making a comparison between two things that are not quite alike:

Nagoya wa Oosaka hodo tooku arimasen.	Nagoya is not as far as Osaka.
Tanaka-san wa Yamada-san hodo kanemochi ja arimasen.	Ms. Tanaka is not as rich as Mr. Yamada.

i. Also use *hodo* to describe situations resulting in extreme, intense, or severe effects:

Kimochi ga waruku naru hodo takusan tabemashita.	I ate so much that I began to feel sick.
Onaka ga itaku naru hodo waraimashita.	I laughed so much that I began to get a stomachache.

j. Use *no yoo ni* [in the likeness of, in the manner of] or *kurai* (or *gurai*) [more or less] when making a

comparison between two things or situations that
are pretty much alike:

Yamada-san wa Eigo ga   Mr. Yamada knows
    Amerikajin no yoo ni   English as well as a
    yoku dekimasu.   native American.
Yamada-san wa Eigo   Mr. Yamada knows
    ga Amerikajin gurai   English as well as
    dekimasu.   [just like] a native
                                     American.

17. THE CLASSES AND FORMS OF VERBS

a. Verb classes:

There are three classes of verbs in Japanese:

Class I—consonant verbs: includes all verbs except
    those in Class II and Class III.
Class II—vowel verbs: includes the majority of verbs
    that, in their plain present form, terminate in *-eru* or
    -iru.
Class III—irregular verbs: *kuru* [come] and *suru* [do].
The base of a *consonant* verb is that part left over after
    the final *-u* has been dropped from the plain present
    affirmative form (= dictionary form). The base
    always ends in a consonant except where there is
    another vowel before the final *-u*.
The base of a *vowel* verb is that part remaining after
    the final *-ru* has been dropped from the plain
    present form. It always ends in either *-e* or *-i*.

b. *-Masu* forms:

-Masu forms (= polite present affirmative forms) are
    formed in the following ways:

Consonant verbs: Drop the final *u* of the dictionary form and add *-imasu*.

Vowel verbs: Drop the final *ru* of the dictionary form and add *-masu*.

DICTIONARY FORM	→	-MASU FORM	
consonant verb			
kaku		*kakimasu*	write
yomu		*yomimasu*	read
vowel verb			
taberu		*tabemasu*	eat
miru		*mimasu*	see

-Masu forms of some respect verbs are formed irregularly:

DICTIONARY FORM	→	-MASU FORM	
irassharu		*irasshaimasu*	go, come, be
ossharu		*osshaimasu*	say
kudasaru		*kudasaimasu*	give
nasaru		*nasaimasu*	do

These respect verbs are consonant verbs. Notice that in their *masu* forms, *r* is dropped. For example, the *-masu* form of *irassharu* is *irasshaimasu*, not *irassharimasu*.

c. The tenses:

In Japanese, a verb form referred to as a "tense" actually describes the *mood* of the action or state.

(1) The present tense (or *-u*-ending form) expresses an *incomplete* action or state and may have several English translations:

| *Hanashimasu* | I speak; I do speak; I will speak |
| *Tabemasu* | I eat; I do eat; I will eat |

(2) The past tense (or *-ta* form) expresses a *completed* action or state. It, too, can have several English translations:

| *Hanashimashita* | I spoke; I have spoken |
| *Tabemashita* | I ate; I have eaten |

The plain form of the past tense is formed from the plain present as follows:

(a) For consonant verbs:
  (i) When the final syllable in the plain present is *-u*, *-tsu*, or *-ru*, drop it and add *-tta:*

PRESENT	PAST	
Kau	*Katta*	I bought
Tatsu	*Tatta*	I stood
Toru	*Totta*	I took

  (ii) When the final syllable in the plain present is *-mu*, *-nu*, or *-bu*, drop it and add *-nda:*

Nomu	*Nonda*	I drank
Shinu	*Shinda*	He died
Yobu	*Yonda*	I called

  (iii) When the final syllable is *-ku* or *-gu*, drop it and add *-ita* in place of *-ku* and *-ida* in place of *-gu:*

| *Kaku* | *Kaita* | I wrote |
| *Isogu* | *Isoida* | I hurried |

(iv) When the final syllable is *-su*, drop it
and add *-shita:*

| *Hanasu* | *Hanashita* | I spoke |
| *Kasu* | *Kashita* | I lent |

(b) For vowel verbs:
Drop the final syllable *-ru* and add *-ta:*

| *Taberu* | *Tabeta* | I ate |
| *Miru* | *Mita* | I saw |

(c) For irregular verbs:

| *Kuru* | *Kita* | I came |
| *Suru* | *Shita* | I did |

The polite form of the past tense is formed from the
polite present (the *-masu* form) by replacing the
final syllable *-su* with *-shita.*

POLITE PRESENT	POLITE PAST	
Ikimasu	*Ikimashita*	I went
Tabemasu	*Tabemashita*	I ate
Mimasu	*Mimashita*	I saw

(3) The tentative (polite: *-mashoo;* plain: *-oo* or
-yoo) expresses an action or state that is not
certain, definite, or completed. It can have several English translations:

| *Yomimashoo.* | I think I will read. Let's read. |
| *Yomimashoo ka?* | Shall we read? |

The plain tentative is formed from the plain
present as follows:

(a) For consonant verbs:
Drop the final *-u* and add *-oo:*

PRESENT	TENTATIVE	
Hanasu.	*Hanasoo.*	I think I'll speak. Let's talk.
Yomu.	*Yomoo.*	I think I'll read. Let's read.

(b) For vowel verbs:
Drop the final *-ru* and add *-yoo:*

Taberu.	*Tabeyoo.*	I think I'll eat. Let's eat.
Miru.	*Miyoo.*	I think I'll see it. Let's see it.

The polite tentative is formed from the polite present by dropping the final *-su* and adding *-shoo*.

POLITE PRESENT	POLITE TENTATIVE	
Hanashimasu.	*Hanashimashoo.*	I think I'll talk. Let's talk.
Tabemasu.	*Tabemashoo.*	I think I'll eat. Let's eat.

d. *-Te* forms:

(1) The *-te* form is formed exactly like the plain past affirmative [see section 17-c-(2), above] except that the final vowel is *-e*. A *-te* form actually has no tense; the "tense" feeling is determined by the "tense-mood," that is, the ending *(-u, -ta, -yoo)*, of the terminal verb.

Kusuriya e itte kusuri o kaimashita.	I went to a drugstore and bought some medicine.

Normally, when there is more than one verb in a sentence, the *-te* form is used for all but the last verb. The pre-*masu* form is sometimes used instead of the *-te* form, but this is considered "bookish."

Kusuriya e itte kusuri o katte uchi e kaette sore o nonde sugu nemashita.	I went to the drugstore and bought some medicine and returned home and took it and went to bed right away.

(2) The *-te* form is also used:

    (a) Adverbially, to modify a verb or adjective:

Isoide ikimashita.	He went hurriedly.
Naite hanashimashita.	He spoke in tears.
Yorokonde shigoto o hikiukemashita.	She took on the job gladly.

    (b) With *kudasai,* to form a request:

Kesa no shinbun o katte kudasai.	Please buy me this morning's paper.

    (c) With *imasu,* to form the progressive:

Hanashite imasu.	I am speaking.
Tabete imasu.	I am eating.

    (d) To form the "stative," which expresses the state resulting from a completed action, (i) add *arimasu* to the *-te* form, or (ii) add *imasu* to the *-te* form. The latter kind is identical with the progressive in form, but not in function. Usually, *arimasu* is used after the *-te* form of a transitive verb, and *imasu* after the *-te* form of an intransitive verb.

Te de kaite arimasu.   It's handwritten. [It is in the state of his having written it by hand.]

Moo kekkon shite imasu.   She is married already. [She is in the state of her being married since she got married.]

PLAIN PRESENT AFFIRMATIVE (DICTIONARY FORM)

CLASS I VERBS (CONSONANT VERBS)	CLASS II VERBS (VOWEL VERBS)	CLASS III VERBS (IRREGULAR VERBS)
hanasu	*taberu*	*suru*
speak	eat	do
will speak	will eat	will do

PLAIN PAST AFFIRMATIVE

hanashita	*tabeta*	*shita*
spoke	ate	did
have spoken	have eaten	has done

POLITE PRESENT AFFIRMATIVE (-*MASU* FORM)

hanashimasu	*tabemasu*	*shimasu*
speak	eat	do
will speak	will eat	will do

POLITE PAST AFFIRMATIVE

hanashimashita	*tabemashita*	*shimashita*
spoke	ate	did
have spoken	have eaten	have done

PLAIN PRESENT NEGATIVE

hanasanai	*tabenai*	*shinai*
do not speak	do not eat	do not do
will not speak	will not eat	will not do

PLAIN PAST NEGATIVE

hanasanakatta	*tabenakatta*	*shinakatta*
did not speak	did not eat	did not do
have not spoken	have not eaten	have not done

POLITE PRESENT NEGATIVE

hanashimasen	*tabemasen*	*shimasen*
do not speak	do not eat	do not do
will not speak	will not eat	will not do

POLITE PAST NEGATIVE

hanashimasen deshita	*tabemasen deshita*	*shimasen deshita*
did not speak	did not eat	did not do
have not spoken	have not eaten	have not done

EXTRA-POLITENESS

NEUTRAL	RESPECT	HUMBLE
hanasu	*ohanashi ni naru, hana-sareru*	*ohanashi suru*

PLAIN *TE* FORM[1]

hanashite	*tabete*	*shite*
speak and ...	eat and ...	do and ...
will speak and ...	will eat and ...	will do and ...

[1] See Section 17-d-(2) above for additional meanings.

POLITE -*TE* FORM[1]

hanashimashite   *tabemashite*   *shimashite*

Note that in the following groups, the "a" lines show the plain form of the verb and the "b" lines show the polite form.

PRESENT PROGRESSIVE AFFIRMATIVE

a. *hanashite iru*   *tabete iru*   *shite iru*

b. *hanashite imasu* he is speaking   *tabete imasu* he is eating   *shite imasu* he is doing

PAST PROGRESSIVE AFFIRMATIVE

a. *hanashite ita*   *tabete ita*   *shite ita*

b. *hanashite imashita* he was speaking   *tabete imashita* he was eating   *shite imashita* he was doing

PRESENT PROGRESSIVE NEGATIVE

a. *hanashite inai*   *tabete inai*   *shite inai*

b. *hanashite imasen* he is not speaking   *tabete imasen* he is not eating   *shite imasen* he is not doing

PAST PROGRESSIVE NEGATIVE

a. *hanashite inakatta*   *tabete inakatta*   *shite inakatta*

---

[1] The polite -*te* form is only used in the most formal conversations. Furthermore, the polite -*te* form is unacceptable in the usages described in 17-(2)-d.

b. *hanashite*   *tabete imasen*   *shite imasen*
   imasen   *deshita*   *deshita*
   deshita   he was not   he was not
   he was not   eating   doing
   speaking

PRESENT STATIVE AFFIRMATIVE

a. *Hanashite*   *Tabete aru.*   *Shite aru.*
   aru.

b. *Hanashite*   *Tabete ari-*   *Shite arimasu.*
   arimasu.   *masu.*   It's done.
   The matter   The meal is   [The work is
   has already   finished.   in the state
   been men-   [The meal is   of my having
   tioned to   in the state   done it.]
   him. [The   of my having
   matter is   eaten it.]
   in the state
   of my hav-
   ing spoken
   about it.]

PAST STATIVE AFFIRMATIVE[1]

a. *Hanashite*   *Tabete atta.*   *Shite atta.*
   atta.

b. *Hanashite*   *Tabete ari-*   *Shite arima-*
   ari-   *mashita.*   *shita.*
   mashita.   The meal   The work
   The mat-   had been   had been
   ter had   eaten.   done.
   been men-
   tioned to
   him.

[1] Usually translated into English by the past perfect.

PRESENT STATIVE NEGATIVE

a. *Hanashite nai.*	*Tabete nai.*	*Shite nai.*
b. *Hanashite arimasen.* The matter has not been mentioned.	*Tabete arimasen.* The meal is not finished.	*Shite arimasen.* It is not done.

PAST STATIVE NEGATIVE

a. *Hanashite nakatta.*	*Tabete nakatta.*	*Shite nakatta.*
b. *Hanashite arimasen deshita.* The matter hadn't been mentioned.	*Tabete arimasen deshita.* The meal hadn't been finished.	*Shite arimasen deshita.* It hadn't been done.

PROVISIONAL AND CONDITIONAL

hatarakeba	*tabereba*	*sureba*
hataraitara	*tabetara*	*shitara*
hataraku to	*taberu to*	*suru to*
hataraku nara	*taberu nara*	*suru nara*
hataraite wa	*tabete wa*	*shite wa*
if I work	if I eat	if I do

18. PARTICLES USED WITH VERBS

The following particles that are used with verbs can also be used with adjectives or the copula. (See also Section 10-g of the Summary of Japanese Grammar for particles used with nouns.)

a. *Bakari desu* =

(1) (Following a -*u* form) does nothing but (something); does only . . .

Sotsugyoo o matsu bakari desu.	I am just waiting for graduation. (I have no more school work to do.)

(2) (Following a -*ta* form) has just done (something); did only (something):

Gohan o tabeta bakari desu.	I have just finished eating.

b. *Dake* = that is just about all; that is just about the extent of it; only; just:

Mita dake desu.	I just took a look at it.
Hanashi o suru dake desu.	I am just going to discuss it. (I won't make any decision yet.)

c. *Ga* – but; in spite of that fact stated above (when preceded by either the plain or polite forms):

Ikimashita ga aemasen deshita.	I went (there) but I couldn't see him.
Kaimashita ga mada tsukatte arimasen.	I have bought it but it hasn't been used.

d. *Ka* = a spoken question mark:

Kyoo wa oisogashii desu ka?	Are you busy today?

e. *Kara* =

(1) (Following a *-te* form) after doing (something);
since doing (something):

Mite kara kimemasu.	I will decide after taking [having taken] a look at it.

(2) (Following any sentence-ending form— *-u*, *-ta*, *-i*) and so, and therefore:

Omoi desu kara watashi ga omochi shimashoo.	It's heavy so I will carry it.

f. *Keredo(mo)*[1] = in spite of that fact stated before; but; however; although:

Isoida keredo ma ni aimasen deshita.	I hurried, but couldn't make it.
Yonda keredomo yoku wakarimasen deshita.	I read it, but I didn't understand it well.

g. *Made* = up to the time of (something)'s happening; until; so far as:

Yamada-san ga kuru made koko ni ori-masu.	I will stay here until Mr. Yamada gets here.

h. *Na* =

(1) (Following a plain present affirmative form) don't do (something). Note that this is never

---

[1] The use of *mo* is optional.

used in refined speech; instead, *-naide kudasai* is used:

Hairu na!	Don't enter!
Hairanaide kudasai.	Please don't enter.

    (2) (Following a sentence-ending form) yeah, that's what it is (used only by men in colloquial speech):

Ii tenki da na!	What fine weather!
Genki da na!	You are in good shape! (You look fine!)

    (3) (Following a verb and used with *ka*) should I? I wonder if I should? (used in colloquial speech):

Dekakeyoo ka na?	Let's see. Shall we go now?
Eiga de mo miyoo ka na.	I guess I will see a movie or something.

i. *-Nagara* = (following a pre-*masu* form, showing that two or more actions or states take place or exist concurrently) while, in the course of:

Arukinagara hanashi-mashoo.	Let's talk as we walk (to that place).
Hatarakinagara ben-kyoo shite imasu.	He is studying while working (he is supporting himself).

j. *Nari* =

    (1) (When used in a parallel sequence) either . . . or . . . ; whether . . . or . . . :

Denwa o kakeru nari   She informed every-
   tegami o kaku nari   body either by phon-
   shite minna ni   ing or writing a
   shirasemashita.   letter.

(2) (When *not* used in a parallel sequence) as soon
    as; the moment (something) has taken place:

Kao o miru nari naki-   He burst into tears the
   hajimemashita.   moment he saw me.

k. *Ni* = the purpose of the "going" or "coming" that is
   expressed (when it follows the pre-*masu* form of a
   verb):

Kaimono o shi ni iki-   He went shopping. [He
   mashita.   went in order to
                             shop.]

l. *Node* = (following a sentence-ending form) and so;
   and therefore:

Amari tsukareta node   I got very tired, so I
   sukoshi yasumitai   would like to [take
   desu.   a] rest.
Okane o   I didn't send the
   harawanakatta node   money for it; that's
   okutte kimasen   why it didn't come.
   deshita.

m. *Noni* = and yet, but, although:

Yonda noni henji ga   I called her but there
   nai.   was no answer.
Itta noni awanakatta.   Although I went there,
                             I didn't see her.

n. *To* =

(1) (Following a present form) whenever:

Hima da to sanpo shi-
masu.

Whenever I am free, I
take a walk.

(2) Acts as an "end quote" when it precedes a verb
meaning "say," "hear," "ask," "think," "believe":

Itsu kimasu ka to
kikareta.

I was asked [as to]
when I would be
coming.

(3) (When it follows a tentative and is in turn followed by *suru*) to be on the point of doing
(something); to try to do (something):

Uchi o deyoo to suru
tokoro e tomodachi
ga kimashita.

Just as I was about to go
out, a friend of mine
came (to visit me).

o. *-Tari . . . -taru suru* =

(1) Sometimes does (something); at other times
does (something else):

Nihon to Amerika no
aida o ittari kitari
shite imasu.

She travels back and
forth between Japan
and the United States.

(2) Does (one thing) and (another):

Hito ga nottari oritari
shite imasu.

Some people are get-
ting on, some are
getting off.

p. Terminal particles:

(1) *Ne* = isn't it? doesn't it?

Erai hito desu ne?	He is a great man, isn't he?

(2) *Sa* = sure it is so (used only by men, slang):

Shitte iru sa!	Of course I know it.

(3) *Wa, wa yo* = a diminutive used only by women:

Sanji ni denwa o kakeru wa (yo).[1]	I will phone you at three.

(4) *Yo* = an exclamatory particle:

Kyoo wa okyakusan ga arimasu yo!	We are going to have a visitor today!

(5) *Zo* = an emphatic particle (used only by men, slang):

Naguru zo!	I'll hit you!

19. NEGATIVES

a. Used with verbs:

(1) Plain negative present—formed from the base of a consonant verb plus the suffix *-anai,* or the base of a vowel verb plus *-nai:*

---

[1] The use of *yo* is optional.

Kaku.	I write.
Kakanai.	I don't write.
Taberu.	I eat.
Tabenai.	I don't eat.

Notice that a verb like *kau* [buy] or *warau* [laugh], whose plain present affirmative ends in two vowels, appends an extra *w* before adding *-anai:*

Kawanai.	I don't buy.
Warawanai.	She doesn't laugh.

(2) Plain negative past—formed from the stem of the negative present (the form without the final *-i*) plus *-katta* (like the plain negative past of an adjective):

Kaita.	I wrote.
Kakanakatta.	I didn't write.

(3) Plain negative tentative:
   (a) For a consonant verb, use the plain present affirmative plus *-mai*.
   (b) For a vowel verb, use the pre-*masu* form plus *-mai*.
   (c) For the irregular verbs, use *komai* and *shimai*.

Kakoo.	I think I'll write it.
Kakumai.	I don't think I'll write it.
Tabeyoo.	I think I'll eat.
Tabemai.	I don't think I'll eat.

b. Used with a copula:

(1) Plain forms:

. . . *da*	It is . . .
. . . *de aru*	It is (formal, bookish) . . .
. . . *ja nai* . . . *de (wa) nai*	It is not . . .
. . . *datta*	It was . . .
. . . *ja nakatta* . . . *de (wa) nakatta*	It was not . . .
. . . *daroo*	It is probably . . .
. . . *ja nai daroo* . . . *de (wa) nai daroo*	It is most probably not . . .

(2) Polite forms:

. . . *desu*	It is . . .
. . . *ja arimasen* . . . *dewa arimasen*	It is not . . .
. . . *deshita*	It was . . .
. . . *ja arimasen deshita* . . . *dewa arimasen deshita*	It wasn't . . .
. . . *deshoo*	It is probably . . .
. . . *ja nai deshoo* . . . *de (wa) nai deshoo*	It is most probably not . . .

c. Used with *i-* adjectives

(1) Plain forms:

Takai.	It is expensive.
Takaku nai.	It is not expensive.

Takakatta.	It was expensive.
Takaku nakatta.	It wasn't expensive.
Takai daroo.	It may be expensive.
Takaku nai daroo.	It is probably not expensive.

(2) Polite forms:

Takai desu.	It is expensive.
Takaku arimasen.	It is not expensive.
Takakatta desu.	It was expensive.
Takaku arimasen deshita. } *Takaku nakatta desu.*	It was not expensive.
Takai deshoo.	It is probably expensive.
Takaku nai deshoo.	It is probably not expensive.

d. Other negative expressions (used with negative predicates):

zenzen	not (at all)
hitotsu mo	nothing
dare mo	no one
doko mo	nowhere
nani mo	nothing
dochira mo	neither . . . nor
kesshite	never
Zenzen wakarimasen deshita.	I did not understand it at all.

20. WORD ORDER

There are two very important rules to remember for word order in declarative sentences:

a. A predicate word (the copula, verb, or adjective used as a predicate) is placed at the *end* of the clause or sentence except when a sentence-ending particle such as *ka* (the question mark particle) or *ne* [isn't it? doesn't it?] is used, in which case the predicate word is usually placed *immediately before* such a particle.

b. A modifier *always precedes the word or clause it modifies:*

(1) An adjective or adjectival phrase (a noun plus *no*) always precedes the noun it modifies.
(2) A prenoun always precedes the noun.
(3) An adverb or adverbial phrase always precedes the adjective, adverb, verb, or copula it modifies.
(4) A modifying clause always precedes the noun it modifies.

For example:

akai booshi	a red hat
ano hito	that person
ano hito no booshi	that person's hat; her (his) hat
ano hito no akai booshi	that person's red hat; her red hat
ookina booshi	a big hat
ano hito no ookina akai booshi	that person's big red hat
katta booshi	the hat she bought
kinoo katta booshi	the hat she bought yesterday
kinoo Matsuya de katta booshi	the hat she bought at Matsuya's yesterday

ano hito ga kinoo no gogo Matsuya de katta booshi	the hat she bought at Matsuya's yesterday afternoon
ano hito ga kinoo no gogo Matsuya de katta ookina akai booshi	that big red hat she bought at Matsuya's yesterday afternoon
ano hito ga kinoo no gogo watakushi to issho ni itte Matsuya de katta ookina akai booshi	that big red hat she bought yesterday afternoon with me at Matsuya's

21. QUESTIONS

The word order for questions is the same as for declarative sentences. The question particle *ka* may or may not be added at the end to show that a question is being asked. For instance:

When *ka* is used, it is not necessary to use the rising intonation. The intonation may remain that of a declarative sentence even though a question is being asked. However, when a question is being asked and *ka* is not used, the rising intonation must be employed, and the last syllable is pronounced with a distinct rise in pitch. (See Lesson 13.)

Ikimasu.	I am going.
Ikimasu?	Are you going?
Ikimasu ka?	Are you going?

See the following section for other words that are used in formulating questions.

22. QUESTION WORDS

There are several words that are used to form questions. Study the list to help you grasp more easily what the words are and how they are used.

QUESTION WORDS	MEANING	NOTES
nan, nani[1]	what thing? what? how many?	For the usage of *nan*, see Lesson 32. The meaning "how many?" applies only when the word is used before a counter.
nannin	how many people?	
ikutsu[1]	what number? how many?	The answer must be a number.
iku-	how many . . . ?	A prefix used only with a counter.
itsu[1]	what time? when?	When used adverbially, it may sometimes be used without a particle.

[1] Notice that this is a noun in Japanese.

Itsu kimashita ka?   When did it arrive?
Itsu hajimarimasu ka?   When does it begin?
Itsu ga ii desu ka?   When would it be good
                              for you?

dare[1]	which person? who?	*dare no:* whose? *dare ni:* to whom? *dare kara:* from whom? *dare to:* with whom?
dore[1]	which thing? which?	Used when there is a choice of more than two.
dochira[1]	which of these two? which direction? which place (polite)?	Used when there is a choice of only two.
dochira e	where to?	
dochira kara	where from?	
dotchi	see above	A variant for the first two meanings of *dochira*.
doko[1]	which place? where?	

Doko ni arimasu ka?   Where is it?
Doko de tabemashita ka?   Where did you eat?

---

[1] Notice that this is a noun in Japanese.

Doko kara kimashita ka?	Where did you come from?	
Doko ga itai desu ka?	Where does it hurt?	
dono	which	A prenoun used when there is a choice of *more than* two. Use *dochira no* when there is a choice of *only* two.
donna	what sort of?	A prenoun used when you are interested in the kind or type of thing being discussed.
doo	how? in what manner?	An adverb.
ikaga	how (polite)?	An adverb; same as *doo* (above) but used in re-fined speech.

23. SOMETHING, EVERYTHING, NOTHING, ANYTHING

Each of the question words appearing in the first col-umn of this table undergoes a change in meaning when it is used together with one of the particles appearing in the other columns. The new meaning is shown for each combination.

TABLE III

QUESTION WORD	+ ka	+ mo (used with affirmative predicate)	+ mo (used with negative predicate)	+ de mo	+ -te mo
nani, nan = what	nani ka = something or other	nani mo ka mo = everything	nani mo = nothing	nan de mo = anything	nani . . . te mo = whatsoever
dore = which one	dore ka = one or the other; anyone	dore mo = all, any	dore mo = no one, not anyone, not a one	dore de mo = whichever it may be; any at all	dore . . . te mo = whichsoever
dochira = which of the two	dochira ka = either one	dochira mo = both	dochira mo = not either one, neither one	dochira de mo = whichever it may be, either one	dochira . . . te mo = whichever
dotchi¹ = which of the two	dotchi ka = either one	dotchi mo = both	dotchi mo = not either one, neither one	dotchi de mo = whichever it may be, either one	dotchi . . . te mo = whichever
doko = which place	doko ka = somewhere or other	doko mo = everywhere; all places	doko mo = not anywhere, nowhere	doko de mo = wherever it may be, any place at all	doko . . . te mo = wherever
dare = which person	dare ka = somebody	dare mo = everybody	dare mo = not anybody, nobody	dare de mo = whoever it may be, anybody at all	dare . . . te mo = whoever

¹ Dotchi is more informal than dochira.

(continued)

TABLE III (continued)

QUESTION WORD	+ ka	+ mo (used with affirmative predicate)	+ mo (used with negative predicate)	+ de mo	+ -te mo
itsu = what time	itsu ka = sometime or other	itsu mo = always	itsu mo = not anytime, never	itsu de mo = whenever it may be; anytime at all	itsu . . . te mo = whenever
doo = how	doo ka = somehow or other; please, by some means or other	doo mo = in every way, very	doo mo = somehow; not; in no way	doo de mo = however it may be; anyway at all	doo . . . te mo = however (one does)
dooshite = why	dooshite ka = somehow or other, for some unknown reason	dooshite mo = by all means, under any circumstances	dooshite mo = somehow or other . . . not; however one tries . . . not	dooshite de mo = by all means; at all costs	—
ikutsu = how many	ikutsu ka = some number, several	ikutsu mo = any number	ikutsu mo = not many, no great number, not much to speak of	ikutsu de mo = however many it may be; any number at all	ikutsu . . . te mo = however many one may
ikura = how much	ikura ka = some amount	ikura mo = any amount; ever so much	ikura mo = not much; no great amount	ikura de mo = whatever amount it may be	ikura . . . te mo = however much it may be one may

24. Even If, Even Though

a. Affirmative:
   Use -*te* plus -*mo:*

Ame ga futte mo iki-masu.	I'll [still] go, even if it rains.
Takakute mo kaimasu.	I'll [still] buy it even if it's expensive.

b. Negative:
   Use -*nakute* plus *mo:*

Ame ga yamanakute mo ikimasu.	I will go [anyhow] even if it doesn't stop raining.
Yasuku nakute mo ka-maimasen.	I don't care even if it's not cheap.

c. Permission:
   Use -*te mo ii desu* for "you may [you have my permission to]"; use -*nakute mo ii desu* for "you don't have to [you have my permission not to; even if you don't, it is all right with me]":

Itte mo ii desu.	You may go.
Ikanakute mo ii desu.	You don't have to go.

d. No matter how, no matter who, no matter how much:
   Use a question word plus -*te mo:*

Donna ni yasukute mo kaitaku arimasen.	I don't want to buy it no matter how cheap it is.
Dare ga shite mo kekka wa onaji desu.	No matter who does it, the result will be the same.

Ikura yonde mo imi ga wakarimasen deshita.	I couldn't understand it no matter how many times I read it.

25. HEARSAY

To express the ideas "I hear that . . ." or "They say that . . ." in Japanese:

a. For the affirmative:
Use a plain affirmative form of a verb, an *i*- adjective, or the copula plus *soo desu:*

Kyoo wa Yamada-san ga kuru soo desu.	I hear that Mr. Yamada is coming to visit us today.
Sapporo de wa yuki ga futta soo desu.	I hear that it snowed in Sapporo.
Takai soo desu.	I understand (that) it's expensive.
Tanaka-san wa byooki da soo desu.	I hear Ms. Tanaka is sick.

b. For the negative:
Use a plain negative form of a verb, an *i*- adjective, or the copula plus *soo desu.*

Rajio no tenki yohoo de wa kyoo wa ame wa furanai soo desu.	According to the weather forecast, it's not going to rain today.
Yamada-san wa konakatta soo desu.	I hear that Mr. Yamada didn't come.
Takaku nai soo desu.	I hear (that) it's not expensive.
Furansugo wa joozu ja nai soo desu.	I hear she is not good at French.

26. SEEMING

You can express the idea of "it seems" or "it seems to me that . . ." in several ways in Japanese:

a. For the affirmative:

(1) Use a plain affirmative form plus *yoo desu:*

Moo shitte iru yoo desu.	It seems to me that he already knows it.
Chotto muzukashikatta yoo desu.	It seems that it was a little difficult.
Minna genki na¹ yoo desu.	It seems that everybody is fine.

(2) Use a plain affirmative form plus *rashii desu:*

Moo shitte iru rashii desu.	It seems to me that he already knows it.
Ano hito wa Amerika e kaetta rashii desu.	It seems that he has gone back to the United States.

However, it is more likely that the sentence with *rashii desu* will be interpreted with the meaning of "hearsay" like *soo desu* in Section 25 than with the meaning of "it seems."

(3) Use an *i*- adjective without the final *-i* or a *na*-adjective without the copula plus *-soo desu:*

Kurushisoo desu.	It seems that he is finding it painful.
Genki soo desu.	It seems that she is fine.

¹ The copula *da* (present affirmative) becomes *na* before *yoo desu.*

b. For the negative:

(1) Use a plain negative form plus *yoo desu:*

Mada shiranai yoo desu.	It seems that he is un-aware of this.
Amari takaku nai yoo desu.	It seems that it is not very expensive.

(2) Use a plain negative form plus *rashii desu:*

Mada shiranai rashii desu.	It seems that he is un-aware of this.
Ano hito wa Nihon e konakatta rashii desu.	Apparently [it seems that] he didn't come to Japan.

(3) Use a negative *i-* adjective without the final *-i* or the negative copula without the final *-i* plus *-sasoo desu:*

Kurushiku nasasoo desu.	He is apparently [it seems that he is] not finding it painful.
Are wa Nakamura-san ja nasasoo desu.	That does not seem to be Ms. Nakamura.

27. IMMINENCE

To express the idea "it appears that . . . will soon happen":

a. For the affirmative:
Use the pre-*masu* form of the verb plus *-soo desu:*

Ame ga furisoo desu ne.	It looks like rain, doesn't it?
Yamada-san wa yamesoo desu.	It looks as if Mr. Yamada is ready to quit.

b. For the negative:
   Use the pre-*masu* form of a verb plus *-soo ja arimasen:*

Ame wa furisoo ja arimasen.	It doesn't look as though it will rain soon.
Nedan wa yasuku narisoo ja arimasen.	It doesn't look as though the price is going down.

28. OBLIGATION AND PROHIBITION

To convey the idea of obligation or impulsion (expressed in English by "should," "must," "ought to," "have to"):

a. For the affirmative:

   (1) Use the negative *-ba* form of a verb, an *i*-adjective, or the copula, plus *narimasen* or *ikemasen* [if you don't do it, it won't do; if not (something), it won't do].
   (2) Use the negative *-te* form plus *wa* plus *narimasen* or *ikemasen.*[1]

---

[1] Notice the use of a double negative.

Ikanakereba narimasen.	
Ikanakereba ikemasen.	
Ikanakute wa nari-	I should (must, have to,
masen.	ought to) go.
Ikanakute wa ikemasen.	
Yoku nakereba narimasen.	
Yoku nakereba ike-	
masen.	
Yoku nakute wa nari-	It should (must, has to,
masen.	ought to) be good.
Yoku nakute wa ike-	
masen.	

b. For the negative:

   (1) Use the affirmative *-te* form of a verb plus *wa* plus *narimasen* [if you do (something), it won't do; if it is (something), it won't do]:

Itte wa narimasen.	I should not (must not, ought not) go.

   (2) Use the affirmative *-te* form of a verb, an *i-* adjective, or the copula plus *wa* plus *ikemasen* or *dame desu:*

Koko de asonde wa ikemasen.	You should not (must not, ought not) play here.
Yasashikute wa dame desu.	It should not be easy.
Kono kaban de wa dame desu.	You should not use this bag. [It should not be this bag.]

c. *Beki desu* [should], *beki ja arimasen* [should not]: *Beki* is a form left over from classical Japanese.

(1) For the affirmative, use the plain present of a verb plus *beki desu:*

Iku beki desu.	I should (must, have to, ought to) go.
Iku beki deshita.	I should have gone.

(2) For the negative, use the plain present affirmative of a verb plus *beki ja arimasen:*

Iku beki ja arimasen.	I should not go.
Iku beki ja arimasen deshita.	I shouldn't have gone.

(3) For warning or prohibition (seen in public signs only), the plain present affirmative of a verb is used with *bekarazu* [don't]:[1]

Hairu bekarazu!	No admission!
Tooru bekarazu!	No trespassing!
Sawaru bekarazu!	Don't touch!

29. PERMISSION

To express the granting of permission, use *-te* plus *mo* plus *ii desu* [you may, it's all right to]:

Kaitakereba katte mo ii desu.	If you want to buy it, you may (buy it).
Uchi e motte kaette mo ii desu.	You may take it home if you wish.
Takakute mo ii desu.	It may be expensive. [Even if it is expensive, it is all right.]

[1] *Bekarazu*, which is a derived form of *beki*, is becoming obsolete in public signs. *-Nai de kudasai* [Please do not—] now is preferred.

*Kono jisho de mo ii
    desu.*

This dictionary will do.
[It is all right to use
this dictionary.]

30. ALTERNATIVES

In statements setting forth a choice of alternatives,
use:

a. *-Tari . . . -tari shimasu* (the *-ta* form plus *ri* followed by the *-ta* form plus *ri suru*):

*Kyoo wa ame ga futtari
    yandari shite imasu.*

Today it has been rain-
    ing off and on.

*Ano hito wa chikagoro
    gakkoo e ittari
    ikanakattari shimasu.*

He has been irregular
    recently in (his) at-
    tendance at school.

*Nichiyoobi no gogo wa
    shinbun o yondari
    terebi o mitari shi-
    masu.*

On Sunday afternoons I
    spend my time doing
    such things as read-
    ing newspapers and
    watching television.

*Hito ga detari haittari
    shite imasu.*

People are going in and
    out.

b. *-Tari shimasu* (a single *-tari* followed by *suru*):

*Eiga e ittari shima-
    shita.*

Among the various
    things (I did), I went
    to the movies. I
    spent my time going
    to the movies and
    doing things like that.

*Miyagemono o kattari
    shimashita.*

I bought souvenirs
    and did (other)
    things like that.

31. PASSIVE, POTENTIAL, AND RESPECT

A verb made up of its base plus -*areru* or -*rareru* may be any one of the following: (1) passive, (2) potential, or (3) respect. (Use -*areru* with a consonant verb and -*rareru* with a vowel verb.) The exact meaning of such a verb is determined by the context in which it is used.

a. Passive:

Watashi wa keikan ni namae o kikaremashita.

I was asked my name by a policeman.

b. Potential:

Nihon no eiga wa Amerika de mo miraremasu.

Japanese movies can be seen in the United States, too. [One can see a Japanese movie in America, too.]

c. Respect:

Itoo-sensei wa kinoo Amerika kara kaeraremashita.

My teacher, Mr. Ito, came back from the United States yesterday.

The passive of some Japanese verbs—most particularly the passive forms of intransitive verbs—means "(something) happened when it wasn't wanted," or "I underwent (something)," or "I suffered from the interference of (something)":

*Densha no naka de
   kodomo ni nakarete
   komarimashita.*

We were embarrassed
by our child, who
cried continuously
while riding on a
train.

*Ame ni furarete sukkari
   nurete shimaimashita.*

We were drenched by
the rain.

32. CAUSATIVE

To form the causative of a verb, add *-aseru* to the base
of a consonant verb and *-saseru* to the base of a vowel
verb. The causative forms of the irregular verbs are
(for *kuru*) *kosaseru* and (for *suru*) *saseru*.

Causative verbs may be used to express the thought
that:

a. X *causes* (makes, forces) Y to do (something)

b. X *allows* (permits, lets) Y to do (something)

Notice that in each instance the element Y is marked
by the particle *ni*.

*Tanaka-san wa
   Yamada-san ni den-
   poo o utasemashita.*

Ms. Tanaka had Mr.
Yamada send a tele-
gram.

*Kodomo ni kimono o
   kisasete kudasai.*

Please have the chil-
dren put on their
clothes.

*Kyoo wa itsu mo yori
   ichijikan hayaku
   kaerasete itadakitai
   desu.*

I would like to have
your permission to
go home one hour
earlier than usual.
[I would like to have
you make me go
home . . .]

A causative can be combined with a passive ending. If the causative ending comes first, the combination means "be made," not "be allowed."[1]

*Ika**serare**mashita.*	I was made to go.
*Tabe**saserare**mashita.*	I was made to eat it.

33. DESIDERATIVES

The desiderative is the grammatical term for verbal expressions that signify a desire to do something.

a. To say, "I want to do (something)," use the pre-*masu* form plus *-tai:*

Kyoo wa kaimono ni iki-tai desu.	I want to go shopping today.
Ima wa nani mo tabe-taku arimasen.	I don't want to eat anything now.

b. To express the idea, "one shows that he/she wants to do (something)," add *-tagaru* to the pre-*masu* form:

Kodomo ga soto e ikitagatte imasu.	The children can't wait to go outside.
Uchi no kodomo wa sono kusuri o nomitagarimasen.	Our child doesn't like to take that medicine. [Our child shows that he doesn't like to take that medicine.]

[1] The combination where the passive ending comes first is possible. In this case, the meaning of the combination does not mean "be made." For example, *naguraresasemashita* means "I made somebody be hit." But such a combination is rare, and awkward.

c. Use the stem (the form without the final -*i*) of an *i*-adjective plus -*garu* to express the meaning that "someone[1] shows outwardly that he/she feels . . .":

Samugarimashita.	He showed that he felt cold.
Hoshigarimashita.	He showed that he wanted to have it.

d. To say, "I want you to do (something) for me," use the -*te* form of a verb plus *itadakitai desu:*

Kono tegami o Eigo ni yakushite itadakitai desu.	I would like you to translate this letter into English for me.
Kore o katte itadakitai desu.	I would like you to buy this for me.

34. To Do (Something) for . . .

a. To say, "Somebody does (something) for me," in the respect form, use -*te kudasaimasu;* in the neutral form, use -*te kuremasu:*

Sono koto wa Yamada-san ga shirasete kudasaimashita.	Mr. Yamada was kind enough to inform me about it.
Shirasete kudasai.[2]	Please let me know.
Ani ga katte kure-mashita.	My older brother bought it for me.

b. Use -*te agemasu* to say "I (or somebody) do (something) for you (him, her)." In the humble form, use

---

[1] Usually not the speaker.
[2] *Kudasai* is a request form of *kudasaimasu*.

-te sashiagemasu. You can use *-te yarimasu* when the receiver of the favor is animals or plants. When the receiver of the favor is a person who is inferior to the speaker, such as a child, *-te yarimasu* can be used, but it is not always appropriate. Thus, it is safer not to use *-te yarimasu* when the receiver of the favor is a person.

Sore wa anata ni katte ageta no desu.	I bought it for you.
Anata ni katte sashiage-mashoo.	I'll buy it for you.
Inu ni katte yarimashita.	I bought it for our dog.

c. Use *-te itadakimasu* to say, "I (or somebody) have you (him, her) do (something)" in the humble form, and *-te moraimasu* in the neutral form:

Yamada-san ni katte itadakimashita.	I had Mr. Yamada buy it for me.
Tomodachi ni yakushite moraimashita.	I had a friend of mine translate it for me.
Yamada-san ni yakushite itadaite kudasai.	Please have it trans-lated by Mr. Ya-mada.

35. MAY, PERHAPS, PROBABLY

To say, "something may (might) happen," add *ka mo shiremasen* after a plain form of a verb, an *i-* adjective, or the copula.

Ame ga furu ka mo shiremasen.	It may rain (but I can't tell for sure).
Shiken wa muzuka-shikatta ka mo shire-masen.	The test might have been difficult.

Tanaka-san wa tenisu ga joozu ka mo shiremasen.[1]	Ms. Tanaka may be good at tennis.

36. IF AND WHEN

a. The use of *to:*

(1) Use *to* between two clauses to show that the second clause follows as a natural result of the first clause. The particle *to* in such a case comes at the end of the "if" or "when" clause:

Ame ga furu to anmari hito ga takusan kimasen.	When it rains, not too many people come.
Kippu ga nai to hairemasen.	If you don't have tickets, you can't get in. [If there isn't a ticket . . .]
Atarashii to takai desu.	When it's new, it's expensive.

(2) Note that the predicate before *to* is *always* in the present form regardless of the tense of the rest of the sentence:

Hima da to sanpo shimashita.	Whenever I had time, I took a walk.

(3) The predicate before *to* usually appears in the plain present form. When *to* is used for "if" or

---

[1] The copula *da* (present, affirmative) is deleted before *ka mo shiremasen.*

"when," the predicate of the main clause (the one following the clause ending in *to*) must be the *-u* or *-ta* form; it can *never* end in *-masyoo* or *-te kudasai*.

b. The use of *-tara:*
   To introduce a condition or a supposition, add *-ra* to the *-ta* form of a verb, adjective, or copula:

Ame ga futtara iki-masen.	If it rains, I won't go.
Denpoo ga kitara denwa o kakete kudasai.	If you get a telegram, please phone me.
Anmari samukattara mado o shimete kudasai.	If it's too cold (for you), please shut the window.
Nihonjin dattara dare de mo ii desu.	Anybody who is a native Japanese will do. [If it's a native Japanese, anybody will do.]

c. The use of *nara:*
   Use *nara* with a plain form of a verb, an *i-* adjective, and the copula to express "if."

Byooki[1] nara yasumu hoo ga ii desu.	If you are sick, you had better rest.
Shiranai nara oshiete agemasu.	If you don't know, I'll teach you.
Yasui nara kaimasu.	If it is inexpensive, I'll buy it.

---

[1] For present affirmative, the copula is deleted.

d. The use of *-ba:*
The *-ba* form is used only for unconfirmed situations. The *-ba* form is formed in the following ways:

Consonant verb:
Drop the final *-u* of the dictionary form and add *-eba*.

furu	→	*fureba*

Vowel verb:
Drop the final *-ru* of the dictionary form and add *-reba*.

miru	→	*mireba*

Irregular verb:

kuru	→	*kureba*
suru	→	*sureba*

i-adjective:
Drop the final *i* of the dictionary form and add *-kereba*.

takai	→	*takakereba*

Negative of a verb, an *i*- adjective, the copula:
Drop the final *-i* and add *-kereba*.

furanai	→	*furanakereba*
takaku nai	→	*takaku na-kereba*
shizuka ja nai	→	*shizuka ja nakereba*

Ame ga fureba ikimasen.	If it rains, I won't go.
Ame ga furanakereba ikimasu.	If it doesn't rain, I will go.
Mireba sugu wakarimasu.	If I take a look at it, I can readily identify it.
Takakereba kaimasen.	If it's expensive, I won't buy it.
Shizuka ja nakereba ikitaku arimasen.	If it is not quiet, I do not want to go.

e. The use of *-te wa:*
   This expression for "if" is most often found in an expression denoting "must" (e.g., "if you don't do . . . , it won't do"):

Soko e itte wa dame desu.	You must not go there. If you go there, it will be no good.
Okane ga nakute wa kaemasen.	If you have no money, you can't buy it.
Yoku benkyoo shinakute wa ikemasen.	If you don't study hard (you must!), it won't do.

37. WHETHER . . . OR . . . , IF . . . OR . . .

a. The uses of *ka:*

   (1) Use *ka . . . ka* in a sentence conveying the meaning "whether or," "if or":

Okane ga aru ka nai ka shirimasen.	I don't know if he has money or not.
Takai ka yasui ka shirimasen.	I don't know if it is expensive or not.

For present affirmative; the copula is deleted:

Suki ka kirai ka kiite kudasai.	Please ask her whether she likes it or dislikes it.

(2) Use *ka doo ka* to express "whether or not," "if or not":

Okane ga aru ka doo ka shirimasen.	I don't know if he has money or not.
Takai ka doo ka shirimasen.	I don't know if it's expensive or not.
Iku ka doo ka shirimasen.	I don't know whether she is going or not.

(3) Use *ka* in a sentence having the sense of "either . . . or":

Suiyoobi ka Mokuyoobi ni kimasu.	She will come on Wednesday or else on Thursday.
Yoshida-san ka mata wa Kida-san ni kite moratte kudasai.	Please have either Mr. Yoshida or Mr. Kida come.

38. NOUN-MAKERS

Certain nouns that appear at the end of a clause convert that entire clause into a noun equivalent. For example:

a. *No* = the one (the time, the person, the place); the act of:

Kesa hayaku uchi e denwa o kaketa no wa Tanaka-san de-shita.	The person who phoned us early this morning was Ms. Tanaka.
Kinoo mita no wa Amerika no eiga deshita.	The one we saw yester-day was an Ameri-can movie.
Kyooto e itta no wa Shigatsu deshita.	It was in April that we went to Kyoto. [The time when we went to Kyoto was April.]
Mainichi yoru osoku made hataraku no wa karada ni warui desu.	Working late night af-ter night is bad for your health.

b. *Koto* = the act of; the experience of:

Hokkaido e itta koto ga arimasu.	I have been to Hok-kaido. [The experi-ence of having gone to Hokkaido exists.]
Nihongo wa hanasu koto wa dekimasu ga yomu koto wa deki-masen.	I can speak Japanese, but I can't read it.

39. IN ORDER TO

a. To say, "one goes or comes in order to do (some-thing)":

(1) Use the pre-*masu* form plus *ni* plus a verb of locomotion such as *ikimasu* or *kimasu*:

Mi ni ikimasu.	I am going there to see it.
Gohan o tabe ni ikimashita.	He went to eat.
Amerika no shinbun o yomi ni kimashita.	I came to read American newspapers.

(2) Use a noun describing an action, plus *ni* plus a verb of locomotion:

Kaimono ni ikimashita.	He went out to shop [for shopping].
Ryokoo ni dekakemashita.	He set out on a journey.

b. To say, "one does (something) for the purpose of doing (something)," the predicate verb can be any verb including a verb of locomotion.

(1) A present-tense verb plus the noun-maker *no* plus *ni* plus a verb:

Kono megane wa hon o yomu no ni tsukaimasu.	I use these glasses for reading books.
Kono basu wa shita-machi e iku no ni benri desu.	This bus is convenient for going downtown.

(2) A present-tense verb plus *tame ni* plus a verb:

Kuruma o kau tame ni okane o karimashita.	I borrowed some money to buy a car.
Tomodachi o miokuru tame ni eki e ikimashita.	He went to the station to see a friend off.

40. REQUESTS, COMMANDS

There are several ways to express a request, command, or wish in Japanese. Use:

a. *-Te kudasai* = please do (something):

   (1) For the affirmative:

Hayaku kite kudasai.	Please come early. Come early.
Yukkuri hanashite kudasai.	Please speak slowly.

   (2) For the negative:

Hayaku konaide kudasai.	Please don't come early.
Yukkuri hanasanaide kudasai.	Please don't speak slowly.

b. *O kudasai* = please give me:

Rokujuunien no kitte o kudasai.	Give me a sixty-two-yen stamp, please.
Mizu o kudasai.	Please give me some water.

c. *Ga hoshii desu* = I want to have (preceded by the noun showing the thing desired):

Puroguramu ga hoshii desu.	I would like a program.
Sake wa hoshiku arimasen.	I don't want any sake.

d. *-Te itadakitai (no) desu (ga)*[1] = I would like to ask you to:

Kore o yonde itadakitai desu.	I would like to ask you to read this for me (but do you have time or would it interfere, etc.).
Eigo de kaite itadakitai no desu ga.	Would you mind writing (may I trouble you to write) this in English?

e. *Yoo ni shite kudasai* = be careful (not) to, try to:

Kono tegami wa hayaku dasu yoo ni shite kudasai.	Please make every effort to send this mail out early.
Kore wa otosanai yoo ni shite kudasai.	Please be careful not to drop this.

f. *-Te choodai* = please do (something):
   This request form is used in an intimate, informal, or relaxed situation.

Katte choodai.	Please buy it.
Sore o totte choodai.	Please pick it up.

g. The plain imperative of a verb:
   Each verb has a form called the "plain imperative," which is constructed by adding *-e* to the base of a consonant verb and *-ro* to the base of a vowel verb. The imperative of the irregular verbs is *koi* for *kuru* [come] and *shiro* for *suru* [do].

[1] The use of *no* and *ga* is optional in this construction.

Ike!   Go!
Miro!   Look at it!

Take note, however, that the plain imperative is used *only* in "rough" speech, and *should not* be used in everyday conversation.

41. ADVERBIAL EXPRESSIONS

a. Formation of adverbial expressions:

(1) Many adverbs are formed by adding *-ku* to the stems (the plain present affirmative minus *-i*) of adjectives:

ADJECTIVE		ADVERB	
takai	expensive	*takaku*	expensively
yasui	cheap	*yasuku*	cheaply
yasashii	easy	*yasashiku*	easily
karui	light	*karuku*	lightly

(2) Some adverbial expressions are formed from *na-* adjectives by using *ni* following the *na-*adjective:

ADJECTIVAL PHRASE		ADVERBIAL PHRASE	
kantan na	simple	*kantan ni*	simply
benri na	convenient	*benri ni*	conveniently
tokubetsu na	special	*tokubetsu ni*	especially
joozu na	skillful	*joozu ni*	skillfully

b. Comparison of adverbial expressions:
   Adverbial expressions can be compared like adjectives (see Section 16 of the Grammar Summary):

POSITIVE	COMPARATIVE	SUPERLATIVE
takaku = expensively	*motto takaku* = more expensively	*ichiban takaku* = most expensively

c. Adverbial expressions of place:
Use *ni* when the verb is *arimasu*, *imasu*, or *sunde imasu*. Use *de* for most other cases.

koko ni, koko de	here
soba ni, soba de	at the side, near
mae ni, mae de	before, in front
ushiro ni, ushiro de	behind
ue ni, ue de	on top
shita ni, shita de	underneath
naka ni, naka de	inside
soto ni, soto de	outside
doko ni mo, doko de mo	everywhere *(with an affirmative verb)*
doko ni mo, doko de mo	nowhere *(with a negative verb)*
tooku ni, tooku de	far
chikaku ni, chikaku de	near
doko ni, doko de	where
soko ni, soko de	there (nearby)
asoko ni, asoko de	there (far off)

d. Adverbial expressions of time:

kyoo	today
ashita, asu, myoonichi	tomorrow
kinoo, sakujitsu	yesterday
ototoi, issakujitsu	the day before yesterday

asatte, myoogonichi	the day after tomorrow
ima	now
sono toki	then
mae ni	before
moto	once, formerly
hayaku	early
sugu	soon, presently
osoku	late
tokidoki	often, from time to time
itsu mo	always
nagai aida	for a long time
. . . tari . . . tari shimasu	now . . . now, sometimes . . . sometimes (See Section 30 of the Grammar Summary).
mada	as yet, still
moo	already *(with an affirmative)*
moo	no longer *(with a negative)*

e. Adverbial expressions of manner:

yoku	well, frequently; studiously; hard
waruku	ill, badly
konna ni	thus, so
onaji yoo ni	similarly
hantai ni	otherwise, conversely
issho ni	together
taihen	much, very
yorokonde	willingly
toku ni	especially
waza to	on purpose, expressly

f. Adverbial expressions of quantity or degree:

takusan	much, many
juubun (ni)[1]	enough
sukoshi	little
motto	more
hidoku	extremely, excessively
amari, anmari	too, too much, too many
sonna ni	so much, so many

42. THE WRITING SYSTEM

The Japanese writing system contains four types of symbols that are usually used together:

a. One set of 46 phonetic symbols called *hiragana*

b. One set of 46 phonetic symbols called *katakana*

c. 1,945 ideographic symbols called *kanji*

d. The letters of the English (or Roman) alphabet, called *Roomaji,* together with the Arabic numerals, which are called *arabiya suuji* or *san'yoo suuji*

Each of the symbols in *hiragana* and *katakana* represents *one syllable,* and each of the forty-six basic syllables of the Japanese language is written with a single symbol, whether in *hiragana* or *katakana* (see Tables IV and VIII, which follow). *Hiragana* symbols are considered to be standard, and are most widely used. Katakana symbols are used primarily for (a) writing "borrowed" words (words derived from Western languages), (b) giving special emphasis to

---

[1] The use of *ni* is optional.

certain words within a sentence, in much the same way that italics are used in English, and (c) writing certain onomatopoeic words.

(1) The hiragana symbols:
Study the charts of *hiragana* symbols on pages 379–382. Compare these charts with Chart I of Table I on page 292. (The syllables in parentheses are only for *katakana*.) Note that the *sound* or *syllable* for each symbol appears in the corresponding square of that chart. For instance, at the point of intersection of vertical and horizontal columns 1 in the chart below, the symbol stands for *ka*.

SPECIAL NOTES FOR
THE *HIRAGANA* SYMBOLS

(a) Note that the first vertical row of symbols (headed "O") shows the symbols for the *vowel syllables only*. In all of the other columns (except the last), each consonant (or semi-vowel)-plus-vowel combination has a new symbol as each stands for a different syllable.

(b) Note, too, that there are *two* symbols for the vowel syllable *o*. The one in column 9 (を) is used *only* to write the particle *o* (the thing acted on, or the direct object); it is *never* used to represent anything else.

(c) Some symbols have a dual function:
    (i) The symbol for *ha* (は) is also used to write *wa* in the following cases:

particle *wa*	これは	kore wa
Konnichi wa.	こんにちは	Hello.
Konban wa.	こんばんは	Good evening.
dewa	では	well then
negative of	しずかでは	It is not quiet.
copula	ありません	

    (ii) The symbol used for *he* (へ) is also
used to write the particle *e* [to,
toward]. The symbol for the vowel *e*
(え) (which appears in the 0 column)
is used to write all other *e*'s.

  (d) Write syllables other than the forty-six
basic syllables covered in the above table
as follows:

    (i) Syllables listed in Chart II of Table I
(see page 293) are written using the
basic symbols plus a diacritical mark
(" or °) on the upper right shoulder of
each symbol, as in Table VI, on page 385.

Table V shows the number of strokes that are necessary to write each of the *hiragana* symbols. In each
chart within the table, the first vertical column shows
the completed symbol; the following columns show
the strokes that make the symbol. Match these left-
hand columns against the symbols in Table IV to read
the symbols. The charts are numbered to correspond
with the vertical columns in Table IV.

    (ii) Syllables that have a *y* in the middle,
e.g., *kya, kyu, kyo, gya, gyu, gyo,* etc.,
are written with special combinations
of two syllables (see Table VII, page
385). This is true also of the syllables

TABLE IV
THE BASIC HIRAGANA SYMBOLS

	0	1	2	3	4	5	6	7	8	9	10
	vowel	k	s	t	n	h'	m	y	r	w	n
1. a	あ	か	さ	た	な	は	ま	や	ら	わ	ん
2. i	い	き	し	ち	に	ひ	み		り		
3. u	う	く	す	つ	ぬ	ふ	む	ゆ	る		
4. e	え	け	せ	て	ね	へ	め		れ		
5. o*	お	こ	そ	と	の	ほ	も	よ	ろ	を	

(left margin label: **v o w e l s**)

cha, chu, cho, sha, shu, sho, ja, ju, jo.
Thus, in writing *kya,* you combine the
symbol for *ki* with the symbol for *ya.*
Note that in forming these special
combinations, the symbols for *ki, shi,
chi, ni, hi, mi,* and *ri* are used as if they
were symbols just for the initial consonant, and not for the consonant-
plus-vowel syllable. And so, to write
kya, you would use the symbol for *ki*
(き), which here would represent the
consonant *k,* plus the symbol for *ya.*
Remember, too, that the second symbol in a special combination must
always be one of the following three:
ya (や), *yu* (ゆ), or *yo* (よ), and that
this second member of the combina-
tion is usually written smaller than the
first and is usually placed slightly to
the right of center in a text written
from top to bottom. Study Table VII
for examples of these special combinations, and compare with Chart III,
Table I, for sound values.

TABLE V

CHART O

Vowels	1	2	3	4
a	あ	ニ	せ	あ	あ
i	い	ハ	い		
u	う	ろ	う		
e	え	ゑ	え		
i'	お	ニ	お	お	お

CHART I

k					
a	か	フ	カ	が	
i	き	ニ	ラ	き	き
u	く	く			
e	け	け	に	け	
o	こ	こ	に		

CHART 2

s					
a	さ	ニ	さ	さ	
i	し	し			
u	す	ニ	す		
e	せ	せ	せ		
o	そ	ソ	そ		

CHART 3

t					
a	た	ニ	た	た	た
i	ち	ニ	ち		
u	つ	つ			
e	て	て	て		
o	と	と	と		

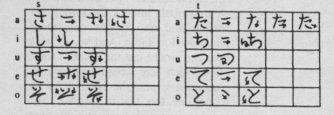

CHART 4

CHART 5

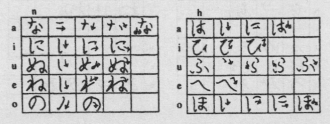

CHART 6

CHART 7

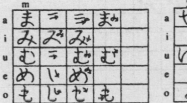
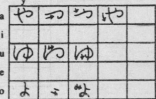

CHART 8   CHART 9

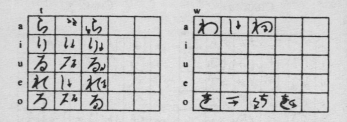

CHART 10

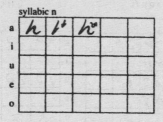

(iii) To write a double consonant other than *nn* in Japanese, you *always* use the symbol for *tsu* (つ), for the first letter, *regardless of the sound that is being doubled,* whether *kk, ss, ssh, tt, tch, tts,* or *pp.* Note that the symbol for *tsu,* when it is used in this way, is frequently written smaller than usual and placed to the right of center in text that is written from top to bottom. In text written horizontally from left to right, however, the symbol for *tsu* is placed either a little above or below the center. Study the examples below. See how the *tsu* symbol is written in place of the first letter in a doubled consonant, which appears here in boldface type:

Chotto	ちょっと	a little
Kekkon	けっこん	marriage
Isshuukan	いっしゅうかん	one week
Ippun	いっぷん	one minute

(iv) See the examples of double vowels:

aa (a-a)	ああ	Oh!
okaasan (*o-ka-**a**-sa-n*)	おかあさん	mother
*oishii (o-i-shi-**i**)*	おいしい	delicious
*kuuki (ku-**u**-ki)*	くうき	air
oneesan (*o-ne-**e**-sa-n*)	おねえさん	older sister

There is one exception to this rule: to write *oo*, you almost always use the symbol for the vowel syllable *u* in place of the second *o*, as illustrated below.

kooshoo (*ko-**o**-sho-**o***)	こうしょう	negotiation
Tookyoo (*to-**o**-kyo-**o***)	とうきょう	Tokyo
*moo (mo-**o**)*	もう	more, not any more (with a negative)
*doozo (do-**o**-zo)*	どうぞ	please
*doozoo (do-**o**-zo-**o**)*	どうぞう	bronze statue

TABLE VI
HIRAGANA WITH DIACRITICAL MARKS[1]

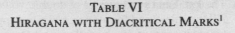

	1 g	2 z/j	3 d	b	5' p	9 v
1-a	が	ざ	だ	ば	ぱ	ゔぁ
2-i	ぎ	じ	ぢ	び	ぴ	ゔぃ
3-u	ぐ	ず	づ	ぶ	ぷ	ゔ
4-e	べ	ぜ	で	べ	ぺ	ゔぇ
5-o	ご	ぞ	ど	ぼ	ぽ	ゔぉ

TABLE VII
COMPLETE LIST OF THE SPECIAL COMBINATIONS

	1 k	2 sh	3 ch	4 n	5 h	6 m	7	8 r	9
1.	きゃ	しゃ	ちゃ	にゃ	ひゃ	みゃ		りゃ	
3.	きゅ	しゅ	ちゅ	にゅ	ひゅ	みゅ		りゅ	
5.	きょ	しょ	ちょ	にょ	ひょ	みょ		りょ	

	g	j			b p				
1.	ぎゃ	じゃ			びゃ ぴゃ				
3.	ぎゅ	じゅ			びゅ ぴゅ				
5.	ぎょ	じょ			びょ ぴょ				

[1] ち and づ are ji and zu, respectively, just as with じ and ず. Usually, じ and ず are used, except for special cases.

(2) The katakana symbols:
All the rules used for writing *hiragana* apply to *katakana* except for the following cases:

(a) Some syllables that are not traditionally Japanese syllables can be used for borrowed words, which are written in *katakana*. Such syllables are shown in parentheses in Table I. They are written as follows:

ti	ティ	*fa*	ファ
tu	テュ	*fi*	フィ
tse	ツェ	*fe*	フェ
		fo	フォ
di	ディ		
du	デュ	*va*	ヴァ
		vi	ヴィ
she	シェ	*ve*	ヴェ
che	チェ	*vo*	ヴォ
je	ジェ		

(b) For the second vowel of a double vowel, use a bar —. In text written vertically, write | . (When *katakana* symbols are used for giving special emphasis to certain words, a bar is not used. Instead, *katakana* symbols are used in the manner of *hiragana*.)

kaado (ka-a-do)	カード	カ ー ド	card
biiru (bi-i-ru)	ビール	ビ ー ル	beer
suupu (su-u-pu)	スープ	ス ー プ	soup
keeki (ke-e-ki)	ケーキ	ケ ー キ	cake
booto (bo-o-to)	ボート	ボ ー ト	boat

Table IX shows the number of strokes that are necessary to write each of the *katakana* symbols. In each chart within the table, the first vertical column shows the completed symbol; the following columns show the strokes necessary to make the symbol. Match these left-hand columns against the symbols in Table VIII to read the symbols. The charts are numbered to correspond with the vertical columns in Table VIII.

TABLE VIII
THE BASIC KATAKANA SYMBOLS[1]

	0	1	2	3	4	5	6	7	8	9	10
	vowel	k	s	t	n	h	m	y	r	w	n
1. a	ア	カ	サ	タ	ナ	ハ	マ	ヤ	ラ	ワ	ン
2. i	イ	キ	シ	チ	ニ	ヒ	ミ		リ		
3. u	ウ	ク	ス	ツ	ヌ	フ	ム	ユ	ル		
4. e	エ	ケ	セ	テ	ネ	ヘ	メ		レ		
5. o*	オ	コ	ソ	ト	ノ	ホ	モ	ヨ	ロ	ヲ	

TABLE IX

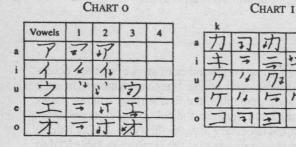

CHART 0

	Vowels	1	2	3	4
a	ア	₹	₹		
i	イ	₹	₹		
u	ウ	₹	₹	₹	
e	エ	₹	₹	₹	
o	オ	₹	₹	₹	

CHART I

k					
a	カ	₹	カ		
i	キ	₹	₹	₹	
u	ク	₹	₹		
e	ケ	₹	₹	₹	
o	コ	₹	₹		

[1] Note that in *katakana*, as in *hiragana*, there are two symbols for the letter *o*.

CHART 2

CHART 3

CHART 4   CHART 5

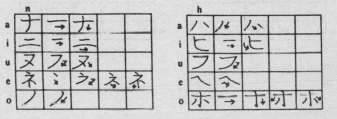

CHART 6

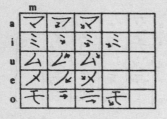

CHART 7

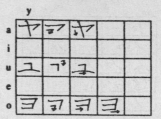

CHART 8

CHART 9

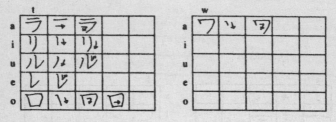

CHART 10

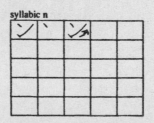

(3) Ideographic symbols (kanji):

A few of the most frequently used ideographic symbols are shown below. These are called *kanji* or, in English, "Chinese characters," because the vast majority of these characters are of Chinese origin, unlike the *hiragana* and *katakana* symbols, which were created in Japan.

SYMBOL	READING	MEANING AND CONTENT
日	*hi* *nichi* *bi* *jitsu*	the sun; a prototype was a stylized picture of the sun: ⊙ This symbol also is used to write -*nichi* in *mainichi* [everyday], *nichi*, and -*hi* in *Nichiyoobi* [Sunday], and it occurs in many other words pertaining to the sun, day, day of the week, etc. Write this figure in the order shown by the arrows:

➤l ⮐ ⊟ ⊟

| 月 | *tsuki*
 gatsu
 getsu | the moon; a stylized picture of the moon; its prototype was more like a crescent: |

☽

This symbol is also used for many other words pertaining to

the moon, such as month (as a duration of time) or name of the month, etc.
The order of writing is:

り 冂 月 月

木　ki
　　moku
　　boku

a tree; a picture of a tree; its prototype had the branches and roots more pictorially drawn: 屮

The order of writing is: ㇐ 十 才 木

一　hitotsu
　　ichi

one: "oneness" is depicted by one line, "two" is 二 , "three" is 三 , but beyond three it is not this simple.
The stroke is written from left to right: ⇒

LETTER WRITING

Formerly, letters were written in accordance with rather rigid forms, but today such forms are seldom used except in formal announcements, such as for weddings, births, and deaths. Instead, ordinary personal correspondence is written without adhering to any particular form.

1. FORMAL LETTERS

a. Salutation:

(1) In a formal letter, it is customary to begin with one of the following highly stylized salutations:
   (a) *Haikei:* corresponds to "Gentlemen," "Dear Sir(s)," or "Dear Madam" [I humbly state . . .]
   (b) *Kinkei:* corresponds to "Gentlemen," "Dear Sir(s)," "Dear Madam" [I reverently state . . .], used mainly by men
   (c) *Haifuku* (used only in reply to a letter): "Gentlemen," "Dear Sir(s)," "Dear Madam" [I reply humbly . . .]

(2) The addressee's name does not appear until the very end of the letter, where it is written in the following order:
   (a) The family name.
   (b) The given name.
   (c) The proper honorific (the most common and useful of which is *-sama,* a formal variation of *-san* [Mr., Mrs., Miss]). (See also the section on complimentary closings, below.)

(3) When a letter in Japanese is written in the English alphabet, it customarily follows the form for an English letter; thus, the addressee's name is used with the honorific -*sama,* and the formal salutation word [see Item (1) above] is omitted.

b. Complimentary close:

(1) First, use one of the following stylized closing remarks:
   (a) *Mazu wa oshirase made.* = Just to inform you (of) the above.
   (b) *Mazu wa goaisatsu made.* = Just to extend my greetings to you.
   (c) *Toriaezu gohenji made.* = Just to answer your letter in a hurry.

(2) Then add one of the following complimentary closings:
   (a) *Keigu.* = Respectfully yours. [I have respectfully stated.]
   (b) *Soosoo.* = Sincerely yours. [In a hurry. Hurriedly.]
   (c) *Kashiko.* = Sincerely yours. [In awe (used by women only).]

(3) After signing your name, place the addressee's name with the proper honorific on a separate line, either flush with the left margin or slightly indented:
   (a) *Yamada Yoshio-sama* = Mr. Yoshio Yamada.

(b) *Yamada Yoshio sensei*[1] = Mr. Yoshio Yamada (used for a minister, priest, doctor, schoolteacher, etc.).

(c) *Yamada Yoshio-dono* = Mr. Yoshio Yamada *(used in official letters)*.

(d) *Yamada Yoshio Shichoo-dono* = (Mr.) Mayor Yoshio Yamada (used for writing to someone we would address as "the Honorable," e.g., a distinguished office-holder: consists of the addressee's name plus his or her official title plus the honorific *-dono* or *-sama*).

---

[1] *Sensei*, unlike *-san* or *-sama*, may be used by itself as a term of address (somewhat like our word "sir"), and consequently is not always appended to the name as a suffix.

2. BUSINESS LETTERS

LETTER 1

> *Peter Paine*[1]
> *104*
> *Tookyoo-to, Chiyoda-ku*
> *Marunouchi Hoteru*
> *Heisei 4 nen*[2]
> *9 gatsu 25 nichi*

104
Tookyoo-to, Chuuoo-ku
Tsukiji 5-3-2
Asahi Shinbun Sha

Japan Quarterly Onchuu:[3]
   Japan Quarterly ichinenbun no koodokuryoo to shite yonsen yonhyaku nijuu en no yuubinkawase o ookuri itashimasu. Ouketori kudasai.

> *Piitaa Pein*
> *(Peter Paine)*[4]

---

[1] It is customary to retain the English name of the writer in the Japanese heading.
[2] *Heisei 4 nen* = the fourth year of the Era of Heisei, corresponding to the year 1992.
[3] *Onchuu* is used when the addressee is a group, such as a company.
[4] Normally, the English name would be signed as in the parentheses.

Marunouchi Hotel
Chiyoda-ku, Tokyo 104
September 25, 1992

Japan Quarterly
Asahi Shinbun Sha
Tsukiji 5-3-2, Chūō
Tōkyō 104

Dear Sir/Madam:[1]
  Enclosed you will find a money order for ¥4,420
for a year's subscription to your magazine *Japan
Quarterly*.

Very truly yours,
Peter Paine

---

[1] In Japanese, it is not necessary to use such a salutation.

LETTER 2

104
Tookyoo-to, Chuuoo-ku
Ginza 4-choome, 2
Sakata Shookai
Heisei 4 nen
8 gatsu 16 nichi

100
Tookyoo-to, Chiyoda-ku
Yuurakuchoo, 1-choome 3
Tanaka shookai Onchuu

Haifuku:
   Otoiawase no shinamono wa saru 8 gatsu 13 nichi
ni machigainaku kozutsumi de hassoo itashimashita.

                            Mazu wa oshirase
                            made.
                            Sakata Yukio

                       Sakata and Co.
                       2, 4-chome, Ginza
                       Chūō-ku, Tokyo 104
                       August 16, 1992

Tanaka and Co.
3, 1-chōme, Yūrakuchō
Chiyoda-ku, Tōkyō 100

Dear Sir/Madam:
   In reply to your recent letter, we wish to advise you
that the merchandise was mailed to you parcel post on
August 13.

                            Very truly yours,
                            Yukio Sakata

3. INFORMAL LETTERS

a. Salutation and content:

(1) Do not use one of the formal salutations described in the preceding section on formal letters.

(2) It is customary to mention the recent weather and climate in your locality.

(3) Inquire into the health of the person to whom you are writing and his/her family.

(4) Go into whatever other topics you want to bring up.

b. Close:

(1) Instead of using any of the complimentary closing remarks described in Item b-(2) of the preceding section on formal letters, close with a stylized remark such as:
   (a) *Dewa mata.* = Well, then again.
   (b) *Gokigen yoo.* = Wishing you good health.
   (c) *Okarada o odaiji ni.* = Keep well. Take good care of yourself.
   (d) *Minasan ni yoroshiku.* = Regards to everyone.

(2) Sign your name on a new line.

c. Examples:
Study the informal letter and thank-you note that follow.

INFORMAL LETTER

Heisei 4 nen
3 gatsu 15 nichi

Azusa sama:

    Otegami ureshiku haiken shimashita.

    Minasama ogenki no yoo de nani yori ni omoimasu.

    Sate watakushidomo no Kyooto hoomon no koto desu ga Shigatsu no hajime ni jikkoo suru koto ni shimashita. Nishuukan taizai no yotei desu. Minasama ni ome ni kakareru no o tanoshimi ni shite imasu.

    Kanai no Irene mo issho ni mairimasu. Shoobai no hoo mo okegesama de umaku itte imasu. Kore ga tsuzuite kureru to ii to omoimasu. Chotto muri na chuumon ka mo shiremasen ga Azusa san mo Shigatsu ni haittara sukoshi te o nuite issho ni ikuraka asoberu yoo ni shimasen ka.

    Konoaida Nomura kun ni attara Azusa san wa doo shite iru daroo to itte imashita. Kare mo shigoto wa umaku itte iru rashii desu.

    Daiji na koto o wasureru tokoro deshita ga Gurando Hoteru ni heya o yoyaku shite moraemasen ka? Shigatsu itsuka desu. Onegai shimasu.

    Ja kyoo wa kore de shitsurei shimasu. Otayori o matte imasu. Okusan ni yoroshiku.

Jakku
(Jack)

March 5, 1992

Dear Azusa:

I was very happy to receive your last letter. I'm glad to hear that all of you are well.

First of all, I expect to spend two weeks in Kyoto at the beginning of April and I'm looking forward to seeing you and your family.

My wife, Irene, is coming with me. Business is pretty good right now. Let's hope it keeps up. Try not to be too busy during the month of April so that we can have some time together. I suppose that's a little difficult for a busy man like you.

The other day Nomura asked about you. His business is going well.

I almost forgot the most important thing. Can you reserve a room for me at the Grand Hotel for April fifth? You'll be doing me a great favor.

I'll stop writing now. I hope to hear from you soon. My best regards to your wife.

Yours,
Jack

THANK-YOU NOTE

Yamada Fujiko-sama:

Kono tabi wa taisoo rippa na okurimono o choodai itashimashite atsuku atsuku orei mooshiagemasu. Hanga ni wa watakushi mo higoro kyoomi o motte ori sono ue ni kondo itadakimashita no wa kyakuma ni kakete yoku choowa itashimasu no de hontoo ni yorokonde orimasu. Arigatoo gozaimashita.

Mazu wa on-rei made.

Robaato Sumisu
Robert Smith

Dear Fujiko Yamada,

I would like to thank you for your delightful present. I have long had an interest in woodblock prints, and I'm glad that the one you gave me matches the other things in my parlor perfectly.

Thank you ever so much.

(Sincerely yours,)[1]
Robert Smith

[1] Note that in Japanese there is no formal closing in a note of this kind.

4. ADDRESSING AN ENVELOPE

For a letter using the Roman letters:

Peter Paine
3-2 Oiwake-chō
Bunkyo-ku, Tōkyō 112

>   602
>   Tanaka Tarō Sama
>   Kyōto Daigaku Igakubu
>   Sakyō-ku, Kyōto-shi

In Japanese writing and using a Japanese envelope:

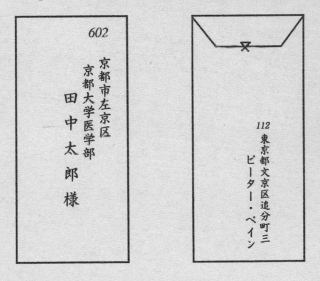